DATE DUE

DE 2000			
NO 12 02			

DEMCO 38-296

EVALUATING MENTAL HEALTH SERVICES

CHILDREN'S MENTAL HEALTH SERVICES

Series Editor
LEONARD BICKMAN,
Peabody College, Vanderbilt University, Nashville

The mental health needs of children have concerned policymakers and professionals for nearly a century. These concerns have intensified in recent years with increasing documentation on the magnitude of the problem and the extent to which children's mental health needs continue to be unmet. Sage's **Children's Mental Health Services Series** is aimed at addressing this need for systematic scholarly analysis of children's mental health needs and the policies and programs that serve them. Through involvement in constructing policy to system development to evaluation design, the esteemed authors of these volumes represent pioneers in the development of systems of care. It is our hope that these contributions will provide a rich basis for thought, discussion, and action.

In this series:

Carol T. Nixon and Denine A. Northrup
Editors

EVALUATING MENTAL HEALTH SERVICES

How Do Programs for Children "Work" in the Real World?

CMHS Children's Mental Health Services, Volume 3

SAGE Publications
International Educational and Professional Publisher
Thousand Oaks   London   New Delhi

eproduced or utilized in any form or by any
copying, recording, or by any information
writing from the publisher.

E-mail: order@sagepub.com

SAGE Publications Ltd.
6 Bonhill Street
London EC2A 4PU
United Kingdom

SAGE Publications India Pvt. Ltd.
M-32 Market
Greater Kailash I
New Delhi 110 048 India

Printed in the United States of America

Library of Congress Cataloging-in-Publication Data

Main entry under title:
Evaluating mental health services: How do programs for children "work" in the real   world?
/ Carol T. Nixon and Denine A. Northrup, editors.
        p.   cm.—(Children's mental health services; vol. 3)
     Includes bibliographical references and index.
     ISBN 0-7619-0795-5 (cloth).—ISBN 0-7619-0796-3 (pbk.)
     1. Community mental health services for children—Evaluation.
   I. Nixon, Carol T.   II. Northrup, Denine A.   III. Series: Children's
mental health services; v. 3.
RJ499.E796   1997
362.2'2'0685—dc20   96-35681

97 98 99 00 01 02 03 10 9 8 7 6 5 4 3 2 1

Acquiring Editor:	C. Deborah Laughton
Editorial Assistant:	Eileen Carr
Production Editor:	Sanford Robinson
Production Assistant:	Denise Santoyo
Typesetter/Designer:	Marion Warren
Indexer:	Cristina Haley
Cover Designer:	Ravi Balasuriya
Print Buyer:	Anna Chin

Contents

How Does Evaluation of
Mental Health Services for
Children Work in the Real World?

CAROL T. NIXON

The present volume is intended to address issues concerning the evaluation of mental health services delivered in communities for children and youth with emotional and behavioral disorders and their families. The chapter authors discuss some of the most recent evaluations examining the effectiveness of systems of care and specific intervention strategies. They also emphasize some of the limitations of evaluation in children's mental health services as well as the implications for future research.

This introductory chapter takes a closer look at the problems experienced in evaluation by the chapter authors and many other researchers. With the ever-present budget ax—particularly in light of recent and highly visible "negative" findings (e.g., Bickman, 1996; Bickman et al., 1995; Weisz, Weiss, & Donenberg, 1992)—not only are programs, serv-

AUTHOR'S NOTE: The author would like to thank Craig Anne Heflinger, Kathleen Maloy, Denine Northrup, Len Bickman, and Lynne Wighton for their thoughtful comments on drafts of this chapter. Furthermore, the editors would like to extend additional thanks to Kathleen Maloy for her efforts in getting this volume off the ground.

ices, and systems of care are under pressure to demonstrate effectiveness, but so too are our evaluation methods and procedures. While describing their individual research efforts, the authors in this volume comment collectively on issues facing researchers conducting mental health services evaluation. In this chapter, I highlight some of the issues that cut across chapters. Although evaluation serves a crucial function, it has some fundamental problems that need to be addressed collectively by researchers, policymakers, and funders to advance the current state of children's mental health services.

The Importance of Evaluation

It has been estimated that 12%-22% of children and youth suffer from a diagnosable mental disorder (Brandenburg, Friedman, & Silver, 1990; Costello, 1989), with some researchers suggesting an increase in prevalence over recent years (Stroul, 1996). It is estimated, however, that only a small proportion of those in need of services receive them, particularly those in non-mental health settings such as schools, primary health care, and juvenile justice facilities (Burns, 1990; Hoagwood, 1994; Saxe, Cross, Silverman, Batchelor, & Dougherty, 1987). Intentions of better addressing this unmet need, in addition to developing and implementing other interventions based on the Child and Adolescent Service System Program (CASSP) principles aimed at improving access, limiting barriers, and providing a continuum of care (see Stroul & Friedman, 1986, 1996), will put further strain on limited financial and human resources.

The evaluation of programs, services, and systems provides a relatively objective means of choosing among alternative programs or services competing for limited resources and informing decisions that affect public policy, both directly and indirectly. Evaluation, assuming that it is of high quality, may provide information about the services that are actually being delivered as compared to those intended, how services are being utilized and by whom, the extent to which services are effective, and the costs of services. In addition, evaluation encourages accountability, cost consciousness, and responsiveness to those in need of and utilizing services. Evaluation can synthesize what is already known, unearth false assumptions, debunk myths, develop new information, and explain the implications of this information for future decision making (Chelimsky, 1995). In fact, as Bickman (1992; see also Bickman, Summerfelt, Firth, & Douglas, Chapter 9, this volume) has pointed out, it may be unethical to continue to provide untested, perhaps invalid, services to children and their families in the name of "treatment."

Yet caution should be exercised in accepting the results of any one evaluation as "truth." For example, the findings of an evaluation are, to some extent, method restricted. In addition, as discussed later in the chapter, a multitude of factors can contribute to null findings when in fact the studied intervention or system does have an effect.

Friedman (Chapter 2, this volume) stresses that numerous evaluations over time, using multiple methods, help to build a solid base of knowledge about serving those children and families in need of mental health services. To make each evaluation as useful as possible, researchers must carefully report evaluation results, even if potentially unpopular, and thoroughly note all constraints and limitations of any study. Indeed, Chelimsky (1995) asserted that "telling the truth about what has been learned is arguably the most important purpose of evaluation" (p. 6). Thus, as evaluators, we are bound ethically to build a solid knowledge base about children's mental health services and perhaps, taking this responsibility a bit further, bound to communicate this knowledge to a diverse audience with a plethora of perspectives, including children with emotional and behavioral disorders, their families, policymakers, providers, funders, insurers, and the public at large.

Theory in Evaluation

Evaluation has been criticized as atheoretical and in dire need of attention to theory at the outset of research efforts (e.g., Bickman, 1987; Boruch & Gomez, 1977; Chen & Rossi, 1983; Weiss, 1983, 1995). Although the field of children's mental health services has been successful in disseminating guidelines for care thought to impact on mental health services delivery, most prominently in the form of CASSP principles (see Cross & Saxe, Chapter 3, this volume; Friedman, Chapter 2, this volume; Stroul & Friedman, 1986, 1996), conceptual frameworks and substantial theory are lacking for mental health service interventions for children and their families, most notably pertaining to the formulation and testing of hypotheses of change in functioning and impairment. In the process of evaluation, researchers explicitly should identify assumptions and theories of change held by program staff and other key stakeholders. Additional efforts need to be devoted to the development of conceptual models that allow exploration of particular components of care for specific segments of the target population. Researchers need to be able to address questions of *what* is effective, *for whom*, and under what *circumstances*. Researchers have tended to focus on the first question while glossing over the second and third, partly due to inadequate sample sizes, statistical power, and funding, thereby limiting exploration of important interaction effects.

Evaluation calls for at least two types of theoretical models. The first represents the development of "general understandings of social phenomena" (Chen & Rossi, 1983, p. 285). It synthesizes the empirical findings in the literature as to how some characteristic, for example, depression, arises and changes over the course of development and identifies interactional variables, such as gender. The second type of model, program theory, pertains to a specific intervention and specifies program resources, activities, and intended outcomes. The first type of theory is nonspecific, applicable to many particular interventions and, most important, is embedded within the program model, linking the pieces—resources, activities, and outcomes—together. It frequently is the "glue" missing in program models, explaining the use of resources and intervention activities to achieve desired outcomes. Moreover, it is from theories of social phenomena that program developers and evaluators construct hypotheses about exogenous and intervening variables and how they potentially may affect outcome variables. Finally, according to Weiss (1995), "Evaluations that address the theoretical assumptions embedded in programs may have more influence on both policy and popular opinion" (p. 69).

Many authors in this volume have stressed the need for greater investment in theoretical models enabling more meaningful investigation of causal linkages between process and outcome, including Attkisson et al. in Chapter 7, Bickman et al. in Chapter 9, and Friedman in Chapter 2. In Chapter 3, Cross and Saxe echo these same concerns due to the rapid implementation of systems of care based on CASSP principles. They note, "There is only a rudimentary sense of why multiple services are appropriate and necessary"—only articulated theories of systems of care in conjunction with outcome research, as "interdependent priorities," are likely to further our knowledge in hopes of improving the quality of services and systems for children with emotional and behavioral disorders.

Stakeholder Participation

Evaluation, in general, has been criticized as *narrow* and *irrelevant* (unresponsive to the information needs of program staff), *unfair* (not considering the needs of service recipients), and *unused* (often not influencing actual decision making about services) (Weiss, 1983). The active involvement of multiple stakeholders—those whose lives are affected directly by the program, services, or system—has been advocated as a mechanism to increase the validity and utility of evaluation results (e.g., Weiss, 1983). Chelimsky (1995) emphasized the importance of involving children with emotional and behavior disorders and their families as coparticipants rather than as "targets" in research studies. They, as well as other relevant stakeholders, are critical in helping to define the problems that plague them and in designing, implementing, and evaluating interventions. Furthermore, the participation of program staff and providers promotes the evaluators' understanding of the "users' milieu" (p. 8), thereby increasing the relevance, breadth, and utility of evaluation results.

Many of the chapter authors make clear their claim that evaluation results are improved by involving stakeholders in the research process. In Chapter 4, Evans and Armstrong emphasize the importance of cultivating a collaborative partnership between researchers, program staff, and policymakers in contributing to the ongoing evaluation of services and thereby enabling policy development. These authors recommend scheduling sufficient time and opportunity for those with different roles to meet; share their own paradigms, languages, assumptions, and concepts; and make site visits so that the "users' milieu" is better communicated and understood. They underscore the importance of bringing other stakeholders (e.g., children with emotional and behavior disorders, their families, service providers, legislators) actively into the research process and note that evaluation results are more likely to be used in decision making when backed by a broad base of support.

In presenting results of an in-depth case study of the decision-making and implementation activities associated with the Tennessee Children's Plan during the first 2 years of its implementation, Maloy (Chapter 6, this volume) again highlights the importance of shared decision making between relevant stakeholders in system reform efforts. In Chapter 5, Meyers and Davis discuss partnerships between private philanthropic foundations and states in reforming systems of care for children with emotional and behavioral disorders and offer similar advice, as do Evans and Armstrong in Chapter 4, for successful collaboration. More-over, Meyers and Davis advance nine desired elements for developing partnerships, including (a) "bottom-up" and "top-down" support cre-ated by the involvement of all relevant stakeholders and thereby help-ing to build a broad base of support to sustain reform efforts, particularly when there is turnover in leadership; (b) the establishment of good working relationships by devoting adequate time and using consultants in the process; (c) attention to the multiple needs and tasks of stakeholders; and (d) specific training for participants to bolster their skills and capacity (e.g., communication skills and systems thinking).

On the basis of their experiences in conducting the Assessing Coor-dinated Care (ACC) study, Farmer, Burns, Guiles, Behar, and Gerber (Chapter 8, this volume) state that it "appears absolutely essential to involve clinical staff in the [research] project to the greatest extent pos-sible." Moreover, they stress that early investment in collaboration, par-ticularly in the study start-up phase, may reduce, or perhaps even prevent, subsequent conflicts between research and program staffs. The authors suggest several concrete mechanisms for increasing collabora-tion, including maintaining an on-site research coordinator, conducting site visits, and holding focus groups. Such mechanisms facilitate com-munication between stakeholder groups, not only making researchers more aware of clinical reality but also giving the research project a "face." For example, addressing providers' concerns related to the re-search design or demands for information can minimize threats to the internal validity of the study; researchers' concerns about treatment integrity, in the form of treatment or services monitoring, can be ap-proached in a less threatening way.

Another mechanism of involving stakeholders, utilized by the Stark County Evaluation Project (SCEP) (see Bickman et al., Chapter 9, this volume), is the use of an advisory committee for feedback about issues related to the design and conduct of a project. The committee for SCEP consisted of representatives of the various child service agencies in the community; yet, the authors note in retrospect that adding parent representatives would have provided not only an overlook but also a valuable perspective. In reality, evaluators have been slow to involve all relevant stakeholders actively, particularly parents and parent advocates. Attkisson et al. (Chapter 7, this volume) stress that family participation must exceed simple involvement in treatment planning to include involvement in the system at large, such as parental participation on committees, councils, and advisory boards.

Problems Encountered in Evaluations in Applied Settings

A number of recent articles have specified threats to internal validity, or the ability to attribute effects to the intervention, and other problems encountered in applied research (e.g., Bickman, 1992; Bickman, Summerfelt, & Foster, 1996; Burns, 1994; Hoagwood, 1994; Lipsey, 1990; Persons, 1991). Here, I briefly discuss a few of the threats to internal validity and other problems encountered in more than one research effort discussed in this volume.

Randomization. Random assignment of subjects to treatment groups typically has been viewed as the "gold standard" in impact evaluation (see Friedman, Chapter 2, this volume). It is the strongest design for controlling threats to internal validity, yet it is difficult to implement in applied settings (for more see, e.g., Bickman, 1992; Hoagwood, 1994). Randomized designs require adequate, longitudinal funding and sufficient start-up time to address procedural problems as well as to ensure that the intervention is adequately developed and stable. Friedman points out that randomized designs should be reserved for special situations and should not be used in initial attempts to evaluate services. He further contends that, except in rare cases (see, e.g., Bickman et al.,

Chapter 9, this volume), randomized designs cannot be used to investigate the effectiveness of community-wide systems of care or initiatives, thus presenting special challenges to evaluators.

Furthermore, the use of randomized designs in applied research typically raises questions from stakeholders. Although Bickman et al.
(Chapter 9, this volume) found fewer objections and more willingness
to be involved in randomized research from high-level administrators
and policymakers, Farmer et al. (Chapter 8, this volume) found intense
feelings about and distrust of randomization reported by clinical
providers and staff, those dealing face to face with children with emotional and behavior disorders and their families. Farmer et al. note that
despite efforts directed at reducing problems concerning the design,
providers' concerns about randomization were never completely alleviated. They speculate that stakeholders' concerns most likely were due
to the design's interference with normal clinical practice, the narrowing
of clinical decision making, and the shift in authority and power. Not
addressed by the chapter authors are the perspectives of children and
youth with emotional and behavior problems or their family members
who have participated in randomized research studies. Similar to the
concerns of Chelimsky (1995) mentioned previously, Heflinger (1987)
noted that the traditional research paradigm views children and their
families as "objects" of study. And although research participants are
told of the research design and provide informed consent before taking
part, randomization robs the participant of his or her freedom of choice
and active role in decision making.

Given the problems of implementing randomized designs, the inap-
plicability to community-wide initiatives, and the ethical concerns
noted above, more attention should be devoted to alternative research
methods. Although a full discussion is beyond the scope of this chapter,
it is important to note that multiple methodologies exist for conducting
viable and useful evaluation without employing traditional scientific
methodology such as randomization (e.g., Coulton, 1995; Weiss, 1995;
H. B. Weiss & Greene, 1995).

Treatment Integrity. A number of evaluators have emphasized the importance of monitoring treatment over the course of evaluation to ensure that the planned treatment did in fact occur (e.g., Burns, 1994;

Heflinger, 1996) and to detail the "black box." Maloy (Chapter 6, this volume), for example, echoes the cautions of many others, in this volume and elsewhere, by emphasizing that reform efforts need to be examined closely to determine whether and in what shape reform actually has occurred *before* purporting to measure its effectiveness. Case studies, such as the one discussed by Maloy, have an important function in evaluation in delineating not only the form of services or system change but also the organizational and environmental contexts in which services take place.

Also in this volume, Friedman (Chapter 2) speaks at length about issues of program implementation, and Farmer et al. (Chapter 8) discuss treatment monitoring in relation to the ACC study. Farmer et al. conclude that a high profile on-site and frequent communications with the clinical staff can help to alleviate some of the distrust and defensiveness that is created by the process of monitoring. Furthermore, consistent monitoring throughout the project is important for overseeing recruitment rates and to ensure early response to problems that might otherwise subsequently threaten internal validity.

Instrumentation. The typical concern raised about instrumentation used in research is about its reliability, validity, and, more recently, sensitivity to change. This last issue has become more prominent with increasing numbers of longitudinal designs because most of the existing instruments in the field have been designed for cross-sectional designs with emphasis on high test-retest reliability. Yet the greater the test-retest correlations for an instrument, the more unreliable are the resulting change scores (Bereiter, 1963). Although many authors acknowledge that insensitivity in measurement potentially contributes to null findings, there has been very little research or in-depth discussion of this issue as it pertains to children's mental health services research. In addition, a need exists for researchers to focus on factors that account for individual differences in change. Thus, it may not necessarily be the change score that is of utmost interest—there may be instances in which a change indicates a *qualitative* change in the construct rather than a *quantitative* change in the amount or degree of it.

Several authors in this volume address other issues of measurement. Bickman et al. (Chapter 9) discuss baseline findings in the SCEP ob-

tained using interactive computerized interviews. While conducting a
more rigorous assessment of their use, the researchers assert that the
feasibility of using interactive computerized assessments was demonstrated. The use of computerized interviews has advantages that
may in turn reduce the financial burden on funders of research, potentially enabling greater sample sizes or more frequent assessments and
longer follow-up phases—all needed to further the current state of the
field.

Finally, in Chapter 10, Canino, Bird, and Canino discuss the methodological challenges in cross-cultural research, including the cultural sensitivity of diagnostic instruments. Just as instruments have typically
been developed for cross-sectional designs, they too have been validated on limited populations. An instrument's validity when utilized
for one population is not necessarily an indication of its validity when
utilized for a population of a different culture. More research is needed
that examines the identification of disability in varying cultures and the
validity of the diagnostic tools used.

Recruitment. Slow recruitment of research participants was encountered by the research teams of both the ACC study and the SCEP (see
Chapters 8 and 9, this volume). Although this problem has been discussed extensively in the literature (e.g., Lipsey, 1990; Sechrest, West,
Phillips, Redner, & Yeaton, 1979), its persistence as a problem, even with
veteran services researchers, should serve as a caution to all evaluators.
Slow recruitment can have serious implications for both internal validity and statistical power and highlights the critical importance of consistent monitoring by research staff. Before beginning evaluation efforts, researchers need to consider the consequences of insufficient
recruitment, prepare plans to address potential problems, and establish
protocols for the ongoing monitoring of recruitment.

Scope of Mental Health
Services Evaluation

The rapid development of systems of care and large-scale service
system reform has created a flurry of research attempting to evaluate
systems as opposed to services. Burns and her colleagues (e.g., Burns &

Friedman, 1990; Farmer et al., Chapter 8, this volume) have pointed to the lack of research on traditional clinical interventions and have advocated for the use of randomized clinical trials (RCTs) to investigate the effectiveness of services. In Chapter 8, Farmer et al. discuss their experiences of one such RCT, the ACC study.

In fact, an argument can be made that the field is in dire need of more basic research, such as the ACC study, as there has been a rush away from more modest aspirations in pursuit of the evaluation of continuums and systems of care. If we follow Chelimsky's (1995) reasoning, although the latter is important, how can we expect such findings to have a large impact on public policy when the more basic link between an intervention and its putative effect has not been established? Furthermore, this failure to demonstrate links between processes and outcome is just the stumbling block that has been noted regarding assessment of quality in mental health services (Salzer, Nixon, Schut, Karver, & Bickman, in press).

In contrast, most of the chapters in this volume present efforts aimed at evaluating systems of care. Cross and Saxe (Chapter 3, this volume) state, "The temptation may be to adopt a 'reductionistic' approach and move away from testing the impact of changing an entire system; undoubtedly, it is simpler to test individual elements. Although some of that sort of research is necessary, it ultimately would be self-defeating. The challenge is to conduct research using systems as a unit of measurement." From a systems perspective (e.g., Ackoff, 1994), the whole is more than the simple sum of its parts. Likewise, the service system has synergy of its own, not defined or understood by simply examining its parts taken alone. Borrowing an analogy provided by Ackoff, an assembly of the best parts chosen from all the existing automobiles (i.e., Mercedes, BMW, Lexus, Acura, etc.) would not necessarily result in the highest quality automobile. In fact, such a car probably would not run— the parts were not designed and developed to function together. The moral of this analogy echoes the assessment of Cross and Saxe expressed above.

Nonetheless, both types of research are critical in advancing the field of children's mental health services. Tests of individual components or basic research are more amenable to highly controlled designs such as randomization. Therefore, internal validity is potentially stronger, allowing more inferences of causality. Given large sample sizes, studies can provide information about interaction effects—what works for whom and under what circumstances. Finally, these studies, over time, components, interventions, can provide the basis for designing system reform efforts.

But it is important for researchers to proceed cautiously, as results from RCTs, positive *or* negative, do not provide the definitive answer. There is still another test—how the components fit together in the system as a whole in successfully leading to desired outcomes. Methodologies have been proposed that extend beyond traditional mainstream experimental design to investigate system change and comprehensive community initiatives (see, e.g., Coulton, 1995; Weiss, 1995; H. B. Weiss & Greene, 1995). Such innovative efforts promise to move the field forward. Although both basic and systems research have a place of their own, neither will further the field unless their separate efforts are well funded, thoroughly reported, and subsequently integrated.

Conclusion

Several factors limit the quality of evaluation efforts and the subsequent contributions to building a strong knowledge base about serving children and youth with emotional and behavior problems and their families. First, there is a serious dearth of longitudinal funding to allow sufficient start-up time for the development, implementation, and stabilization of the interventions, services, and systems being studied. Funders, among others, often underestimate the amount of time needed to realize significant improvements in outcome (Schorr, 1994).

Second, although the array of funding mechanisms is broadening, there still exist fundamental biases in the review of proposals for extramural funding. For example, with the current shift to results-based accountability, there are pressures to avoid efforts that pose measurement difficulties and do not promise quick results (Schorr, 1994). Funders often prefer traditional scientific research methods, emphasizing, for example, strong internal validity and low risk of Type I errors. The result is "cookie cutter" evaluations of little innovation that less often provide new information or fill gaps in existing knowledge.

Third, researchers too often fail to heed the threats and warnings detailed in the literature are overlooked because of insufficient time or resources allowed by funding. Moreover, although the involvement of children and families in research has been emphasized, evaluation efforts typically have not actively involved relevant stakeholders in all aspects of the research process.

To further the field, researchers must take on the responsibility of innovation and creativity in evaluation by drawing from a broader range of methodologies as have the researchers represented in this volume. Opening the channels of communication with stakeholders, reporting results in a meaningful way, and utilizing feedback are critical to overcome the problems discussed in this chapter and elsewhere.

References

Ackoff, R. L. (1994). *The democratic corporation: A radical prescription for recreating corporate America and rediscovering success.* New York: Oxford University Press.

Bereiter, C. (1963). Some persisting dilemmas in the measurement of change. In C. W. Harris (Ed.), *Problems in measuring change* (pp. 3-20). Madison: University of Wisconsin Press.

Bickman, L. (Ed.). (1987). *Using program theory in evaluation.* San Francisco: Jossey-Bass.

Bickman, L. (1992). Designing outcome evaluations for children's mental health services: Improving internal validity. *New Directions for Program Evaluation, 54,* 57-68.

Bickman, L. (1996). Reinterpreting the Fort Bragg Evaluation findings: The message does not change. *Journal of Mental Health Administration, 23*(1), 137-145.

Bickman, L., Guthrie, P. R., Foster, E. M., Lambert, E. W., Summerfelt, W. T., Breda, C. S., & Heflinger, C. A. (1995). *Evaluating managed mental health services: The Fort Bragg experiment.* New York: Plenum.

Bickman, L., Summerfelt, W. T., & Foster, M. (1996). Research on systems of care: Implications of the Fort Bragg Evaluation. In B. A. Stroul (Ed.), *Children's mental health: Creating systems of care in a changing society.* Baltimore, MD: Paul H. Brookes.

Boruch, R. F., & Gomez, H. (1977). Sensitivity, bias, and theory in impact evaluation. *Professional Psychology, 8,* 411-434.

Brandenburg, N., Friedman, R., & Silver, S. (1990). The epidemiology of childhood psychiatric disorders: Prevalence findings from recent studies. *Journal of the American Academy of Child and Adolescent Psychiatry, 29,* 76-83.

Burns, B. J. (1990). Mental health service use by adolescents in the 1970s and 1980s. *Journal of the American Academy of Child and Adolescent Psychiatry, 30,* 144-149.

Burns, B. J. (1994). The challenges of child mental health services research. *Journal of Emotional and Behavioral Disorders, 2,* 254-259.

Burns, B. J., & Friedman, R. M. (1990). Examining the research base for child mental health services and policy. *Journal of Mental Health Administration, 17,* 87-98.

Chelimsky, E. (1995). Preamble: New directions in evaluation. In R. Picciotto & R. C. Rist (Eds.), *Evaluating country development policies and programs: New approaches for a new agenda* (New Directions for Evaluations, No. 67, pp. 3-12). San Francisco: Jossey-Bass.

Chen, H., & Rossi, P. H. (1983). Evaluating with sense: The theory-driven approach. *Evaluation Review, 7*(3), 283-302.

Costello, E. J. (1989). Developments in child psychiatric epidemiology. *Journal of the American Academy of Child and Adolescent Psychiatry, 28*, 836-841.

Coulton, C. J. (1995). Using community-level indicators of children's well-being in comprehensive community initiatives. In J. P. Connell, A. C. Kubisch, L. B. Schorr, & C. H. Weiss (Eds.), *New approaches to evaluating community initiatives: Concepts, methods, and contexts* (pp. 173-199). Washington, DC: Aspen Institute.

Heflinger, C. A. (1987). Psychotherapy research ethics: Continuing the debate on controlled clinical trials. *American Psychologist, 42*(10), 957.

Heflinger, C. A. (1996). Implementing a system of care: Findings from the Fort Bragg evaluation project. In L. Bickman (Ed.), *The Fort Bragg experiment* [Special issue]. *Journal of Mental Health Administration, 23*(1), 16-29.

Hoagwood, K. (1994). Introduction to the special section: Issues in designing and implementing studies in non-mental health care sectors. *Journal of Clinical Child Psychology, 23*, 114-120.

Lipsey, M. W. (1990). *Design sensitivity.* Newbury Park, CA: Sage.

Persons, J. B. (1991). Psychotherapy outcome studies do not accurately represent current models of psychotherapy: A proposed remedy. *American Psychologist, 46*(2), 99-106.

Salzer, M. S., Nixon, C. T., Schut, J., Karver, M., & Bickman, L. (in press). Quality as a relationship between structure, process, and outcome: A conceptual framework for evaluating quality. In L. Bickman & M. S. Salzer (Eds.), *Evaluation review* [Special issue]. *Quality of care in human services.* Thousand Oaks, CA: Sage.

Saxe, L., Cross, T. P., Silverman, N., Batchelor, W. F., & Dougherty, D. (1987). *Children's mental health: Problems and treatment.* Durham, NC: Duke University Press. (Originally published by Office of Technology Assessment, U.S. Congress, Washington, DC)

Schorr, L. B., in collaboration with Farrow, F., Hornbeck, D., & Watson, S. (1994). The case for shifting to results-based accountability. *The Improved Outcomes for Children Project.* Washington, DC: Center for the Study of Social Policy.

Sechrest, L. B., West, S. G., Phillips, M. A., Redner, R., & Yeaton, W. (1979). Some neglected problems in evaluation research: Strength and integrity of treatments. In L. Sechrest, S. G. West, M. A. Phillips, R. Redner, & W. Yeaton (Eds.), *Evaluation studies review annual* (Vol. 4, pp. 15-35). Beverly Hills, CA: Sage.

Stroul, B. A. (1996). Introduction: Progress in children's mental health. In B. A. Stroul (Ed.), *Children's mental health: Creating systems of care in a changing society.* Baltimore, MD: Paul H. Brookes.

Stroul, B. A., & Friedman, R. M. (1986). *A system of care for severely emotionally disturbed children and youth.* Washington, DC: Georgetown University Child Development Center, CASSP Technical Assistance Center.

Stroul, B. A., & Friedman, R. M. (1996). The system of care concept and philosophy. In B. A. Stroul (Ed.), *Children's mental health: Creating systems of care in a changing society.* Baltimore, MD: Paul H. Brookes.

Weiss, C. H. (1983). The stakeholder approach to evaluation: Origins and promise. In A. S. Bryk (Ed.), *Stakeholder-based evaluation* (New Directions for Program Evaluation, No. 17, pp. 3-14). San Francisco: Jossey-Bass.

Weiss, C. H. (1995). Nothing as practical as good theory: Exploring theory-based evaluation for comprehensive community initiatives for children and families. In J. P. Connell, A. C. Kubisch, L. B. Schorr, & C. H. Weiss (Eds.), *New approaches to evaluating community initiatives: Concepts, methods, and contexts* (pp. 65-92). Washington, DC: Aspen Institute.

Weiss, H. B., & Greene, J. C. (1995). An empowerment partnership for family support and education programs and evaluations. *Family Science Review, 5,* 131-148.

Weisz, J. R., Weiss, B., & Donenberg, G. R. (1992). The lab versus the clinics: Effects of child and adolescent psychotherapy. *American Psychologist, 47,* 1578-1585.

2

Services and Service Delivery Systems for Children With Serious Emotional Disorders

Issues in Assessing Effectiveness

ROBERT M. FRIEDMAN

Since the publication of *Unclaimed Children* in 1982 by Knitzer, the children's mental health field has undergone considerable change (Friedman, 1996). In this chapter, I focus particularly on factors in the children's mental health field that have produced the changes in the types of services provided to children with serious emotional disorders and their families and the changes in the service delivery systems that provide the support for these services. I also examine the role of research and evaluation on the effectiveness of services and systems of care in bringing about these changes. The challenges that researchers and evaluators face in increasing their contribution to the improvement of services and systems of care also are considered. With this foundation,

AUTHOR'S NOTE: The author is appreciative of the comments and suggestions made by Al Duchnowski, Marcela Gutierrez-Mayka, Mario Hernandez, and Krista Kutash.

I conclude by advocating for a comprehensive knowledge development strategy for the field in which a broad range of research and evaluation methods and designs are used.

I do not seek to review all of the benefits of research and evaluation since the publication of *Unclaimed Children*. Rather, I focus on changes in service delivery and systems of care and the impact of research and evaluation on effective services and systems.

Changes Since *Unclaimed Children*

Following the publication of *Unclaimed Children*, the National Institute of Mental Health (NIMH) initiated its Child and Adolescent Service System Program (CASSP) (Stroul & Friedman, 1986). Through CASSP, states were provided with modest resources to improve their capacity specifically to serve children with serious emotional disturbances and the families of these children. The focus on this particular target population—children with the most serious disturbances and their families—represented a major change in the public children's mental health field (Friedman, Kutash, & Duchnowski, 1996). States throughout the country prioritized this particular population as well, and children with the most serious disturbances remain the highest priority of most public children's mental health systems.

In 1986, CASSP produced a monograph on community-based systems of care (Stroul & Friedman, 1986). This model provided a set of principles and values for service delivery systems; described a range of services that should be included within such a system; provided a multiagency focus for the system; and emphasized the need for organized, integrated systems of care and not just isolated programs. This monograph also built on work done in places such as North Carolina (Behar, 1985), Florida (Friedman, 1983), Alaska (Burchard, Burchard, Sewell, & VanDenBerg, 1993; VanDenBerg, 1990), Illinois (Dennis, 1992; Stroul & Goldman, 1990), and Vermont (Burchard & Clarke, 1990; Yoe, Bruns, & Burchard, 1995) to emphasize the importance of individualized services that respond to the strengths and needs of each child and his or her family.

Additional emphases during the 1980s were on the need to develop culturally competent services (Cross, Bazron, Dennis, & Isaacs, 1989) and to bring parents and professionals into a productive partnership (Duchnowski, Berg, & Kutash, 1995; Friesen & Koroloff, 1990). Taken together, the message of the 1980s was the need to develop multiagency, community-based systems of care based on parent-professional partnerships that provided individualized, culturally competent, and comprehensive services to effectively serve children with serious emotional disturbances and their families. Although there remains much need for continued improvement in the field, clearly there has been substantial change with regard to both the development of systems of care and the use of new service delivery approaches (Duchnowski & Friedman, 1990; Stroul et al., 1996).

Factors Contributing to Change

What role has research and evaluation played in bringing about these changes? What type of research and evaluation has contributed most to the changes? Have those studies that have been best controlled made the greatest contribution? These are some of the questions to be considered in this section.

A Framework for Examining Changes

A multidimensional framework offered by Hoagwood, Hibbs, Brent, and Jensen (1995) can be used as a tool for analyzing the contributions of research and evaluation to the changes discussed above. In a recent article discussing issues of efficacy and effectiveness in child and adolescent psychotherapy, the authors offered a model with three continuous dimensions. One of these dimensions has to do with the degree to which internal or external validity is the primary focus of the effort. Internal validity issues have to do with the extent to which the research or evaluation design makes it possible for a clear relationship to be drawn between the independent variable (or intervention) and the dependent variables (or outcomes). External validity focuses on the generalizability of the findings beyond the conditions of the study.

A related distinction is between "scientific rigor and social relevance" (Brown, 1995, p. 221)—that is, to what extent have new services originated with practitioners, administrators, or policymakers in the field, who are primarily concerned with providing service, as opposed to researchers and evaluators, who are external to the service delivery system and apply as much scientific rigor to the process as they can to advance knowledge by providing as clear an answer as possible about service effectiveness?

The second dimension offered by Hoagwood et al. (1995) examines the nature of the intervention that is being studied, that is, the degree to which the intervention is structured. Interventions vary from highly structured treatments that may involve just a single modality to less structured treatments involving multiple approaches.

The third dimension is an outcome dimension. It examines the extent to which the study or program is focused on different types of outcomes, including clinical outcomes, broader indicators of functioning and adaptation, community, or systemic outcomes.

Application of the Framework

A brief historical examination of the public children's mental health field using these dimensions suggested by Hoagwood et al. (1995) may be helpful in understanding the factors that have contributed to change. One of the earlier innovative services was the Homebuilders program, a complex, multidimensional, home-based service intervention in which staff have very small caseloads and work intensively with families for a limited time period (Kinney, Madsen, Fleming, & Haapala, 1977). This model was first developed and tested in Tacoma, Washington, as part of an effort to reduce unnecessary out-of-home placements. The initial article describing the model presented data primarily on a systemic outcome measure—the number of out-of-home placements—using a nonexperimental evaluation design. The model was consistent with the value of providing family-based services and striving to keep families together if at all possible. The Edna McConnell Clark Foundation promoted refinement, training, and dissemination of this model (Edna McConnell Clark Foundation, 1985), which has now spread broadly across the United States despite continuing debates about the adequacy of the empirical support for its effectiveness and the absence of controlled studies using random assignment of participants (Rossi, 1992; Wells & Beigel, 1991).

The Homebuilders intervention is a complex, multifaceted intervention and requires intensive, specialized training before being applied. The tasks of ensuring high-quality implementation of this complex intervention and of assessing the extent to which implementation has been well done raise important issues for researchers and evaluators. It cannot be assumed, for example, that a program purporting to provide services in keeping with the Homebuilders model is actually doing so. Furthermore, this lack of knowledge about the integrity of implementation serves as a barrier to conducting appropriate studies of the program model or theory. This problem reappears constantly with multimodal interventions at the more complex end of the intervention dimension (degree of structure) proposed by Hoagwood et al. (1995).

In the late 1970s and early 1980s, one of the most significant developments in the children's mental health field was a class action lawsuit brought against the state of North Carolina (Behar, 1985). This lawsuit (known as the Willie M. lawsuit), brought on behalf of a class of youngsters with serious emotional disturbances or neurological disorders who also were violent, resulted in a settlement that required the state of North Carolina to appropriately serve all youngsters in this class in the least restrictive setting possible. The state was not permitted to reject a youngster as inappropriate for treatment if he or she met the conditions of class membership; nor could the state eject a youngster from services. This became known as the "no reject, no eject" policy and presented a new challenge to mental health professionals. Suddenly, services could not be denied to those youngsters who were often the least responsive to traditional interventions.

In response to this lawsuit, North Carolina developed community-based systems of care that emphasized individualized services, coordinated by case managers. The term *wraparound* was coined to describe a process of supporting children in the services through wrapping services around them rather than surrounding them with institutional walls. This innovation was developed by policymakers in the field and involves complex interventions that cannot be reduced to a high level of structure. Perhaps the most compelling finding from the experience with the Willie M. lawsuit was that youngsters who were previously believed to need treatment in secure residential settings often could be effectively maintained in the community with a wide range of therapeutic and supportive services. Because no youngster who met the criteria for membership in the class covered by the lawsuit could be denied service, there was no possibility of identifying a comparable control or comparison group in North Carolina for this intervention. Yet, despite a lack of high internal validity in evaluations, there has probably been no other intervention that has so influenced the children's mental health field in developing community-based systems of care, with case management and wraparound services as key features.

An additional systemic intervention developed in the early 1980s was the children's system of care of Ventura County, California (Jordan & Hernandez, 1990). This system targeted children with serious emotional disturbances who were already in out-of-home placements or at risk for such placements and focused primarily on systemic rather than clinical outcome measures. The idea for the system originated with administrators and policymakers in Ventura County. Systematic data collection was built into the operation of this innovative system and the evaluation focused on the extent to which the community succeeded in reaching quantitative goals and objectives that were agreed on by the county and legislative leaders in California. Because the intervention was systemic and countywide, again there was no possibility of using a comparison group within the area. The intervention was a complex one programmatically, involving many services and close collaboration between four systems—mental health, child welfare, special education, and juvenile justice. As the intervention evolved, the program administrators increasingly emphasized that the core of the intervention was not the specific services that were provided but a collaborative planning process that had to take place among multiple agencies.

The Ventura planning model has now been replicated in several counties in California, and an additional external evaluation has included a comparison of these special counties with other counties in California on broad systemic outcomes (for a detailed discussion, see Attkisson et al., Chapter 7, this volume; see also Attkisson, Dresser, & Rosenblatt, 1993). The Ventura planning model has had a national impact as well, influencing the development of systems of care in many communities as well as the development of the Mental Health Services Program for Youth of the Robert Wood Johnson Foundation (Beachler, 1990) and the Children's Mental Health Services Program of the U.S. Center for Mental Health Services (MACRO International & University of South Florida, 1995).

The movement toward individualized care, which received an important contribution from the North Carolina activities in response to the Willie M. lawsuit, also benefited from the activities of the Kaleidoscope Program in Chicago (Dennis, 1992) and the Alaska Youth Initiative (Burchard & Clarke, 1990; VanDenBerg, 1990). Both of these efforts also originated in the field with practitioners, administrators, and policymakers. The trademark of each of these programs is the unique constellation of services provided to each youngster and family, based on a comprehensive and participatory process of identifying strengths and needs in multiple life domains. Neither of these efforts was evaluated through the use of designs that promoted high internal validity. Rather, evaluation efforts focused on individual case studies (Burchard et al., 1993) and the achievement of systemic outcomes (reduction in out-of-home or out-of-state placements). Yet these efforts have continued to gain momentum and influence across the country, not only in children's mental health but also in related fields.

As indicated earlier, information about each of these innovations and findings was incorporated in material on systems of care beginning with a monograph by Stroul and Friedman (1986) and including a number of special reports (Stroul & Goldman, 1990; Stroul, Goldman, Lourie, Katz-Leavy, & Zeigler-Dendy, 1992). This description and dissemination, made possible through CASSP, provided a set of values and principles about service delivery to children with serious emotional disturbances and their families. These values and principles emphasized, for example, that systems of care should be child centered and community based, that children should have access to a comprehensive array of services, that services should be individualized in accordance with the unique needs and potential of each child, and that families should be full participants in all aspects of planning and delivery of services. A conceptual framework of the service delivery system also was provided in which the child and family were the centerpiece of a system of care that provided functional services in the following areas: mental health, social services, education, health, vocational training, recreation, and operations, including case management (Stroul & Friedman, 1986).

Summary and Conclusions

This brief history and analysis is based partly on my involvement as a participant-observer in the process and partly on discussions specifically on this topic with other participants representing the practitioner, policymaker, and research communities. I specifically looked at innovations in service delivery, such as the Homebuilders model, case management, individualized care with wraparound services, and innovations in service delivery systems, such as the North Carolina system following the Willie M. lawsuit and the Ventura County, California, model.

Based on this analysis, it appears that for the first stage of system change that took place in the children's mental health field during the 1980s, the major contributing factors were

- The development of service delivery and system of care innovations by practitioners, administrators, and policymakers in the field
- Program and system evaluation findings that are encouraging but include no controlled studies using randomized assignment to interventions
- A strong emphasis on data collection and evaluation of systemic outcome measures, such as number of children in out-of-home or out-of-state placements, rather than on clinical or functional measures of child behavior
- The development of statements of values and principles on the one hand and conceptual frameworks on the other hand to summarize the field experiences of the innovative service delivery and system of care innovations and provide a heuristic model for planners, policymakers, practitioners, and evaluators

If this analysis of the factors leading to expansion of new service and system of care models is correct, and if, in fact, research studies and evaluation efforts that have been focused primarily on internal validity have had relatively little influence on the assessment of effectiveness and on the growth in the field, what are the implications for the children's mental health field and for research and evaluation?

It should be considered first that the absence of well-controlled research and evaluation studies leaves the children's mental health field at risk. It is possible, for example, that the field has been moving in the wrong direction based on findings from studies that lack appropriate rigor. It also may be that the field is moving in an appropriate direction but now has developed past the stage where relatively weak program evaluation designs provide sufficient data for policymakers, particularly as financial resources grow tighter and tighter in many states and competition for limited resources increases. Therefore, it may be that without more conclusive findings there will be a decrease in funding for existing services even if the field is moving in the right direction.

Given each of these possibilities, and their negative consequences for the field, there can be little doubt that there is a need for more research and evaluation that meets appropriate internal and external validity standards. Yet, it must be recognized that there are also risks in studies that appear to meet appropriate standards. Bickman and Heflinger (1995) listed three reasons why evaluations may result in failure to find an effect. The first of these is that the program theory is wrong; the second is that the program has not been adequately implemented; and the third is that the evaluation has not been conducted appropriately. Burns (in press) also emphasized the risk of failing to find an effect when it is in fact there due to methodological problems that obscure the effectiveness of the intervention. Finally, Hernandez indicated that the lack of clarity of assumptions and operational definitions inhibits the ability to conduct adequate evaluations (M. Hernandez, personal communication, January 1996). In addition to these risks, there are special challenges in conducting research and evaluations in applied settings. These are further discussed later in the chapter.

Failure to find effects because of methodological issues can have an enormous impact on a field, sometimes rapidly reversing progress that has taken many years to achieve. This is particularly the case when studies appear to have met high standards of internal validity and the methodological shortcomings (which are often inevitable in field research) are not obvious. This is especially true at the present time, when the public and many policymakers are questioning whether it is worthwhile to maintain the same level of support for human services. It is important in the children's mental health field in light of the findings of Weisz and his colleagues (e.g., Weisz, Weiss, & Donenberg, 1992), who have found no evidence from studies conducted in clinics that psychotherapy for children is effective. In addition, Bickman and his colleagues (Bickman, 1996; Bickman et al., 1995) concluded from an evaluation of a major demonstration project that there was no evidence of improved clinical outcomes for children served in a continuum of care as compared to traditional services. Because of the importance of this issue, in the next section I examine three issues that present special challenges in this type of research and evaluation and have a great effect on the potential impact (positive or negative) that research and evaluation may have.

Theory, Implementation, and Design: Special Challenges

It should be noted first that for purposes of this discussion there is little benefit in distinguishing between research and evaluation. As Knapp (1995) pointed out in a discussion of methodologies for examining comprehensive collaborative services for children and families, both research and evaluation "are concerned with systematic learning about the design, conduct, and impacts of a form of social intervention aimed at a broad range of human needs" (p. 6).

Theories of Change

Bickman (1987) pointed out that a program theory is "the plausible and sensible model of how the program is supposed to work" (p. 5). Weiss (1995) indicated that the concept of grounding evaluation in theories of change is based on the assumption that social programs are all based on a theory of how and why the program will work, whether the theory is explicitly stated or not. She further points out that the evaluation should surface those theories and identify all of the assumptions that are built into a program. Unless this is done, researchers cannot determine whether failure to find positive results from an intervention is due to an inaccurate theory.

With all of the changes that have taken place in the children's mental health field since the early 1980s, there has been much talk about values and concepts but very little talk about theory. What is required to bring about positive changes in youngsters with serious emotional disturbances, for example? What features of individualized care or systems of care are necessary for change to take place? How do changes at the systemic level impact on the quality or effectiveness of services received by children and their families?

There are several ideas emerging from CASSP that form at least the beginnings of potential theories of change, but there has been very little refinement or testing of these theories. For example, after a qualitative study involving in-depth interviews with children, parents, and practitioners, Whitbeck concluded that what is essential to effective service delivery is access, voice, and ownership (Robinson & Whitbeck, 1993; Whitbeck, 1993). All key participants must feel that they have access to the process and that they have a voice in determining what will happen. If this is the case, then they will have ownership in the process, according to this theory, and positive change will be facilitated. VanDenBerg (1992) offered a similar idea. He indicated that the key feature of successful intervention is that all of the key individuals—child (if of appropriate age), parents, other family members and members of the natural helping network, educators, mental health professionals, and so on—come together to offer their perspectives, listen to each other, and agree on a plan of action. VanDenBerg indicated that the specifics of the plan of action may be less important than the process of involving all of the key people and reaching agreement. Malysiak (1995) has offered a related theory for wraparound services. She indicated that the key to success may be the active engagement of the family in the process as a collaborator and decision maker and the use of a strength-based, ecologically oriented approach.

What are the implications of these theories of change? Surely, if any or all of these theories are accepted as the basis for an intervention designed to have an impact on the functioning of the children served, then it is essential that the evaluation include data collection about the extent to which key participants feel that they were adequately involved in the process and committed to the agreed-on plan of action. Yet, this information rarely is collected and when it is the findings raise serious questions. For example, in a descriptive study of participation in service planning meetings, Nyberg (1992) indicated that parents spoke very little, and when they did speak they frequently received no response. Bickman et al. (1995) reported that in the Fort Bragg demonstration sample only 48% of parents participated in the initial treatment planning meeting, compared to 39% in the comparison sites.

There are other bases for developing theories of change as well. For example, Fraser, Pecora, and Haapala (1988) interviewed staff and parents who had successfully completed a Homebuilders intervention. Both staff and parents were asked to identify the critical features of success. Staff most frequently referred to a moment of therapeutic intervention that they believed to be especially meaningful, whereas parents more frequently talked about some activity by staff that they as parents believed went above and beyond the call of duty and helped them accept the commitment of staff to helping. Noteworthy staff activities included responding promptly to requests for help, regardless of the time of day, and waiting in long lines with parents to help them receive special services. Dennis (1992), VanDenBerg (1992), and Burchard and Clarke (1990) have emphasized the importance of "unconditional commitment" as an important contributor to positive change. They have indicated that youngsters with serious problems typically have been discharged from several services or programs because of their behavior and an important element of securing a positive commitment from the child is for the staff to make a commitment to remain with the child regardless of his or her behavior. This is consistent with reports from youngsters that positive relationships were often the most important part of the intervention to them and change took place only when they realized that their therapist, case manager, or counselor was going to stick by them regardless of what they did. Such reports provide additional data from which to propose a theory of change. Although it is beyond the scope of this chapter to review the literature on psychotherapy and behavior change strategies, there is certainly empirical support for many of these concepts already in the literature.

An important aspect of stating a theory of change is indicating the population to which the theory applies. It may be, for example, that a system of care is more important for youngsters with serious problems who require multiple services than it is for youngsters with less serious problems or for youngsters who require only a single service. In fact, one of the debates in interpreting the findings from the Fort Bragg Evaluation (Bickman, 1996; Bickman et al., 1995) has to do with whether the theory should be tested on all participants in the evaluation sample, regardless of how serious their problems were or what services they received, or only on youngsters with serious emotional disorders (Friedman & Burns, 1996).

Regardless of the specific theories of change proposed, to shed more light on issues of service and system effectiveness researchers and evaluators need to be clear about their theories and include mechanisms for assessing the accuracy of the theories. Weiss (1995) offered four major reasons for theory-based evaluation:

1. It concentrates evaluation attention and resources on key aspects of the program.
2. It facilitates aggregation of evaluation results into a broader base of theoretical and program knowledge.
3. It asks program practitioners to make their assumptions explicit and to reach consensus with their colleagues about what they are trying to do and why.
4. Evaluations that address the theoretical assumptions embedded in programs may have more influence on both policy and popular opinion. (p. 69)

Description of the Intervention and Assessment of Its Implementation

The logical next step after stating the program theory is describing the intervention developed from the theory. In experimental terms, the intervention is the *independent variable*.

The intervention must be defined and described in sufficient detail and comprehensiveness so that it is possible to determine if it is being appropriately applied in the study of concern and, ultimately, so that it can be replicated. This task becomes increasingly difficult as the field moves from relatively unidimensional interventions of a clinical nature to more complex, multidimensional interventions, whether clinical or systemic in nature. Although an important role remains for research to test unidimensional interventions (e.g., new medications), the clinical or systemic interventions that have been developed specifically to serve children with serious emotional disturbances are by their nature much more complex. This shift from interventions that represent unidimensional changes to those that are multifaceted represents one of the most important shifts in the field and one of the most important challenges to researchers and evaluators (Friedman, 1989; Usher, 1995). Schorr (1995) pointed out that the very characteristics that are likely to make services effective—they are comprehensive, individualized, flexible, and so forth—make them more difficult to describe and to evaluate.

One of the risks in research and evaluation is that erroneous conclusions will be drawn about the ability of interventions to lead to a positive outcome as a result of studies in which standard, fixed interventions are used for problems requiring more individualized and comprehensive interventions. Although such standard and fixed interventions should not be expected to produce strong improvements in youngsters with serious and complex problems, studies employing such fixed interventions often receive extra attention in meta-analyses and literature reviews because they have good internal validity (Kazdin, 1987).

An additional concern is the frequent lack of thoroughness with which investigators describe the intervention that they are studying. This shortcoming with regard to description of the intervention, as significant as it is, is modest in relation to the shortcomings with regard to assessment of the adequacy of the implementation of the intervention. This is a particular challenge for individualized interventions; although the task of assessing adequacy or "fidelity" of implementing the intervention is clearly more difficult for individualized interventions than for interventions for which there is a standard way of intervening, the task of assessing adequacy is no less important. Unless this task is done, it will not be possible to determine the cause of failure to obtain positive outcomes.

An exception has been the work of Henggeler and his colleagues in testing multisystemic therapy (Henggeler & Borduin, 1990, 1995; Henggeler, Melton, Smith, Schoenwald, & Hanley, 1993). First, a theory and set of principles is presented as a foundation for the therapy. Second, the intervention is described, including the manner in which therapists were selected and trained. Third, the fidelity or integrity with which the intervention was administered is assessed by an intensive process of supervision and case review. Fourth, if it is determined that particular therapists consistently failed to properly apply the intervention, their data are not included in the data analysis. For example, in one recent report Scherer, Brondino, Henggeler, Melton, and Hanley (1994) indicated that "data for two of the therapists ($n = 13$) who are no longer with the project were omitted when integrity checks indicated that they had seriously and continually violated the treatment protocol"

(p. 203). This approach of describing the theory and intervention, assessing the implementation, and discarding data in instances where the intervention is not appropriately applied permits a clear test of the intervention. This is one approach to assessing the adequacy of implementation that rarely has been used in the assessment of the effects of multifaceted services for children with serious emotional disorders.

Some variation on this approach is necessary when the intervention involves changing the overall service delivery system and investigators seek to determine if the systemic intervention has an impact on the functioning of individual children and families. An example is the work of Groves (1994), who assessed the impact of systemic level changes on the way individual children and families were served. To do this, Groves (1994) systematically and intensively studied a sample of children and families. The approach he and his colleagues used involved the development of a structured case protocol designed with input from the key stakeholders in the system about the principles and practices they believed to be essential for effective care. This design process has the effect that Weiss (1995) referred to as helping stakeholders be more explicit about their theory of change, the principles and practices that operationalize that theory, and the performance standards for the application of the principles and practices.

The protocol developed by Groves (1994) calls for interviewing children, parents (both foster parents and biological parents), case managers, therapists, and other key individuals involved with the youngster as well as reviewing the case record. This is done by trained, professional interviewers for a random sample of youngsters in the targeted system of care; the performance of the system is assessed by rating the application of the appropriate principles and practices.

Such an approach is being used statewide in Tennessee (Lee, 1994; O'Neal, 1995) and also is being incorporated by the Florida Mental Health Institute in evaluations of the Urban Child Mental Health Initiative of the Annie E. Casey Foundation (Friedman & Hernandez, 1993) and the Comprehensive Mental Health Services Program for Children of the Center for Mental Health Services (MACRO International & University of South Florida, 1995). These procedures are still in a relatively early stage of development, and additional work needs to be done on reliability and validity issues. The use of intensive studies with structured protocols and trained interviewers is, however, one promising approach for assessing implementation of particular service level interventions, of system level interventions, and of the manner in which the theory of change proposes that service and system changes are related to child and family outcomes.

It is important to recognize that in this intensive case approach just described, the unit of analysis is not really the child or the family. Rather, each child or family serves as a test of how well the system is implementing the explicitly desired principles and practices. The issue is not determining the effectiveness of any particular service, be it a day treatment program, case management, psychotherapy, or whatever. Rather, in keeping with the principles typically described for systems of care, the issue is to determine how well the system overall responds to the needs and strengths of the children and families served. For youngsters with serious, multiple, and long-lasting needs, that system response clearly involves multiple services and systems, partnership with families, and involvement of others in a child's natural helping network.

Morrissey, Johnsen, and Calloway (1995) appropriately indicated that one of the main challenges in the field is finding ways to test and evaluate the connection between system changes, changes in treatment interventions, and child and family functioning. The approach used by Groves (1994) is one attempt to assess implementation of a new intervention by looking specifically at a sample of children and families and determining if the agreed-on features of the intervention have been applied. It should be noted that Morrissey and his colleagues (Johnsen, Morrissey, & Calloway, 1995; Morrissey, 1992; Morrissey et al., 1995) have done extensive work on examining service delivery networks. Their approach is one way of assessing whether the interventions in the service delivery system have resulted in the necessary changes in the structure of the system, although it falls short of assessing the impact of the system changes at the level of the child and family as they interact with the system.

A third approach to assessing adequacy of implementation is illustrated in the work of Bickman and his colleagues (1995) in their evaluation of the Fort Bragg demonstration project. They used multiple methods to assess both quality of the interventions and adequacy of implementation. These methods included interviews with participants in the system; assessment of the quality of key components of the overall system, such as case management; network analysis of the relationship between agencies in the community; and review of performance in relation to standards by an outside accrediting group (the Joint Commission on the Accreditation of Health Care Organizations). Although these approaches are all useful, unlike the approaches used by Henggeler and his colleagues (Henggeler & Borduin, 1990, 1995; Henggeler et al., 1993) and Groves (1994), they do not directly examine what happens at the level of interaction of the child and family with the overall service delivery system. Unless this more direct focus is taken, it is difficult to know if changes at the system level are really being translated into the desired changes at the level of the child and family.

A fourth approach that is increasing in frequency is the use of focus groups as a means of getting input from key stakeholders on the implementation of the intervention. Focus groups are being used, for example, in the evaluation of both the Urban Child Mental Health Initiative (Friedman & Hernandez, 1993) and the Comprehensive Mental Health Initiative for Children (MACRO International & University of South Florida, 1995). Such an approach would seem to be a useful complement to other approaches. At this point, it is not possible to determine, however, the degree of congruence between information gained from a particular source through focus groups (e.g., youngsters, parents, practitioners) and the information gained from the same source through intensive case reviews. Will there be consistency between the more global reports gained in a group setting and the more specific reports gained in a one-to-one interview? This has yet to be determined.

The Comprehensive Mental Health Services Program for Children has contributed a fifth approach to assessing the adequacy of implementation. MACRO International and the University of South Florida (1995) have developed a structured protocol for assessing the quality of the overall system of care. This protocol is used by trained professionals to conduct interviews with multiple stakeholders in a community and review data and documents from that community. The protocol examines two general qualities of the system: the infrastructure and the actual delivery of services. The protocol development involved input from experts in the field, who were called on to make explicit the features of an effective system of care. This procedure has had an initial application in demonstration sites across the country but remains in early stages of development; if adequate reliability and validity can be demonstrated, it would seem to be a very useful part of assessing interventions at the system of care level.

Assessment of the quality of the system of care is particularly important in the evaluation of a multisite demonstration program, such as the Comprehensive Mental Health Services Program for Children. It is to be expected that sites differ in level of development of systemic infrastructure and actual service delivery. Because the theory underlying this particular demonstration program is that positive outcomes for children and families result from strong system infrastructures and delivery of services that incorporate CASSP principles and practices, it should be expected that outcomes for children and families will be better in those sites that have implemented both aspects of the intervention adequately. Through the use of this system assessment procedure, along with other mechanisms such as focus groups, stakeholder interviews, and case studies, it will be possible to determine which sites are at the highest level of system development and service delivery and are, therefore, the best test of the system of care theory.

This approach also will permit separate conclusions to be drawn about the theory of a system of care and the actual demonstration project. The theory will be supported if those sites, no matter how few, that implement the intervention appropriately and achieve a high level of service delivery in accordance with the expressed principles and practices have the best outcomes for children and families. If only a few sites achieve these outcomes, however, the demonstration may be ineffective for whatever combination of reasons (e.g., inadequate amount of time to develop the system, difficulty in obtaining the needed collaboration, inadequate funding).

The Comprehensive Mental Health Services Program for Children illustrates another issue in assessing implementation of the intervention. Successful applicants in this grant program received funding with virtually no time to plan. The system development and service delivery activities were to begin immediately. This is a similar circumstance to the research demonstration programs funded by the Center for Mental Health Services (Kutash, Duchnowski, & Sondheimer, 1994). Grantees were initially given just a 3-year period to both implement and evaluate the intervention. In both of these cases, the decisions about the amount of time available were made not for professional but for political reasons. Yet, such limits have great impact on the potential to achieve the stated goals. The development of innovative services, and especially of systems of care, inevitably requires time; unless there is adequate time for an intervention to be appropriately implemented, the evaluation of the intervention may be problematic. Yet, because an internally valid evaluation is a prerequisite for funding and there generally is a limited time to conduct the evaluation, there is a risk that data will be collected prematurely, that is, before the intervention has been adequately implemented (Burns, 1994).

A related issue in services research and evaluation must also be considered. As program administrators know well, services and programs are rarely static entities. They are constantly undergoing change, due to internal organizational changes or external changes in the community in which the program operates. As Patton (1994) pointed out, evaluations are frequently divided into two general categories: summative and formative. Summative evaluations are designed to assess the overall effectiveness of a program or system in meeting its goals, whereas formative evaluations are designed to describe the process of program development. Implicit in this notion, however, is the belief that after an initial start-up period, programs reach a "steady state" in which they are genuinely a fixed entity that is ready for a summative evaluation. But as Patton (1994) indicated, program designers

> never expect to arrive at a steady state of programming because they're constantly tinkering as participants, conditions, learnings, and context change. They don't aspire to arrive at a model subject to summative evaluation and generalization. Rather, they aspire to continuous progress, ongoing adaptation, and rapid responsiveness. . . . They don't value traditional characteristics of summative excellence such as standardization of inputs, consistency of treatment, uniformity of outcomes and clarity of causal linkages. They assume a world of multiple causes, diversity of outcomes, inconsistency of interventions, interactive effects at every level—and they find such a world exciting and desirable. (p. 313)

The challenge to evaluators and researchers in the context of the developmental nature of interventions is to avoid a single assessment of adequacy of implementation and to make evaluation an ongoing process and report changes as they take place. These changes, of course, must be related to the outcomes achieved by the participants who were served at different points in time.

Research Design

The developmental nature of program and system development obviously has implications for research and evaluation design. The "gold standard" in services research and evaluation is using experimental designs in which participants are randomly assigned to conditions. One illustration of the esteem in which this design is held comes from Hollister and Hill (1995), who stated, "For quantitative evaluators random assignment designs are a bit like the nectar of gods: once you've had a taste of the pure stuff it is hard to settle for the flawed alternatives" (p. 134).

The use of randomized design to determine the effectiveness of particular services, such as multisystemic therapy or case management with wraparound, is certainly possible and doable (Clark et al., 1994; Evans et al., 1994; Scherer et al., 1994), although there are a number of risks. According to Burns (in press), among the situations that can contribute to a failure to find an effect when it is there include the following methodological problems: (a) sample size is inadequate; (b) outcome measures may not be sensitive to the wide variety of disorders of children with serious emotional disturbances, or may not be developmentally appropriate or sensitive to change; (c) as already indicated, implementation of both the experimental and control interventions requires constant monitoring and may not be carried out as intended; (d) such studies often require multiple years to enroll and follow the needed number of youngsters, during which time it is not unusual for there to be changes in the external environment that affect the intervention; and (e) it is difficult to enlist and maintain the cooperation of the clinicians who are providing the intervention. Burns (1994, in press) noted that because controlled studies involve a demanding set of requirements and are costly to conduct, they should be reserved for special situations. Moreover, they should be used with high-cost, high-risk interventions, such as alternatives to hospitalization and residential placement.

Thus, random designs should not constitute the first effort to evaluate an intervention. The most reasonable approach is to wait until an intervention has reached an acceptable level of implementation and other evaluative data suggest that it is impacting favorably on participants before launching the more costly and rigorous controlled study. Unfortunately, however, proposals to do less rigorous program evaluations as a prelude to controlled studies often are not looked on favorably by potential funders, particularly government funders. Nor are such funders likely to provide the resources to allow the developmental time needed for new interventions to reach a level of implementation that is appropriate for a rigorous controlled study. As a consequence, the pressure is on researchers and evaluators to propose controlled studies prematurely. Such premature studies do the interventions a disservice; often yield results that are, at best, hard to interpret; and raise skepticism about the potential value of research and evaluation.

In determining the effectiveness of particular services, although the realities of finding appropriate funding are a major stumbling block, determining appropriate methodology, at least, seems achievable. The desirable approach is to allow services adequate time to reach a high level of implementation, to gather data on level of implementation over time, to also gather data on child and family outcome over time (using pre-post and other types of time-series designs, for example), and then to design and implement a more rigorous controlled study when (and if) the preliminary evaluation results are encouraging and the level of implementation of the intervention is appropriate.

Although the course is certainly not easy from a methodological or a practical standpoint, it presents a different challenge than evaluating the effectiveness of community-based systems of care.

Where the unit of analysis is the overall community-based system, it is not feasible to use a design that includes random assignment of children or families, regardless of the intervention's stage of development. In discussing comprehensive community-wide initiatives, Hollister and Hill (1995) indicated,

> Community-wide programs present special problems for evaluators because the "nectar of the gods"—random assignment of individuals to program treatment and to a control group—is beyond their research. The central problem of impact evaluations, creating a reasonable and convincing counter factual (what would have happened in the absence of the program intervention), remains a major challenge. (p. 158)

Given the inability to use the "gold standard" to evaluate the effectiveness of community-wide interventions and an increased focus in children's mental health and other related systems on the need for community-wide interventions, one development has been a shift from asking questions such as that posed above by Hollister and Hill (what would have happened in the absence of the program intervention?) to a broader knowledge development focus. Brown (1995) described this as placing "less emphasis on discovering the one, objective truth about a program's worth and more attention to the multiple perspectives that diverse interests bring to judgment and understanding" (p. 204). This focus often involves the use of multiple methods, including both qualitative and quantitative; the gathering of information from multiple sources; a more participatory model of interaction between evaluators and those sources of information, be they administrators, practitioners, parents, or youngsters among others; and a more developmental approach to studying the process of change.

Knapp (1995), in talking about the evaluation of comprehensive, collaborative services for children and families, emphasized the need for studies to be strongly conceptualized (particularly presenting a clear theory of action), descriptive (including both qualitative and quantitative data), comparative (looking across communities), and constructively skeptical. He emphasized the importance of research and evaluation "that trace backward from the experiences, behavior, perceptions, and status of service recipients" (p. 12) as a means of determining how or if system level changes impact at the level of the child and family. The intensive case methodology described earlier (Groves, 1994) is one strategy for doing this.

Yin (1994), the major leader in case study approaches to evaluation, has predicted that methodologically and conceptually there will be a gradual integration of quantitative and qualitative evaluation methodologies. He specifically listed such quantitative methods as quasi-experiments, surveys, true experiments, and quantitative analysis of archival records and such qualitative methods as case study research, ethnography, participant-observation, fieldwork, and life histories. Such a variety of methods and approaches cannot entirely avoid some of the selection biases and confounds that may make interpretation of the data difficult. But in a field in which it is generally acknowledged that interventions must be sensitive to the community and cultural context in which they take place, the issue of determining at a high level of probability that a particular community-wide intervention leads to a certain set of outcomes may not be the most relevant issue. Instead, it may be more helpful to make general assessments of the extent to which findings "converge" on a particular conclusion and to advance knowledge through gathering ongoing and comprehensive data of multiple types from multiple sources.

Brown (1995) indicated, "What is important is that a research and demonstration context is created in which evaluators are provided with the resources they need and are encouraged to work with community initiatives to develop and try out new ways of learning about how these initiatives work and how their long-term impacts can be enhanced" (pp. 218-219). She advocated moving beyond evaluation to simply determine the impact of a particular intervention to creating a "learning culture" that encourages and incorporates a range of strategies both for generating knowledge and for improving practice.

Conclusions

This analysis of issues related to assessing effectiveness of services and service delivery systems leads to several conclusions.

1. It is apparent that most of the changes in services and service delivery systems since the beginning of the 1980s have originated with practitioners in the field. These changes have been supported by program evaluations that primarily have used system outcome measures rather than child or family outcome measures. Moreover, changes have occurred despite the absence of research and evaluation efforts with tight designs and high internal validity. It may be that the absence of the constraints of such designs has contributed to the successful expansion of the models or it may be simply that the field has not yet progressed to the point for conducting rigorous tests of the effectiveness of these models.

2. Although those in the field have emphasized the values and principles that should serve as a foundation for the development of services and service systems, there has been very little attention to theories of change. This lack of attention to program theory serves as an obstacle to research and evaluation on effectiveness and also may be holding back overall progress in the field.

3. Investigators have similarly placed very little emphasis on describing the interventions to be tested and assessing the adequacy of the implementation of these interventions. The task of assessing implementation is clearly a difficult one because the interventions are complex, individualized, and multifaceted and often occur at both the service and the system levels. Yet until the issue of assessing implementation is addressed seriously, progress in determining effectiveness through rigorous research and evaluation studies will be limited.

4. As investigators in the field move to examine interventions that are system- or community-wide, randomized designs become inapplicable. Even with studies of the effectiveness of particular services that are not community-wide, there are important restrictions on the applicability of randomized designs. This presents a challenge to those in the field to develop and use other methodologies. Such approaches should begin with clear conceptualizations of the theory of change, include a thorough assessment of the adequacy of the intervention (not just from a single point in time or static perspective but from a developmental perspective), and include multiple methods and information gathered from multiple sources. The methods may need to be both quantitative, including such alternatives to randomized field trials as quasi-experimental designs, and qualitative to enable better understanding of the overall impact of the intervention while also determining how it affects the children and families who are served. It may not be possible for investigators in such studies to draw clear inferences about causality. Knowledge grows incrementally, however, and studies that provide an opportunity to determine how and if different methods converge on the same finding can do a great service to the field.

5. It is hoped that funding sources, be they government agencies or foundations, will invest in the types of long-term studies that are critical to studying the development of new interventions, assessing the adequacy of their implementation, and determining their impact through multiple methods. If studies are not properly funded and conducted, the field runs the dual risk of failing to gain needed practical knowledge and coming up with misleading conclusions that can set the field back.

The challenge of developing new service and system of care approaches to better support children with serious emotional disturbances and their families has been an enormous one. It has proceeded more rapidly than the research and evaluation field, and as a result, there is much knowledge about effectiveness, particularly about child and family functioning, that needs to be gathered. The pace of change at the community level, and certainly at a governmental level, suggests that this situation of service change moving more rapidly than evaluations can keep up with is only going to increase. If knowledge development through systematic research and evaluation efforts is going to progress as is needed, the field of research and evaluation needs to move rapidly and creatively to develop and test new strategies and refine existing strategies for determining effectiveness.

References

Attkisson, C. C., Dresser, K., & Rosenblatt, A. (1993). Service systems for youth with severe emotional disorder: System of care research in California. In L. Bickman & D. Rog (Eds.), *Creating a children's mental health system: Research, policy, and evaluation* (pp. 236-280). Newbury Park, CA: Sage.

Beachler, M. (1990). The Mental Health Services Program for Youth. *Journal of Mental Health Administration, 17,* 115-121.

Behar, L. (1985). Changing patterns of state responsibility: A case study of North Carolina. *Journal of Clinical Child Psychology, 14,* 188-199.

Bickman, L. (Ed.). (1987). *Using program theory in evaluation.* San Francisco: Jossey-Bass.

Bickman, L. (1996). Reinterpreting the Fort Bragg evaluation findings: The message does not change. *Journal of Mental Health Administration, 23*(1), 137-145.

Bickman, L., Guthrie, P. R., Foster, E. M., Lambert, E. W., Summerfelt, W. T., Breda, C. S., & Heflinger, C. A. (1995). *Evaluating managed mental health services: The Fort Bragg experiment.* New York: Plenum.

Bickman, L., & Heflinger, C. A. (1995). Seeking success by reducing implementation and evaluation failures. In L. Bickman & D. Rog (Eds.), *Children's mental health services: Research, policy, and evaluation* (pp. 171-205). Thousand Oaks, CA: Sage.

Brown, P. (1995). The role of the evaluator in comprehensive community initiatives. In J. P. Connell, A. C. Kubisch, L. B. Schorr, & C. H. Weiss (Eds.), *New approaches to evaluating community initiatives* (pp. 201-225). Washington, DC: Aspen Institute.

Burchard, J. D., Burchard, S. N., Sewell, R., & VanDenBerg, J. (1993). *One kid at a time: The case study evaluation and implementation of the Alaska Youth Initiative Demonstration Project.* Washington, DC: Georgetown University Press.

Burchard, J. D., & Clarke, R. T. (1990). The role of individualized care in a service delivery system for children and adolescents with severely maladjusted behavior. *Journal of Mental Health Administration, 17,* 48-60.

Burns, B. J. (1994). The challenges of child mental health services research. *Journal of Emotional and Behavioral Disorders, 2,* 254-259.

Burns, B. J. (in press). What drives outcomes for emotional and behavioral disorders in children and adolescents? In D. M. Steinwachs, L. Flynn, & D. Norquist (Eds.), *Using outcomes to improve care: New directions in mental health services.* San Francisco: Jossey-Bass.

Clark, H. B., Prange, M. E., Lee, B., Boyd, L. A., McDonald, B. A., & Stewart, E. S. (1994). Improving adjustment outcomes for foster children with emotional and behavioral disorders: Early findings from a controlled study on individualized services. *Journal of Emotional and Behavioral Disorders, 2,* 207-218.

Cross, T. L., Bazron, B. J., Dennis, K. W., & Isaacs, M. R. (1989). *Towards a culturally competent system of care*. Washington, DC: Georgetown University Child Development Center, CASSP Technical Assistance Center.

Dennis, K. (1992, April). *The history of wraparound and the role of families*. Paper presented at the First Annual Wraparound Conference, Pittsburgh, PA.

Duchnowski, A. J., Berg, K., & Kutash, K. (1995). Parent participation in and perception of placement decisions. In J. M. Kauffman, J. W. Lloyd, T. A. Astutu, & D. P. Hallahan (Eds.), *Issues in the educational placement of pupils with emotional or behavioral disorders* (pp. 183-196). Hillsdale, NJ: Lawrence Erlbaum.

Duchnowski, A. J., & Friedman, R. M. (1990). Children's mental health: Challenges for the nineties. *Journal of Mental Health Administration, 17*, 3-12.

Edna McConnell Clark Foundation. (1985). *Keeping families together: A case for family preservation*. New York: Author.

Evans, M. E., Armstrong, M. I., Dollard, N., Kuppinger, A. D., Huz, S., & Wood, V. M. (1994). Development and evaluation of treatment foster care and family-centered intensive case management in New York. *Journal of Emotional and Behavioral Disorders, 2*, 228-239.

Fraser, M. W., Pecora, P. J., & Haapala, D. A. (1988). *Families in crisis: Final report on the family-based intensive treatment program*. Salt Lake City: University of Utah, Social Research Institute.

Friedman, R. M. (1983, August). *The status of children's mental health services and policy in Florida*. Paper presented at the Children's Mental Health Conference, Tampa, FL.

Friedman, R. M. (1989). Service system research: Implications of a systems perspective. In P. Greenbaum, R. M. Friedman, A. Duchnowski, K. Kutash, & S. Silver (Eds.), *Children's mental health services and policy: Building a research base—Conference proceedings* (pp. 1-6). Tampa: University of South Florida, Florida Mental Health Institute.

Friedman, R. M. (1996). Child mental health policy. In B. L. Levin & J. Petrila (Eds.), *Mental health services: Public health perspective* (pp. 234-248). New York: Oxford University Press.

Friedman, R. M., & Burns, B. (1996). The evaluation of the Fort Bragg Demonstration Project: An alternative interpretation of the findings. *Journal of Mental Health Administration, 23*, 128-136.

Friedman, R. M., & Hernandez, M. (1993, October). *Special challenges in evaluating multisite system reform efforts: A focus on mental health services*. Paper presented at the Fifteenth Annual Research Conference of the Association for Public Policy Analysis and Management, Washington, DC.

Friedman, R. M., Kutash, K., & Duchnowski, A. J. (1996). The population of concern: Defining the issues. In B. A. Stroul (Ed.), *Children's mental health: Creating systems of care in a changing society* (pp. 69-96). Baltimore, MD: Paul H. Brookes.

Friesen, B., & Koroloff, M. (1990). Challenges for child and adolescent mental health. *Health Affairs, 11*, 125-136.

Groves, I. (1994). *Performance and outcome review*. Tampa: University of South Florida, Florida Mental Health Institute.

Henggeler, S. W., & Borduin, C. M. (1990). *Family therapy and beyond: A multisystemic approach to treating the behavior problems of children and adolescents*. Pacific Grove, CA: Brooks/Cole.

Henggeler, S. W., & Borduin, C. M. (1995). Multisystemic treatment of serious juvenile offenders and their families. In I. M. Schwartz & P. AuClaire (Eds.), *Home-based services for troubled children* (pp. 113-130). Lincoln: University of Nebraska Press.

Henggeler, S. W., Melton, G. B., Smith, L. A., Schoenwald, S. K., & Hanley, J. H. (1993). Family preservation using multisystemic treatment: Long-term follow-up to a clinical trial with serious juvenile offenders. *Journal of Child and Family Studies, 2,* 283-293.

Hoagwood, K., Hibbs, E., Brent, D., & Jensen, P. (1995). Introduction to the special section: Efficacy and effectiveness in studies of child and adolescent psychotherapy. *Journal of Clinical and Consulting Psychology, 63,* 683-687.

Hollister, R. G., & Hill, J. (1995). Problems in the evaluation of community-wide initiatives. In J. P. Connell, A. C. Kubisch, L. B. Schorr, & C. H. Weiss (Eds.), *New approaches to evaluating community initiatives: Concepts, methods, and contexts* (pp. 127-172). Washington, DC: Aspen Institute.

Johnsen, M. C., Morrissey, J. P., & Calloway, M. O. (1995, November). *Structure and change in child mental health services delivery network.* Paper presented at the annual meeting of the American Public Health Association, Washington, DC.

Jordan, D. D., & Hernandez, M. (1990). The Ventura Planning Model: A proposal for mental health reform. *Journal of Mental Health Administration, 17,* 25-47.

Kazdin, A. E. (1987). Treatment of antisocial behavior in children: Current status and future directions. *Psychological Bulletin, 102,* 187-203.

Kinney, J., Madsen, B., Fleming, T., & Haapala, D. (1977). Homebuilders: Keeping families together. *Journal of Consulting and Clinical Psychology, 45,* 667-673.

Knapp, M. S. (1995). How shall we study comprehensive collaborative services for children and families? *Educational Researcher, 24,* 5-16.

Knitzer, J. (1982). *Unclaimed children: The failure of public responsibility to children and adolescents in need of mental health services.* Washington, DC: Children's Defense Fund.

Kutash, K., Duchnowski, A. J., & Sondheimer, D. L. (1994). Building the research base for children's mental health services. *Journal of Emotional and Behavioral Disorders, 2,* 194-197.

Lee, J. (1994). The C-Port pilot test procedures. *The Advocate, 5,* 4-7.

MACRO International & University of South Florida. (1995). *Evaluation of the Comprehensive Mental Health Services Program for Children with Severe Emotional Disturbances: Overview of the evaluation.* Atlanta, GA: Macro International.

Malysiak, R. (1995). *Same as it ever was? The hope and challenge for the wraparound model.* Paper presented at Building on Family Strengths, the Sixth Annual National Conference on Research and Services in Support of Children and Their Families, Portland State University, Portland, OR.

Morrissey, J. P. (1992). An interorganizational network approach to evaluating children's mental health service systems. In L. Bickman & D. Rog (Eds.), *Evaluating mental health services for children* (pp. 85-98). San Francisco: Jossey-Bass.

Morrissey, J. P., Johnsen, M. C., & Calloway, M. O. (1995, November). *Evaluating performance and change in mental health systems serving children and youth: An interorganizational network approach.* Paper presented at the annual meeting of the American Public Health Association, Washington, DC.

Nyberg, T. (1992, March). *Family service planning teams: An initial survey.* Paper presented at the annual conference A System of Care for Children's Mental Health: Expanding the Research Base, Tampa, FL.

O'Neal, L. (1995). The children's plan outcome review team. *The Advocate, 5,* 1-7.

Patton, M. Q. (1994). Developmental evaluation. *Evaluation Practice, 15,* 311-319.

Robinson, R. A., & Whitbeck, J. (1993). Facilitating tailored care for children with severe emotional disturbance in their communities: Fifteen case studies. In K. Kutash, C. J. Liberton, A. Algarin, & R. M. Friedman (Eds.), *A system of care for children's mental health: Expanding the research base, 5th annual research conference proceedings* (pp. 255-261). Tampa: University of South Florida, Florida Mental Health Institute.

Rossi, P. (1992). Strategies for evaluation. *Children and Youth Services Review, 14*, 167-191.

Scherer, D. G., Brondino, M. J., Henggeler, S. W., Melton, G. B., & Hanley, J. H. (1994). Multisystemic family preservation therapy: Preliminary findings from a study of rural and minority serious adolescent offenders. *Journal of Emotional and Behavioral Disorders, 2*, 198-206.

Schorr, L. B. (1995, September). *New approaches to evaluation: Helping sister Mary Paul, Geoff Canada, and Otis Johnson while convincing Pat Moynihan, Newt Gingrich, and the American public.* Presentation at the Second Annual Research/Evaluation Conference, Annie E. Casey Foundation, Baltimore.

Stroul, B. A., & Friedman, R. M. (1986). *A system of care for severely emotionally disturbed children and youth.* Washington, DC: Georgetown University Child Development Center, CASSP Technical Assistance Center.

Stroul, B. A., Friedman, R. M., Hernandez, M., Roebuck, L., Lourie, I. S., & Koyanagi, C. (1996). Systems of care in the future. In B. A. Stroul (Ed.), *Systems of care for children and adolescents with severe emotional disturbances: From theory to reality* (pp. 591-612). Baltimore, MD: Paul H. Brookes.

Stroul, B. A., & Goldman, S. K. (1990). Study of community-based services for children and adolescents who are severely emotionally disturbed. *Journal of Mental Health Administration, 17*, 61-77.

Stroul, B. A., Goldman, S., Lourie, I., Katz-Leavy, J., & Zeigler-Dendy, C. (1992). *Profiles of local systems of care for children and adolescents with severe emotional disturbances.* Washington, DC: Georgetown University Child Development Center, CASSP Technical Assistance Center.

Usher, L. (1995, September). *Outcomes.* Presentation to the Second Annual Research/Evaluation Conference, Annie E. Casey Foundation, Baltimore, MD.

VanDenBerg, J. (1990). The Alaska Youth Initiative: An experiment in individualized treatment and education. In A. Algarin, R. M. Friedman, A. J. Duchnowski, K. M. Kutash, S. E. Silver, & M. K. Johnson (Eds.), *2nd annual conference proceedings: Children's mental health services and policy: Building a research base* (pp. 59-72). Tampa: University of South Florida, Florida Mental Health Institute.

VanDenBerg, J. (1992, April). *Modifying categorical services.* Paper presented at the First National Wraparound Conference, Pittsburgh, PA.

Weiss, C. H. (1995). Nothing as practical as good theory: Exploring theory-based evaluation for comprehensive community initiatives for children and families. In J. P. Connell, A. C. Kubisch, L. B. Schorr, & C. H. Weiss (Eds.), *New approaches to evaluating community initiatives: Concepts, methods, and contexts* (pp. 65-92). Washington, DC: Aspen Institute.

Weisz, J. R., Weiss, B., & Donenberg, G. R. (1992). The lab versus the clinics: Effects of child and adolescent psychotherapy. *American Psychologist, 47*, 1578-1585.

Wells, K., & Beigel, D. E. (Eds.). (1991). *Family preservation services: Research and evaluation.* Newbury Park, CA: Sage.

Whitbeck, J. (1993, April). *Beyond the numbers: Practical research.* Paper presented at the Second National Wraparound Conference, St. Charles, IL.

Yin, R. K. (1994). Discovering the future of the case study method in evaluation research. *Evaluation Practice, 15,* 283-290.

Yoe, J. T., Bruns, E., & Burchard, J. (1995). Evaluating individualized services in Vermont: Behavioral and service outcomes. In C. J. Liberton, K. Kutash, & R. M. Friedman (Eds.), *A system of care for children's mental health: Expanding the research base, 7th annual research conference proceedings* (pp. 9-14). Tampa: University of South Florida, Florida Mental Health Institute.

Many Hands Make Mental
Health Systems of Care a Reality

Lessons From the Mental Health
Services Program for Youth

THEODORE P. CROSS

LEONARD SAXE

Mental health care for children is undergoing profound change with fundamental tenets about how services should be provided being challenged by advocates, policymakers, and researchers (cf. Institute of Medicine, 1989; National Commission on Children, 1991). Efforts are nevertheless maturing to implement new types of coordinated community-based services (see Friedman, 1994; Knitzer, 1993), and there is substantial interest in determining how to enhance provision of effective and efficient care for children with mental disorders. In the present chapter, we describe findings from the evaluation of a national demonstration of children's mental health service systems and reflect on the state of development of systems of care. Our focus is on the feasibility of efforts to manage mental health care and the variety of ways in which system of care principles are applied in different communities.

In 1988, the Robert Wood Johnson Foundation (RWJF) initiated a national demonstration, the Mental Health Services Program for Youth (MHSPY), to test the operationalization of a set of principles about the provision of mental health care (Beachler, 1990; Cole & Poe, 1993; England & Cole, 1992; Saxe, Cross, Lovas, & Gardner, 1995). The goal of RWJF was to demonstrate the feasibility of coordinated systems of care to integrate services across a community's child-serving agencies. The theory was that coordinated community-based services could reduce reliance on out-of-home placements of children and make more efficient use of limited mental health resources. MHSPY fostered the idea that one could harness better the efforts of many in the community—an idea that was ripe to be implemented. The evolving consensus that children were being poorly served by a fragmented service system made the effort even more imperative (Knitzer, 1982; Saxe, Cross, Silverman, & Batchelor, 1987). Political changes that emphasized devolution of responsibility from agencies to local communities and limits on the growth of health and social services made MHSPY's premises even more compelling. The emergence of managed health care provided a parallel model. The ideas behind MHSPY began as innovative but have now been widely disseminated and become accepted wisdom about care for children with serious emotional disturbances.

MHSPY was successful in part simply by dint of having been established. The creation of a system of care at MHSPY sites made clear that managing children's mental health care was feasible and provision of community-based service was more than a rhetorical possibility (see Saxe et al., 1987). Systematic assessment of MHSPY adds detail and an explanatory framework to this accomplishment. The details suggest that although systems of care are feasible, much remains to be learned about how to deliver therapeutically effective care that is financially viable. No single model of care appears to provide the best care. The key seems to be the adaptation of the system to the needs of the children and their families. A central ingredient appears to be the availability of funds that can be used flexibly for a continuum of services and interventions specially tailored to the needs of children and families.

Consensus About the Problem

Prior to the development of MHSPY, the deplorable state of services for children with mental disorders was repeatedly documented by advocacy organizations and government agencies. The Children's Defense Fund (CDF) report *Unclaimed Children* (Knitzer, 1982) was one of the first in a series of systematic assessments of children's mental health services. Knitzer noted that among the 2 million U.S. children with severe emotional disturbances (SED), few received adequate mental health services. The report identified fragmentation of services as a core problem and urged development of coordinated systems of care.

In 1986, the Congressional Office of Technology Assessment (OTA) conducted a study on children's mental health problems (see Saxe et al., 1987) that documented the substantial gap between the numbers of children in need of treatment and those who actually receive treatment. It was conservatively estimated that 12% of children had a diagnosable mental disorder, yet only a small proportion of these children received appropriate services. The existing system of care focused most resources on a small number of children placed in residential settings, with the majority of children unable to access appropriate care.

The documented need for services led to calls for the development of community-based systems of care to provide effective services to children with serious emotional disorders. The essential ingredient of these programs is placing children (and families) at the center of a managed care system and ensuring that a wide spectrum of community-based services is available as needed. Such system of care models have now been widely disseminated and federal and state mandates require communities to reorganize their services to provide less fragmented and more appropriate care.

Child and Adolescent
Service System Program

The principal federal initiative to promote children's mental health care systems is the Child and Adolescent Service System Program (CASSP) (Day & Roberts, 1991). CASSP was established in response to the perceived fragmentation of services provided to children with severe emotional disorders. Children typically receive services from multiple agencies, including child welfare, juvenile justice, education, and mental health services, and coordination across agencies is problematic (Stroul & Friedman, 1986). CASSP promoted systems of care to coordinate services, involve family members as partners, and promote individualized care provided in the least restrictive setting possible.

The CASSP philosophy posed an extraordinary challenge to public children's service systems. They were called on simultaneously to coordinate multiple, often entrenched, public agencies; to avoid hospitalization; to provide a continuum of care with a menu of intermediate services (some of which needed to be created); to involve families; and to provide case management, individualize care, and be culturally competent. The development of systems of care was initially slow and focused on the organizational level. CASSP, created in 1984, promulgated system of care principles and funded states to plan and implement interagency organizational development. Policy and organizational structures developed in many states, but in other states, services remained categorical and fragmented. Inadequate development of the system of care at the local level and lack of funding for community-based services hindered implementation.

Through CASSP, the system of care conceptual model (Stroul, 1993; Stroul & Friedman, 1986) guided efforts to change children's mental health care in virtually all states. By stressing the importance of a full array of services and integration of the efforts of multiple child-serving agencies, new emphasis was given to systems as active agents to provide effective children's mental health care. This model also promoted quality of care and focused attention on creating effective and efficient services.

Developing comprehensive child- and family-focused care has tremendous appeal, but some contend that the theory has not been articulated (see, e.g., Bickman, 1996a, b), and there have been many questions about the feasibility of the theory. Systems of care require behaviors that have *not* been characteristic of human service agencies: cooperation rather than competition among agencies, flexible use of monies, treatment planning based exclusively on the individual needs of children and families, strong family involvement in decision making, and culturally sensitive policy and intervention. With so much system change required, feasibility is understandably a primary question.

CASSP has had a profound effect on how states organize care for children and families dealing with emotional disorders, yet there is little evaluative data on the effectiveness of the resulting systems (Bickman, 1996, in press; Weisz, Weiss, & Donenberg, 1992). CASSP principles continue to drive reorganization of systems of care and provide important conceptual direction for developing systems, but they have been based on limited research evidence. Moreover, there is a paucity of outcome data about the effectiveness of these systems.

Fort Bragg Demonstration

The Fort Bragg Child and Adolescent Mental Health Demonstration provided a coordinated continuum of children's mental health care at Fort Bragg, North Carolina, beginning in June 1990 (Behar, 1996; Bickman et al., 1995). The continuum of care was designed to offer a wide range of services to be more responsive to the needs of children and families and avoid unnecessarily restrictive treatments, such as psychiatric hospitalization. The demonstration emphasized intermediate services such as in-home crisis stabilization, after-school group treatment, therapeutic homes, and crisis management to help fill the gap between outpatient psychotherapy and institutional treatment. The demonstration was conducted as a quasi-experiment in which care provided at Fort Bragg was compared with care provided at two other military bases.

Care provided at the demonstration expanded dramatically and tripled the number of children served at baseline, far outstripping the number of children having access to care in two comparison sites. Implementation was difficult at first because providers were apparently responding to pent-up demand; nevertheless, the evaluation found that by the third year services were of high caliber and implemented according to the program model. Children in the demonstration were less likely to use hospital and residential treatment, but also less likely to use outpatient treatment only; intermediate services were more frequent. Children in the demonstration had significantly more therapy visits and longer time in treatment. Clinical outcomes, however, were generally no different. Children at both the demonstration and comparison sites improved, but the demonstration did not lead to better scores on mental health measures. Moreover, the demonstration was more expensive, spending 1.5 times more money per child than the comparison, though this could not necessarily be attributed to the model of care used (Behar, 1996; Bickman et al., 1995).

The Fort Bragg evaluation has achieved notoriety because it challenges widely held beliefs about the superiority of a continuum of care approach for improving children's mental health outcomes. Several aspects of the evaluation need to be noted, however (see also Bickman, 1996a, b; Cross, 1996; Friedman & Burns, 1996; Saxe & Cross, in press). First, the evaluation showed that a comprehensive continuum of care could be developed, something that had not been empirically demonstrated. Second, the demonstration significantly increased access to services for children in need. Third, children in the demonstration and the comparison *both* improved to comparable degrees. The Fort Bragg project has raised serious questions about the system of care model. It reaffirmed the capacity of the model to increase access to care and maintain children outside of hospitals and residential treatment, but the lack of superiority in clinical outcomes and inflated costs have led both to calls for more research and attention to cost control within systems of care.

Center for Mental Health Services Program

The Center for Mental Health Services, an office in the federal Substance Abuse and Mental Health Services Administration (SAMHSA), funded a national demonstration of children's mental health systems of care in 22 sites across the country, the Comprehensive Community Mental Health Services Program for Children with Serious Emotional Disturbances (CMHS Services Program). Influenced by both MHSPY and the Fort Bragg Demonstration, this program is the first federal initiative to fund services according to a system of care model. Funding supports both system development and service delivery, and a national evaluation is in progress.

Mental Health Services Program for Youth

MHSPY was designed to demonstrate that systems of care could be implemented in local communities and radically change the delivery of care to children with serious emotional disturbance (SED) (Beachler, 1990; Cole & Poe, 1993; England & Cole, 1992; Saxe, Gardner, & Cross, 1993; Saxe et al., 1995). The demonstration was explicitly aimed to change how care was organized and financed in eight sites across the country that represented diverse geographic and demographic areas. Projects were joint endeavors between state and local agencies and so are identified by the state name, even though most projects focused on specific local communities. The sites were as follows:

- California—San Francisco
- Kentucky—Bluegrass region
- North Carolina—Smoky Mountain and Blue Ridge Area Programs
- Ohio—Cleveland and East Cleveland
- Oregon—Multnomah County (Portland area)
- Pennsylvania—Delaware County (north of Philadelphia)
- Vermont—entire state
- Wisconsin—Dane County (Madison area)

MHSPY provided funds for services but also required that each site establish a state-local partnership to develop the system of care, implement case management, and generate financial reforms. Each site was funded to serve approximately 200 of the children with the most severe emotional disturbance in that particular area. All of the projects involved collaborations among mental health; child welfare; education; and, with one exception, juvenile justice. Sites aimed to avoid hospitalization and keep children in the community through the establishment of an expanded continuum of care in each community, implementation of case management with an individualized care philosophy, and financing to promote this model of alternative care. Project development was devoted to the establishment and elaboration of interagency coordination and the creation and expansion of community-based services. New and expanded services included therapeutic foster care; crisis intervention; independent living programs; intensive home visiting; and other services intended to provide flexible, intensive interventions in the community.

Evaluation of MHSPY

The evaluation of MHSPY was designed to assess how changes in the organization and financing of mental health care can improve the provision of care to children with SED. The primary unit of analysis was the system of care. The evaluation was thus focused on the administrative and financial structures and processes that support the delivery of care. The evaluation emphasized description of the diversity of forms of an effective system of care and how implementation of systems of care varies across sites in response to differences in population, geography, financing, administrative and legal structures, and local history.

The evaluation had three distinct components (see Saxe et al., 1995):

1. *Organizational and Financial Assessment.* Detailed case studies were developed on each of eight sites to understand in depth how care was organized and financed. Site documents were reviewed and site visits conducted including interviews, focus groups, and observation.

2. *Client Information System.* Client information systems were developed for all of the sites. The information system was designed to provide data about client demographics and problems, treatment plan, services provided, and annual status on several outcome variables. The original plan to develop a common client information system for all the sites proved infeasible; instead, sites used their own data systems and data were integrated by the national evaluation team (see Cross, Gardner, & Friedman, 1993; Hallfors, Cross, & Roan, 1993).

3. *Clinical Assessment Conferences.* Conducted by expert clinicians on a sample of cases at each site (see Solnit, Adnopoz, & Fallon, 1993), the clinical assessment conference provided an analysis of the quality of care and an appraisal of the contribution of the interagency system of care to the child's treatment. Several cases were reassessed a second or third time over the 5-year demonstration period.

Feasibility

A primary evaluation question concerns the feasibility of widespread development of systems of care. Many obstacles could hinder implementation. A system of care requires coordination of multiple children's service agencies, which are often at odds in states and local communities. It requires the availability of a continuum of community-based services, which often have not been developed. It requires the capacity to develop and follow through on treatment plans involving multiple services. It requires changes in attitudes about the appropriateness of community-based care, the level of family involvement, and the use of care that is individualized and culturally competent. Changes in financing to support new models of care are also necessary. Despite successes in individual communities (e.g., Ventura County, California; see Jordan & Hernandez, 1990), systems of care had never before been created on a systematic, widespread basis. Our initial analysis, therefore, concerns whether it is feasible to implement systems of care.

The data from the evaluation converged to support the hypothesis that systems of care were indeed feasible with the appropriate organizational and financial support. Most elements of the system of care were implemented in the sites, even though some gaps in the systems remain and system development continues. Moreover, the systems of care were stable. The structures and services created by MHSPY almost invariably remained after the project was completed.

Community-Based Care. A major tenet of the system of care philosophy is providing care in the community. MHSPY aimed to maintain children at risk of psychiatric hospitalization in the community while still providing for their multiple, often intensive, service needs. The data provide evidence that the demonstration accomplished this goal. Service data from the client information system demonstrated that hospitalization and residential treatment rarely were used during the 1- to 2-year periods per site during which services were tracked. For most sites, the percentage of MHSPY children in residential or hospital treatment was 5% or less during the 1- to 2-year treatment period studied (except in Kentucky, where 10% were hospitalized at the beginning of treatment and 8% at 12 months of treatment). Low levels of hospitalization and residential treatment were achieved in MHSPY despite the fact that many of the children and youth had histories of residential or hospital treatment; because of the way they were selected, most were at high risk for placement or hospitalization (England & Cole, 1992), yet the rates of hospitalization and residential treatment were significantly below what one would have expected for the population.

Evidence from the client information system suggests that the continuums of care were maintained during the periods studied. There was substantial consistency within a site across the treatment period in the array of services. The percentages of clients receiving specific services remained fairly stable from the first 3-month time point to the end point of data collection. Therapy remained consistently frequent; brief interventions usually remained relatively frequent; within each site, the available intermediate services were maintained at the same level of utilization throughout the period studied; and residential and hospital treatment were consistently low. There were important exceptions, of course. Not surprisingly, evaluation and screening services (the Early and Periodic Screening and Treatment Program [EPSDT] in Pennsylvania) tended to decline with longer duration of treatment. In Kentucky, the use of brief interventions tended to decline with time in treatment. In Vermont, residential treatment declined but therapeutic foster care increased over time in treatment. North Carolina—Blue Ridge experienced a slight increase in hospitalization. Nevertheless, the overall trend was toward consistency.

Changes in financing services were instrumental in providing a wider range of services and a fit between families' and children's needs and services. In response to MHSPY's emphasis on innovation and the movement toward change in financing, sites made changes, often radical, that continued when MHSPY ended. Many of the new and expanded services developed by MHSPY sites were based on such financing innovations as pooled funding, wraparound funds, and innovative use of federal entitlements (see discussion of financing below).

Systems Development. MHSPY also actively changed the system of child-serving agencies in each site to improve access to care, increase coordination of multiple services, ensure appropriateness, and increase availability and flexibility of financing. Data from the Organizational/Financial Assessment provide detail about the nature of changes. The general trend over the 5-year program was toward ever greater interagency coordination and close working relationships between different child-serving agencies.

During MHSPY, existing interagency structures in Kentucky and Vermont consolidated and extended their influence on care philosophy and practice. They developed new services, implemented training programs in system of care models, and tried innovative financing methods. Interagency working groups emerged from the central interagency structures to deal with specific issues such as training, outcomes, programming, case review, and technical assistance to local communities.

By the project's end, Vermont was discussing redefining interagency teams to serve a wider range of children and changing the governance structure in some communities so that interagency collaboration would be extended to the day-to-day management of services. The California, North Carolina, Ohio, Oregon, Pennsylvania, and Wisconsin sites all formed new local interagency groups during MHSPY for such functions as case review, program development, and management of specialized services.

One striking accomplishment was the staying power of the elements of the systems of care developed by projects. In every site but Pennsylvania, most of the services and structures created by MHSPY survived beyond the end of funding from RWJF. Even Pennsylvania maintained several organizational and program structures begun through MHSPY although the site withdrew from the project at midpoint. Sites replaced foundation funds from a variety of sources. Innovations at the Ohio site were supported by the county mental health board. Several innovations developed through MHSPY were directly or indirectly incorporated in managed mental health care plans developed by the states; for example, the Carolina Alternatives model in North Carolina.

Despite substantial development of services and systems, the sites fell short of ideal systems of care. One issue was the difficulty of establishing services to cover more than a few well-chosen points on the continuum of care. Typically, each site had at least some gaps in the continuum of care. North Carolina, for example, continually struggled to deal with a lack of residential treatment programs. Although systems of care are community based, there still is a need for residential treatment for a small number of children. In several sites, some child-serving agencies remained essentially outside the interagency systems of care and financing innovations often produced limited funding pools or supported services for a limited number of children. At project end, each site was still working to implement system of care principles fully.

The MHSPY data demonstrate that it is possible to maintain children with SED in the community through a variety of intermediate services and committed, creative interdisciplinary treatment teams, but that it requires substantial investment and willingness to tackle daunting obstacles, and sites may still have significant gaps in their systems. These data provide evidence that these MHSPY sites did indeed provide many elements of the system of care described in Stroul and Friedman (1986).

The vast majority of children were maintained in community settings; they received multiple, diverse services of varying intensity and restrictiveness; and services were maintained over the duration of treatment. It should be noted, however, that these data were not adequate to test fully whether systems of care were implemented, even in the sites covered; for example, we lack complete data on interventions from child welfare, juvenile justice, and education to provide a comprehensive picture of the functioning of a system of care. To the extent measured, however, it appears that sites had substantial success in establishing systems of care.

Application

In addition to showing the feasibility of systems of care, MHSPY demonstrated important lessons about how to apply the system of care principles to actual communities. In strategies of application, the eight sites share striking commonalities. At the level of actual implementation of system changes, however, diversity and sharp contrast characterize the sites.

The sites generally aimed to implement a similar menu of services, had comparable approaches to interacting with families, and used similar financing schemes. MHSPY's National Program Office was active in disseminating strategies, and the sites were receptive to using them. Several sites had similar histories of traditional children's mental services (e.g., reliance on outpatient therapy) as well as reliance on CASSP (e.g., the development of interagency organizational structures) that influenced the development of the systems of care under MHSPY (Lovas, Cross, Gardner, & Saxe, 1994).

Yet the sites varied substantially in nearly every element of design and implementation. Each site underwent a process of implementation influenced by its particular history, demography, and politics. Sites varied in

- Specific objectives for system changes
- Particular population labeled as the most seriously disturbed
- Services specialized in and utilized
- Methods of coordinating services
- Interaction of state and local professionals

- Methods of financing services
- Structure of systems

The evaluation data demonstrate that application was not straightforward, but involved a series of choices with many individual steps. In this section, we discuss the process of application of the system of care principles and the significant variation in how they were applied.

Community Context. Many common service elements were recognizable across sites, although the continuums of services across sites differed. All sites expanded their range of services and provided individualized care through case management and, to a lesser extent, wraparound services. The particular services that were developed varied by site, and the distribution of use of specific services differed greatly.

One commonality was the use of multiple services. Over a year of treatment, the mean number of services across sites provided, in addition to case management, ranged from 3.9 to 7.4, and the percentage of clients who received three or more services, in addition to case management, ranged from 82% to 99%. Interventions within a site varied in intensity and restrictiveness, from outpatient services to several different intermediate care services such as therapeutic foster care, group homes, and independent living programs. Both brief and longer-term interventions were used with some frequency, and both therapeutic and support services (recreation, basic needs, transportation) were also frequent. As noted above, inpatient and residential treatment were generally rare.

By design, case management was universal throughout the MHSPY program. Whatever other services children and their families received, they always had a case manager to manage their service plan, to help advocate for their interests, and to provide support and week-to-week problem solving. Often, case managers performed the same functions as a discrete service; for example, they provided parent support and education; arranged for help with basic needs; did brief home-based interventions; and in some cases, even helped provide recreational opportunities. Case managers often had access to flexible funds to organize individualized interventions that would not necessarily be recorded as a discrete service. Case management clearly played an enormous role in sites' efforts to create change for children and families.

Despite the common use of case management, the role of case managers varied across sites (see also Geismer, 1994). In Oregon, case managers had an especially prominent role. Clinically trained, they managed the array of services, oversaw therapeutic planning, and controlled each child's capitated allotment. Similarly, in Ohio, case managers played a strong part because they came from the Positive Education Program (PEP), which had a strong history of creative, individualized care that predated MHSPY. In Vermont, on the other hand, local treatment and interagency teams played a stronger role, and case managers gained ideas and authority from their participation in the teams. In the California project, case managers came from different service agencies and brought distinct skills into the project. The Wisconsin sites provided great diversity in case management, because case managers came not only from the parent service organization but also from six other private agencies: an African-American service agency, an outdoor skills-building program, an agency that works primarily with juvenile justice-involved youth, and three multiservices agencies.

In all sites, the majority of clients received some form of outpatient therapy, and this usually remained consistent across duration of treatment. Thus, despite growing awareness in the children's mental health field over the past 15 years of the limitations of outpatient therapy, the sites here consistently found it useful as one of a package of services. All sites also seemed to have at least one frequently used intensive, intermediate service in between outpatient services and residential or hospital treatment, designed to prevent placement outside the community. But the specific intermediate services used varied by site. Sites tended to specialize in one or two intermediate services. Kentucky, for example, provided home-based services to up to 53% of children and Pennsylvania to as many as 46%, whereas Vermont and North Carolina (specifically the Blue Ridge area) provided this service to no more than 5% of MHSPY children. North Carolina (Blue Ridge) and Wisconsin provided crisis services to 20% or more of children, but crisis service as a distinct intervention was rarely identified by other sites. Vermont employed therapeutic foster care for 21% or more of clients, but other sites used this service rarely. Often, a basic similarity underlay these interventions—providing substantial, strength-building support in the community by a professional offering a flexible, individualized re-sponse—but the models for doing this were specific to the site and depended on the particular needs, imagination, history, and skills of those in that site.

Other commonalities in service development existed. Five of eight MHSPY sites expanded crisis services because of the special risks and often-unpredictable course of treatment for children with SED. Five sites increased their level of home-based services to bring services to people proactively and intervene more effectively by helping people change their home environments directly. Six sites tried to expand thera-peutic foster care, but with mixed success. Therapeutic foster care pro-vides a home for children with SED and provides foster parents with additional professional support and resources. Sites often faced diffi-culty recruiting special foster parents or involving private provider agencies. Kentucky, North Carolina, Ohio, and Vermont expanded therapeutic foster care, but Oregon and Wisconsin could only try in-stead to support regular foster care with special, added services and money for individualized care. Most sites reached out to families of children with SED and increased parent education, parent support, and respite services (designed to provide temporary care for children and thus give parents a respite). Although many of the interventions devel-oped by the MHSPY sites were similar, the sites used several different approaches to expanding services, including

- Development of interagency public programs
- Development of community-based services among private provider agencies
- Utilization of wraparound services

Examples of each method follow.

Collaboration between public children's services agencies often pro-duced new service programs for children and families. In Vermont, mental health and education providers collaborated on a new program to provide mental health services in the schools using mental health personnel and education dollars, matched by Medicaid. A similar pro-gram was implemented to place mental health staff in local child wel-fare offices. The MHSPY project in San Francisco brought together staff from multiple service agencies in one organization providing case management and individualized care. In North Carolina, mental health and education services collaborated to develop a day treatment program, and interagency development of services is now common throughout the state.

Several MHSPY projects succeeded in expanding the variety of services available in the community by working with private agencies. In several cases, however, sites had to overcome resistance among private agencies to a community-based, individualized care approach, and the difficulty of engaging private agencies in the process remains an issue. The California MHSPY project negotiated "minicapitations" for neighborhood-based agencies. This strategy was expected to generate greater interest and make sure new programs serving the SED population were culturally sensitive. In North Carolina, a new pool of private providers emerged in response to Carolina Alternatives (the capitated Medicaid program for managed mental health care for children and adolescents), developed during the final years of MHSPY, because the pool of eligible providers was no longer limited to community mental health centers (CMHCs) and psychiatrists. In Ohio, agencies that had previously provided residential treatment services extended their role to offer specialized and therapeutic foster care as well.

After struggling to implement a structured system of care for SED children and youth through much of its grant period, Wisconsin's Children Come First ultimately obtained a wide range of services from several private nonprofit providers, as described above. Through this approach, Wisconsin expanded case management services, built on existing strengths of the service community, and improved its capacity to provide individualized services.

On other hand, the Oregon site could not engage private agencies successfully during MHSPY; few agencies responded to requests for proposals, and the proposals received were often inadequate. Oregon had to turn to a wraparound approach to cope with its lag in service development and ultimately heightened interest among providers and encouraged agencies to expand their own options to avoid being left out of the system. Although this was not the intended use of wraparound funds, realistically this often may be the result in overburdened systems lacking a full continuum of care and is better than the alternative of not providing for needs at all. The California MHSPY project in San Francisco also implemented a wraparound approach in response to difficulties in persuading private nonprofit providers to develop new services.

Innovation helped create diversity in the service programs. For example, California recruited several neighborhood agencies to create "packages" of services to offer families. Kentucky developed an outreach service to help children in private child care. By the end of MHSPY, North Carolina had developed a project to coordinate naturally occurring sources of support in the community and formal human services. The Vermont Department of Mental Health created collaborative service programs in the schools and child welfare offices. Wisconsin created a cadre of case aides providing diverse services and worked with a residential treatment center to provide limited residential stays with children maintaining their community activities and contacts with regular case workers while in residence.

System Models. MHSPY required considerable system development to achieve progress toward the system of care philosophy. Again, there was commonality on general aims, strategies, and trends of system development, but the specific system models employed diverged greatly.

One commonality was the general trend toward increased interagency action in the local community, at the state level, or both. Staff in several sites reported a process in which the different organizations in the systems of care gradually became more engaged and more likely to work together productively. Sites went through a learning process in which local agencies absorbed system of care principles that were previously little known. One issue in Vermont was the difficulty early in the program of persuading children's mental health agencies in some counties to use the network of interagency structures that had been developed and to try harder to serve children and youth in the community. In Ohio, the child welfare agency and private agencies that traditionally had contracts for residential beds only gradually developed an investment in a more community-based system of care. Kentucky implemented an extensive training program to educate participants in the system of care philosophy. This helped promote the relationship between the mental health and education agencies by reducing educators' concern about bearing sole responsibility for funding services for children identified through special education as having SED.

In part, interagency relationships flourished because MHSPY projects had funds and services to offer and case managers with skills in individualized care for cases that other agencies found difficult to manage. In Ohio, for example, child welfare workers came to rely on MHSPY case managers because they were able to provide substantial support to clients, design individualized services, and apply flexible Medicaid in numerous situations. In California, empowered by control over capitated Medicaid funds, MHSPY was able to develop a culturally sensitive, individualized model of care of working with neighborhood agencies to create packages of services to meet the individual needs of clients.

Diversity was evident in almost every aspect of the organization of these systems. For example, the California project, located in San Francisco, developed an autonomous organization staffed by workers donated by multiple child-serving agencies. The cultural and professional diversity of the organization mirrored that of San Francisco itself. This interagency organization has developed considerable presence within the target neighborhoods. In Vermont, in contrast, the system was based on a network of interagency teams based in the public agencies. These start with treatment teams centered on individual families, continuing to local interagency teams, and progressing to a state interagency team. There is substantial interaction between local and state teams. In Ohio, the system was based on the partnership of a strong county mental health board allied with a well-regarded, innovative private agency that follows Hobbs's (1982) reeducation model. In Wisconsin, the project created a private nonprofit organization expressly designed to implement a prepaid, capitated managed care program, obtaining services from a number of private nonprofit providers.

Financing Structures. The development of systems of care required money beyond what the RWJF provided, and, indeed, financing innovations to support systems were a planned component of the demonstration. Funding for systems of care has to be flexible, so that various nontraditional services and multiple service providers of varied disciplines can be supported. The MHSPY sites accessed several sources of flexible funds, particularly Medicaid funds, made more flexible by waivers eliminating certain federal requirements.

MHSPY sites' financial initiatives fit the conceptual scheme outlined by Meyers (1994), identifying four basic approaches to financing: (a) redeploying funds, (b) maximizing federal financing, (c) decategorizing funding streams, and (d) raising revenue. Often, sites found resources for new services by redirecting funds reserved for hospital and residential treatment to community-based services. Sites became expert at securing funds for community-based services through federal entitlement programs, primarily Medicaid and social security. Several sites won federal grants for demonstration programs of innovative mental health services that paralleled or extended the MHSPY projects. Sites developed flexible sources of funding by pooling money from multiple agencies for special programs and individualized care. In several cases, states, counties, or municipalities augmented RWJF grants with matching funds to extend the system of care to a wider range of clients or to add to the continuum of care. By project's end, most sites were continuing to support innovations developed during MHSPY using new state and local appropriations, new sources of federal reimbursement, new foundation or government grants, and new methods of pooling existing funds.

During the demonstration, each site tried to increase interagency collaboration to finance services in new ways that would have been difficult for any agency individually. The results were often substantial and occasionally dramatic. One strategy was to pool a portion of state or local appropriations for children's mental health care, often for individualized services. The Oregon project based its financial plan on state-level pooling of state and local funds, thereby obtaining significant amounts of money from the county, participating school districts, state and local child welfare agencies, the state mental health agency, and the state Medicaid office. The two MHSPY communities in North Carolina eliminated the majority of categorical service programs, making available funds more adaptable to children's needs. Long-term funding commitments from four different agencies kept the Kentucky project operational after termination of MHSPY foundation support. Other states' efforts were more modest: Pennsylvania created a blended funding pool by charging dues to each of the participating agencies in the county. Kentucky, Vermont, and Ohio also created interagency funding pools for wraparound services from agency service funds. Funding pools for these services had limitations, however. In two sites, funds were either frozen or discontinued, and concerns emerged about agency ownership of funds.

Nevertheless, financial collaboration became the norm in several sites and funds were pooled in various ways to pay for services. The degree of collaboration varied: In some cases, financial collaboration was the basis for funding services in a system of care; in others, even limited interagency funding pools were difficult to maintain. Collaboration seemed to prove most effective when it was supported by a pre-MHSPY history, when agencies worked together to secure funds from federal entitlement programs, and when joint financial planning was supported and encouraged by interagency structures and expectations. Financial collaboration seems likely to continue because of sites' success.

Interagency collaboration was also integral to sites' initiatives to obtain new support from federal entitlement programs. Meyers (1994) noted, "The difficulty of coordinating activity among agencies or levels or government" (p. 50) was a major obstacle to using federal entitlements to fund new children's mental health services programs. Building on a core of interagency and state-local relationships, MHSPY sites were able to overcome this problem. In programs in Vermont and North Carolina, education and child welfare agencies furnished school system dollars to provide a Medicaid match for mental health services. North Carolina became the only state to access Title IV-A funds from social security using a collaborative state plan of the mental health and child welfare agencies. Considerable interagency planning and collaboration have been necessary to implement Carolina Alternatives, a Medicaid capitated payment system intended to wed the system of care approach to services with a managed care approach to financing.

The MHSPY sites' initiatives to obtain more funding from federal entitlements constituted the single most successful change in financing and made the largest, most substantial contribution to revenues. Working collaboratively, as noted above, most sites successfully increased federal payments for children's mental health services using Medicaid (Title XIX) and social security (Titles IV-A and IV-E). For example, the North Carolina sites increased Medicaid billing more than fivefold between 1990-1991 and 1992-1993. States that previously had waivers and options, such as Pennsylvania and Vermont, increased the range of services covered during MHSPY. In Pennsylvania, family-based mental health services, mental health crisis planning, and intensive case management became reimbursable. Greater use of federal entitlements for providing care in MHSPY sites was promoted by (a) the advancement of systems of care; (b) the development of new community-based services; (c) the spread of the CASSP philosophy of care; (d) greater attention to financing, in response to economic realities and aided by technical assistance from MHSPY's National Program Office; and (e) the development of interagency organizational structures. For example, the development of Bluegrass/Kentucky IMPACT allowed more creative and extensive use of the rehabilitation services option that had been obtained earlier and Kentucky increased Medicaid reimbursement. California and North Carolina added the rehabilitation services option during MHSPY.

The most dramatic change in use of federal entitlements was several MHSPY states' development of the Medicaid 1915(a) option. Section 1915(a) gives states the option to contract with a health maintenance or service organization or other service agency to provide prepaid or capitated services to Medicaid recipients within a specific area for "services not included in the state plan." The organization receives a fixed amount of dollars per child that can be used flexibly for whatever services meet the child's individual needs. The 1915(a) option provides maximum flexibility because there is little stipulation about what services are used and it makes other waivers and options superfluous. Unlike standard Medicaid reimbursement, however, which is dispensed per service with no limit per child, capitated funds available through 1915(a) are limited by child. Thus, use of 1915(a) was somewhat controversial and has generated substantial concern about the need to set capitation rates high enough to allow for the often-heavy service load of children with SED. Yet this approach also creates excitement because of the possibility of reducing costs per child and using funds flexibly, without the addition of substantial administration, paperwork, or case management effort per child. The MHSPY site in Dane County, Wisconsin, used the 1915(a) option as the financial cornerstone of its revamped project. With a substantially altered system of financing, a pool of money to match Medicaid was developed through redirection of state psychiatric hospitalization funds, county residential treatment monies, and other sources. Ohio implemented the 1915(a) option early in the project. This project was then able to use capitated monies to help replenish a pool of local agency funds for individualized services that had been exhausted early on. Several sites that have not yet implemented the 1915(a) option are planning to do so.

In the last years of the demonstration, new financing plans involving capitation and managed care became central to several MHSPY projects. Several sites were at the forefront of states that developed managed care plans for children's mental health services. The project in Dane County, Wisconsin, implemented the most striking change. Using 1915(a) and a pool of state and county funds diverted primarily from hospital and residential treatment, the project contracted with a capitated managed care organization to provide services through private nonprofit providers while deemphasizing the role of public children's service agencies. The revamped MHSPY project achieved substantial reductions in the per-child cost of mental health care, although the dramatic changes in the organization of care were somewhat controversial. The Oregon project developed a capitated system based on a large, diverse pool of money from state and local sources, including school districts, child welfare agencies, mental health organizations, and the state Medicaid office. The San Francisco project developed its own capitation plan modeled after the 1915(a) Medicaid option using local, state, and federal Medicaid funds. The capitation plan became the major financing strategy and included innovations such as provision of minicapitations to community agencies for neighborhood systems of care that provided culturally appropriate traditional and alternative services. North Carolina inaugurated Carolina Alternatives, a substantial statewide 1915(b) capitated managed care program with capitation rates set at levels sufficient to provide an adequate system of care for children with SED.

Securing greater federal entitlements for community-based care and using them creatively in flexible, capitated, managed care programs were among the most visible and dramatic changes in care in the MHSPY sites. These developments exemplified the MHSPY approach of simultaneously developing the children's services system of care and finding new ways to fund the coordinated, community-based, individualized services that are central to the treatment philosophy of the program.

Ideals and Reality. The experience of the MHSPY communities makes clear that systems of care take a variety of shapes and comprehensive services can be implemented in multiple ways. It is difficult at this stage in the development of care systems to specify what an ideal system should be. The general characteristics of the demonstration systems typically included (a) case management, usually with some less-than-optimal flexible, wraparound funds; (b) an array of traditional outpatient services (e.g., therapy, evaluation, consultation); (c) brief interventions (e.g., crisis services and respite care); (d) a small number of intermediate services of moderate intensity (but not the whole array of theoretically possible services); and (e) hospitalization or residential treatment for a small number of children who needed it. In reality, it appears that not all the points in the continuum of care in these sites were covered by specific services; instead, a few services were consistently provided at diverse points in the continuum of care and other service needs were addressed through pragmatic and innovative case management and the availability of flexible funds.

That no "right" way exists to develop systems of care, even though systems share common elements, is not surprising given how dramatically communities differed. MHSPY sites were very different communities, with differing target populations, existing services, histories of organizational coordination, leadership, degree of state involvement, and availability of resources. These differences reflected adaptation to different geography, demography, and political history and varying previous experiences with systems of care. A previous evaluation report details how, for example, a site's history of involvement in CASSP predicted the course of development of the system of care during the MHSPY project (see Lovas et al., 1994; Lovas, Glass, & Cross, 1993). The findings from MHSPY suggest that efforts to develop generic models of systems of care may be misguided and should be viewed skeptically.

MHSPY has been a catalyst for a substantial amount of change in the organization and financing of children's mental health services in several major regions of the country. Moreover, the influence of MHSPY is likely to grow, as the results of innovations become disseminated within MHSPY states and the Comprehensive Community Mental Health Services Program for Children.

MHSPY seems to have had durability and influence, unlike other programs for children (cf. Schorr, 1989), and several factors seem responsible. First, MHSPY provided direct services that were flexible and responsive to families' needs. MHSPY projects' work with children and families excited the imagination of people who care about children and are committed to a community-based approach. Second, most of the states in the program had a history of planning and development of interagency coordination through grants from CASSP. MHSPY was a logical extension and implementation of existing plans. Third, the state-local partnership that was part of every MHSPY project increased the program's influence. In each state, the local project demonstrated changes in services affecting children and families, and the state was involved to advocate for or help write new legislation, to spread innovations to new communities, and to represent the project with other state agencies and legislators. State administrators also were invested through the considerable work they had to do to bring about many of the financial innovations of MHSPY. Fourth, financing innovations MHSPY developed made it possible to spread the program and service innovations to new places. New sites could adopt MHSPY innovations in care because methods of financing these innovations were provided along with them. Finally, MHSPY is congruent with a larger movement in our society toward increasing local control, building on strengths, and valuing families.

Although understanding MHSPY and evaluating its impact is undoubtedly made difficult because it was implemented differently in eight sites, the variety of ways in which the concept was operationalized is also the program's strength. Flexibility seems to have been a key element in the program; the ability of clinicians to adapt treatment to individual family needs and the ability of communities to adapt the program to their own needs is, perhaps, the hallmark of the demonstration.

Implications

Systems of care that require community resources to provide comprehensive services to children with serious emotional disorders are now an established fact. MHSPY, which was developed after a decade of advocacy, accumulating research evidence, and expert views on the need for system reform (see, e.g., England & Cole, 1992; Saxe et al.,

1987), bridged the gap between rhetoric about children's mental health care and implementation. MHSPY played an essential role in helping to demonstrate that ideas about systems of care were feasible and in making clear that parents, professionals, and bureaucratic agencies could work together to reorganize care. But the variety of ways in which MHSPY was operationalized by those who participated in the RWJF demonstration make clear that the system of care construct needs to be refined. And we have yet to demonstrate that reorganizing treatment systems improves the efficiency and effectiveness of care provided to children. Developing the theory of systems of care and conducting outcome research are interdependent priorities.

Construct

To the extent that a theory of systems of care exists, it is embodied in the principles of the system of care described by Stroul and Friedman (1986). These principles, focusing on maintaining children in community settings and providing multiple, diverse services of varying intensity and restrictiveness, were adopted and adapted by each of the MHSPY sites. Yet the principles represent more of an orientation to care than specific operating procedures. The MHSPY experience suggests that wide variation is to be expected in the operationalization of the principles. Although some variation is undoubtedly healthy and may be part of the essential construct, as the concept matures it should be possible to specify better the conditions for appropriate and effective care.

Part of the difficulty with specification of the principles is that the logic remains fuzzy. We accept the concept of community-based care in part because we believe that hospitalization is harmful and cost-inefficient (cf., Saxe et al., 1987), but we are not clear about how we can provide supportive environments for children in the community. A particular difficulty is that we lack agreement about the responsibilities of families and professionals—how should all of the "hands" that need to be involved in helping children work together? Furthermore, there is only a rudimentary sense of why multiple services are appropriate and necessary. This is not to critique the concept of community-based comprehensive services but to say that the underlying theory needs to be better explicated if we are going to be able to understand how to better develop systems of care.

Research

Further refinement and dissemination of systems of care ideas necessarily will have to be accompanied by systematic research that demonstrates the impact of these new delivery systems. Accountability is increasingly a concern of those who fund health and social services and systems of care; given the costs associated with services, they will be intensively scrutinized. Conducting research will in part depend on investigators being able to explicate the construct better. The role of families, different professionals, and the settings where care is provided will have to be systematically studied. The temptation may be to adopt a "reductionistic" approach and move away from testing the impact of changing an entire system. Undoubtedly, it is simpler to test individual elements, but although some of that sort of research is necessary, it would ultimately be self-defeating. The challenge is to conduct research using systems as a unit of measurement. A variety of methodologies will need to be used, including methods for meta-analysis of multiple evaluations.

Conclusion

Experience with RWJF's MHSPY demonstration perhaps proves the adage that with wisdom comes ignorance and the more one knows, the more one realizes there is to know. Although MHSPY was successful in demonstrating that systems of care can be implemented, the demonstration also makes clear how much more needs to be learned about providing services to children with serious emotional disorders. Services to children are being revolutionized as we find ways to coordinate the activities of all those who have responsibility for children, and we are perhaps on the threshold of even greater change. Research on children's mental disorders played a central role in bringing about these changes, and new research will help us move even further toward effective ways of aiding all children with serious emotional disorders.

References

Beachler, M. (1990). The mental health services program for youth. *Journal of Mental Health Administration, 17*, 115-121.

Behar, L. B. (1996). Policy implications of the evaluation of the Fort Bragg Child and Adolescent Mental Health Demonstration Project. *Journal of Mental Health Administration, 23*(1), 118.

Bickman, L. (1996a). Reinterpreting the Fort Bragg evaluation findings: The message does not change. *Journal of Mental Health Administration, 23*(1), 137-145.

Bickman, L. (1996b). A continuum of care: More is not better. *American Psychologist, 51,* 689-701.

Bickman, L., Guthrie, P. R., Foster, E. M., Lambert, E. W., Summerfelt, W. T., Breda, C. S., & Heflinger, C. A. (1995). *Evaluating managed mental health services: The Fort Bragg experiment.* New York: Plenum.

Cole, R. F., & Poe, S. L. (1993). *Partnership for care: Systems of care for children with serious emotional disturbances and their families.* Washington, DC: Washington Business Group on Health.

Cross, T. P. (1996). *The Fort Bragg evaluation project: An overview of the controversy* (Monograph for the Technical Assistance Center on the Evaluation of Children's Mental Health Systems, Judge Baker Children's Center). Boston, MA: Technical Assistance Center.

Cross, T. P., Gardner, J. K., & Friedman, C. (1993). Implementation of a management information system for children's mental health care: Lessons from a national demonstration. *Research and Evaluation in Group Care, 3*, 10-13.

Day, C., & Roberts, M. C. (1991). Activities of the Child and Adolescent Service System Program for improving mental health services for children and families. *Journal of Clinical Child Psychology, 20*(4), 340-350.

England, M. J., & Cole, R. F. (1992). Building systems of care for youth with serious mental illness. *Hospital and Community Psychiatry, 43*, 630-633.

Friedman, R. (1994). Restructuring of systems to emphasize prevention and family support. *Journal of Clinical Child Psychology, 23*(Suppl.), 40-47.

Friedman, R., & Burns, B. J. (1996). The evaluation of the Fort Bragg project: An alternative interpretation of the findings. *Journal of Mental Health Administration, 23*(1), 128-136.

Geismer, M. R. (1994). *Between rhetoric and reality: Implementation of case management for children and adolescents with severe emotional disturbances.* Doctoral dissertation, Brandeis University, Waltham, MA.

Hallfors, D., Cross, T., & Roan, C. (1993). Case data (MIS). In L. Saxe, J. Gardner, & T. Cross (Eds.), *Evaluation of the Mental Health Services Program for Youth: Interim report.* Section III, pp. 1-23. Waltham, MA: Brandeis University, Heller School, Family and Children's Policy Center.

Hobbs, N. (1982). *The troubled and troubling child: Re-education in mental health, education and human services programs for children and youth.* San Francisco: Jossey-Bass.

Institute of Medicine. (1989). *Research on children and adolescents with mental, behavioral, and developmental disorders: Mobilizing a national initiative* (Report of a study by a committee of the Institute of Medicine, Division of Mental Health and Behavioral Medicine). Washington, DC: National Academy Press.

Jordan, D., & Hernandez, M. (1990). The Ventura planning model: A proposal for mental health reform. *Journal of Mental Health Administration, 17*(1), 26-47.

Knitzer, J. (1982). *Unclaimed children.* Washington, DC: Children's Defense Fund.

Knitzer, J. (1993). Children's mental health policy: Challenging the future. *Journal of Emotional and Behavioral Disorders, 1*(1), 8-16.

Lovas, G. S., Cross, T. P., Gardner, J. K., & Saxe, L. (1994). *Developing infrastructure and implementing change: The road to better systems of care for children's mental health.* Unpublished manuscript. (Available from the Family and Children's Policy Center, Heller School, Brandeis University, Waltham, MA 02254)

Lovas, G., Glass, A., & Cross, T. P. (1993). Organizational/financial assessment. In L. Saxe, J. Gardner, & T. Cross (Eds.), *Evaluation of the Mental Health Services Program for Youth: Interim report.* Section II, pp. 1-263. Waltham, MA: Brandeis University, Heller School.

Meyers, J. C. (1994). Financing strategies to support innovations in service delivery to children. *Journal of Clinical Child Psychology, 23* (Suppl.), 48-54.

National Commission on Children. (1991). *Beyond rhetoric: A new American agenda for children and families* (Final report of the National Commission on Children). Washington, DC: Government Printing Office.

Saxe, L., & Cross, T. P. (in press). A cup half-full: Interpreting the Fort Bragg children's mental health demonstration. *American Psychologist.*

Saxe, L., Cross, T. P., Lovas, G. S., & Gardner, J. K. (1995). Evaluation of the Mental Health Services Program for Youth demonstration: Examining rhetoric in action. In L. Bickman (Ed.), *Creating a children's mental health service system: Policy, research and evaluation* (pp. 206-235). Thousand Oaks, CA: Sage.

Saxe, L., Cross, T. P., Silverman, N., & Batchelor, W. F., with Dougherty, D. (1987). *Children's mental health: Problems and services.* Durham, NC: Duke University Press. (Originally published by the Office of Technology Assessment, U.S. Congress; OTA-BP-H-33; Washington, DC: Government Printing Office)

Saxe, L., Gardner, J. K., & Cross, T. P. (Eds.). (1993). *Evaluation of the Mental Health Services Program for Youth: Interim report.* Waltham, MA: Brandeis University, Heller School, Family and Children's Policy Center.

Schorr, L. B. (1989). *Within our reach: Breaking the cycle of disadvantage.* New York: Anchor/Doubleday.

Solnit, A. J., Adnopoz, J., & Fallon, T. (1993). Clinical assessment conferences. In L. Saxe, J. Gardner, & T. Cross (Eds.), *Evaluation of the Mental Health Services Program for Youth: Interim report.* Section IV, pp. 1-67. Waltham, MA: Brandeis University, Heller School, Family and Children's Policy Center.

Stroul, B. A. (1993). *Systems of care for children and adolescents with severe emotional disturbances: What are the results?* Washington, DC: Georgetown University Child Development Center, Child and Adolescent Service System Program Technical Assistance Center.

Stroul, B. A., & Friedman, R. M. (1986). *A system of care for severely emotionally disturbed children and youth.* Washington, DC: Georgetown University Child Development Center, Child and Adolescent Service System Program Technical Assistance Center.

Weisz, J. R., Weiss, B., & Donenberg, G. R. (1992). The lab versus the clinic: Effects of child and adolescent psychotherapy. *American Psychologist, 47,* 1578-1585.

The Development of a State's Perspective on Keeping Children in the Community

Strategies for Change

MARY E. EVANS

MARY I. ARMSTRONG

In 1990, Burns and Friedman published an article on examining the research base for children's mental health services and policy. That article, which has become required reading in the field, noted several roles for researchers, including identifying effective community-based demonstrations of services, initiating partnerships between university researchers and policymakers, and providing a sound research base on which to make policy and programmatic decisions. In this chapter, we describe the development of a partnership between policymakers and researchers at the state level in New York and examine the ways in which these two parties have worked together to develop a vision and a plan for keeping children in communities.

AUTHORS' NOTE: The authors thank Elizabeth Pease for her assistance in preparing this manuscript and Richard C. Surles, who worked with them to develop an outline for this chapter.

Over the past several years, New York State has used a number of strategies to shape a policy framework for serving children with serious emotional disturbance (SED) and their families. This policy focuses on developing a community-based, family-centered system of care that enables children with SED to remain in the community. Strategies that have been employed include the use of

- Data to inform policy decisions
- The formal authority of the state mental health office to redesign regulations
- Changes to develop reimbursement mechanisms
- Program evaluation and research to foster and to evaluate policy change
- Resource allocation, crisis, and controversy as opportunities to reshape the system

In this chapter, we highlight some of the policy-related strategies used to redirect New York State's children's mental health system and present a case study of a collaboration between policymakers and researchers. In this case study, we examine the use of program evaluation to shape the development of a new program model, Children and Youth Intensive Case Management (CYICM). The creation of this new model was followed by a research demonstration grant focused on the outcomes associated with Family-Centered Intensive Case Management and those of treatment foster care. This research project, known as Project FIRST, in turn has further influenced the development of policy and the refinement of program models.

Policy-Related Strategies

During the period 1960-1980, the mental health system generally offered only two alternatives for children: inpatient treatment and outpatient clinic treatment. Most inpatient treatment was highly restrictive, stigmatizing, and costly; clinic treatment was limited in the level of support it offered children and their families. Thus, many children with SED were referred to the child welfare or juvenile justice systems and usually lacked adequate access to mental health treatment.

Service need often was identified as a result of service availability and frequently produced even greater inequity in resource allocation. Fragmentation between inpatient and community-based services also contributed to a lack of information on children and adolescents presenting for psychiatric emergency and inpatient services. Without data on the characteristics and service needs of these high-risk children and their families, planning an appropriate array of community-based programs and services was problematic. Faced with a legacy of heavy reliance on inpatient care, the New York State mental health authority, the Office of Mental Health (OMH), devoted increased attention to the gap between the need for comprehensive child mental health services and service availability. OMH researchers used a number of strategies to inform and support the policy shifts necessary to move toward a more community-based service system and to create more parity in resource allocation. These strategies included using existing databases for analysis; creating a minimum database on children using community-based services; and conducting targeted policy analyses, program evaluation studies, and research demonstrations. These strategies will be highlighted in greater detail throughout the chapter.

Data to Inform Policy Decisions

Beginning in 1988, the state mental health office gave priority to better understanding the characteristics and service needs of children and adolescents appearing for emergency and inpatient services. Data were sought both to inform policy decisions regarding the array of alternative community-based services and to validate the assumption that children were being placed inappropriately in inpatient care. Making use of a targeted, time-limited study approach, during a 7-month period in 1989 all state-operated inpatient programs were asked to submit case summaries of children 8 years of age and under. Seventy case summaries were received and analyzed using a standard protocol (New York State Office of Mental Health, 1989). The case review protocol, a joint effort of policymakers and evaluators in the central office of OMH, included such factors as age at admission, referral source, environmental stressors surrounding admission, child behaviors associated with admission, child welfare history, mental health history, immediate prior mental health contacts, and family status.

A number of statewide patterns emerged from the data. Many children came from chaotic family situations, including physical or sexual abuse, and had experienced serious school problems. Seventy percent of the children's families had prior child welfare involvement (child protective services, foster care, etc.). In reviewing past mental health contacts, 37% indicated no recent mental health contact. Clearly, many children admitted to inpatient programs had not been screened or seen by mental health providers. Many children had been admitted in response to family conditions and need for services. The state mental health office used this information to direct attention to the actual service needs of children being admitted to inpatient programs and to highlight the necessity for creating community-based alternatives for young children and improving access to existing alternative services.

Formal Authority of the New York Mental Health Authority to Redesign Regulations

New York had few alternatives to state-operated inpatient programs that could respond to the clinical and behavioral characteristics of children with SED and their families. Before appropriate alternatives could be developed, the role of inpatient care in a community-based service system needed to be clarified. First, a shift in policy was made to target state-operated inpatient programs primarily for adolescents and to establish an intermediate length of stay (30-180 days).

State criteria for licensing acute inpatient programs (up to 30 days length of stay) in local general hospitals also were altered in a number of ways to articulate a new policy framework. Using program guidelines, the state mental health office redesigned regulations for the children's inpatient certificate of need (CON) programs. CON programs are state regulatory mechanisms that require review of designated capital and service capacity expansion plans before such inpatient expansion may be initiated. Planning agency approval is based on review of the project against a set of planning criteria and a finding of community need. CON programs provide states with a mechanism to achieve policy goals related to cost, quality, and accessibility of mental health services.

In 1988, the Mental Health Services Council (a statutory advisory group to the OMH commissioner that reviews and makes recommendations on all CON recommendations) advised that a moratorium be imposed on the development of new children's psychiatric beds. The reason for this recommendation was that New York's CON regulations lacked sufficient criteria for determining whether additional children's beds were needed for any particular geographic area. The state mental health office responded by issuing emergency regulations to impose the recommended moratorium and by undertaking an intraagency effort to reshape regulations governing the development of children's inpatient beds. This effort focused on an examination of the values and principles on which inpatient care for children should be based. Issued in 1989, the revised CON regulations link specific programmatic criteria to the quantitative assessment of the number of beds needed in each geographic area. The number of beds is derived by researchers from existing data on service utilization, program capacity, demographic factors of individual county populations, and a special study that was conducted on the needs of children receiving services. To obtain approval, new applicants for children's beds must demonstrate that the proposed program is consistent with both the programmatic principles and the assessment of unmet need in a particular area of the state.

The programmatic criteria, based on the state's policy goals regarding the role of inpatient treatment in a community-based system of care, include a criterion that children should be admitted to inpatient care only during periods of most critical need and after less restrictive alternatives have been considered. The state office also relied on a policy position developed by the American Academy of Child and Adolescent Psychiatry. The academy deems that acute inpatient care is appropriate for children who require crisis stabilization or intensive short-term treatment and medical intervention and cannot be cared for outside a structured, 24-hour setting. The CON criteria also state that acute inpatient care should be provided in small, designated children's units in local general hospitals, close to the child's family and home community, and that program accessibility must be ensured by the provider through appropriate screening and evaluation mechanisms accessible to the community. Furthermore, the inpatient program must ensure linkages with other service providers, both mental health and other programs providing services to children and their families, and discharge plans should specify postdischarge services and arrangements including clinical, school, family supports, residential, social services, health care, and substance abuse services, as needed.

Strategic Changes to Develop Reimbursement Mechanisms

New York also has used its regulatory authority to redirect the role of children's outpatient treatment programs, based on the premise that children with SED can be successfully treated in the community if they and their families have access to an array of services. For a child, an array of supports, including clinical and service supports for the family, is as important as individual treatment. One dilemma in providing access for clinical supports is that most programs have been dependent on a fee-for-service billing structure and require service provision at licensed sites. Child and family outpatient services sometimes need to be offered at a variety of sites, including homes and schools where children grow and develop. Thus, consultation and problem-solving assistance to non-mental health professionals working with children in schools and community recreation programs are essential. As part of an overall reform of New York's outpatient programs, several modifications were introduced to children's clinics. These modifications permitted some clinic visits for children to be offered on-site in homes and schools and required that clinical support services be available for families. In addition, a mechanism for offering consultation for non-mental health professionals was provided.

The regulatory changes for children's clinic treatment programs also include financial incentives. Medicaid for clinic visits with collaterals, including families, is now reimbursed at the same rate as clinic visits for the identified client. Reimbursement mechanisms are available for clinical consultation with collaterals and for providing family support groups. A limited percentage (25%) of clinic visits for children can be off-site if the visits are necessary to maintain the children in outpatient programs.

Program Evaluation and Research to
Foster and Evaluate Policy Change

As new program models were being designed, funded, and implemented based on the changes in regulation and financing, the Bureau of Evaluation and Services Research at OMH was developing a minimum data set that could be used to describe all children admitted to and discharged from eight different program types across the state. The data set would provide information about proximal outcomes such as length of stay, changes in restrictiveness of living environment, and changes in symptoms and functioning. The instruments used for the minimum data set were constructed using standards recommended by the Mental Health Statistics Improvement Program (Leginski et al., 1989). Instructions about how to complete these forms were prepared, providers in the five regions of the state were trained in their use, and the forms were distributed. The resulting data have provided information for discussions with policymakers regarding the target population served in each program model, average length of enrollment in particular services, and some of the outcomes experienced by children enrolled in the programs.

Also at this time, the bureau developed and initiated evaluations of three program models: CYICM; Home-Based Crisis Intervention (HBCI), an in-home intensive crisis intervention program; and Family-Based Treatment (FBT), New York's model of treatment foster care. As data from the minimum data set became available, they were used in these evaluations for analytic purposes and to provide a frame for the selection of samples of enrolled children for more detailed study. For example, the minimum data set provided the frame from which a 30% sample of cases was selected for a longitudinal study of the child outcomes associated with CYICM.

Resource Allocation, Crisis, and Controversy
as Opportunities to Reshape the System

Consistent with changes in regulation and the acquisition of data to inform policy decisions, all new budgetary requests for children for the past 4 years have been to support the care of children in the community. The articulated budget priority is to develop an array of programs in each service area that includes a local fixed point of responsibility to access emergency services, family support services, both clinic treatment and day treatment programs, and community-based residential options. On a public policy level, the limiting of resource requests to community services has sometimes been questioned by advocates, families, and providers of inpatient care. The many problems associated with adult deinstitutionalization sometimes become an issue as children's mental health policy shifts to a community-based system. The public dialogue created by concern has been an opportunity to refine thinking on what is best for children with SED. The refinement in thinking has resulted in a number of structural innovations in child-serving systems that facilitate individualizing care for children most in need to services from multiple agencies. An example of such a structural innovation is the development of the Coordinated Children's Service Initiative, a three-tiered (case level, county level, and state level) structure and process that engages parents and professionals in identifying and overcoming barriers to the provision of individualized care.

At the same time that resource allocations for community-based services are being made, the state mental health office has been working to respond strategically to crisis to achieve positive outcomes. Most recently, New York, as well as other northeastern states, has experienced a severe fiscal crisis requiring major cutbacks in state government. Faced with the mandate to reduce both programs and employees, the New York State mental health office has attempted to use the fiscal crisis as an opportunity to reshape the children's system. Consulting the OMH database on hospital use showed that the number of annual admissions to state-operated children's inpatient programs in New York increased 25%, from 1,412 in 1977 to 1,758 in 1994. The median length of stay decreased over 59%, from 70 days in 1979 to 29 days in 1994, however. Given the decrease in length of stay, the average daily census in state-operated children's hospitals decreased 37%, from 766 in 1979 to 481 in 1994. This change in utilization can be attributed to the priority given to the development of alternatives to state-operated inpatient care, such as CYICM, children's community residences, FBT foster care, HBCI, and acute inpatient units in local general hospitals. The data on reduced demand for long-term inpatient programs permitted the state mental health office to reduce bed capacity without a reduction in access to state inpatient care. Prevalence estimates, developed by the researchers, guided bed reduction decisions with the goal of a more equitable resource distribution statewide.

Using the above information as context, a case study related to the development of New York's approach to case management is presented below. This case study illustrates how the minimum data set, program evaluation outcomes, and a research demonstration grant have contributed to the interplay between researchers and policymakers at multiple levels over time. This interaction, in turn, has resulted in the case management program.

Children and Youth Intensive
Case Management as a Case Study

Children and Youth Intensive Case Management (CYICM) is an intensive, client-centered service provided to children and youth under 18 years of age who have SED. The program is targeted at children and youth who have a history of, or who are at risk for, out-of-home placement, including those at risk for repeated or lengthy psychiatric hospitalizations. The program goal is to keep children in their natural homes, schools, and community environments. The specific services provided by intensive case managers are dictated by the needs of each child and delivered within the context of the family or community setting. Using Robinson's (1991) paradigm, the New York State case management model can be classified as an Expanded Broker Model, which includes assessment, planning, linking, and advocating on behalf of the client. Case managers also are encouraged to advocate for systems change when that is necessary to provide the most efficacious care to children with SED and their families.

Because CYICM is a statewide program that is meant to be sensitive to local environments, the process of enrolling children varies somewhat across settings. The general process for enrollment of children referred for CYICM includes a review by an interagency committee. Names of children are entered on a roster according to their level of need for this service, so that those with the greatest need are enrolled in the program first when a vacancy occurs (New York State Office of Mental Health, 1989).

CYICM programs provide care 24 hours per day, 7 days a week, and each intensive case manager has a caseload of 12 children. (Prior to 1995, caseload size was 10 children.) Intensive case managers can access flexible annual service dollars to purchase individualized services or develop new programs for the target population of children. Depending on the fiscal year, flexible service dollar amounts have ranged from $1,000 to $2,000 per child.

A three-pronged effort is being used to assess the effectiveness of CYICM. The first effort is focused on program monitoring, utilizing the minimum data set previously described to help determine if the intended target population is being served and how long children are remaining in services. The second effort is program evaluation, examining the service utilization of program enrollees in greater detail through comparisons of enrolled children and a nonequivalent comparison group of similar children who are not enrolled. In addition, a random sample of 30% of the children enrolled over time in the program has been studied intensively to assess changes in their needs for services and functioning. The final effort being used to assess the effectiveness of CYICM is the development of research projects, including Project FIRST, to answer more generic questions about case management that are of interest not only in New York but also to researchers and policymakers across the country.

This case study is focused on the program evaluation effort and examines the needs, service use, symptoms and functioning, and patterns of state hospital use of children before and after enrollment in CYICM. In the minimum data set, data are available for 3,336 children who have been enrolled in intensive case management since 1988. On the basis of these data, the typical child served was 12 years of age, non-Hispanic white (61%), male (67%), in the custody of a natural parent (77%), and living in a single-parent household (49%). Furthermore, the typical child had Medicaid coverage (65%), was in a special education placement (57%), and was referred to CYICM by a mental health program (67%). At the time of intake, the child displayed an average of 5.8 problem behaviors and symptoms, was functionally impaired in 2.5 of 5 areas, and had a psychiatric hospital or other out-of-home placement twice before.

Outcomes of the Evaluation

In this section, we outline some of the outcomes associated with enrollment in the program. Additional detail is available in Evans, Banks, Huz, and McNulty (1994) and Evans, Huz, McNulty, and Banks (in press). Data have been obtained from analysis of the 30% random sample of children and their families.

Service Needs. The service needs of the sample of children and their families were measured at enrollment and at discharge or 3 years if the child was still enrolled in the program. To date, there is a sample of 162 children who have been discharged from the program. Figure 4.1 shows that the medical (t [1, 161] = 2.23, $p < .05$), educational (t [1, 161] = 2.00, $p < .05$), and recreational (t [1, 161] = 4.71, $p < .001$) needs of the children that were identified at baseline had decreased significantly at discharge or follow-up. Children continued to have high unmet need for social support and showed slightly higher, although not statistically significant, unmet needs for mental health services.

Symptoms. The average number of symptoms per child decreased from 5.7 to 3.1 (t [1, 161] = 9.35, $p < .001$). Significant decreases were noted in aggression, suicidal behavior, sexual acting out, cruelty to animals and others, and psychotic symptoms.

Functioning. The Child and Adolescent Functional Assessment Scale (CAFAS) (Hodges, 1990) was used to measure children's functioning at enrollment and at discharge. Note that lower CAFAS scores indicate better functioning. Figure 4.2 shows that CAFAS scores generally declined, but significantly so only for Behavior (t [1, 161] = 2.59, $p < .05$). There was no significant change in caregivers' ability to provide care. This was expected because CYICM is child focused, not family focused.

Hospitalization. A suitable comparison group was not available for our sample of children in CYICM; therefore, a single-group pre- and postintervention analytic strategy was used to examine the possible differences in hospitalization that might be associated with CYICM. We believed that one measure of the effectiveness of CYICM would be success in keeping children out of restrictive settings such as state hospitals.

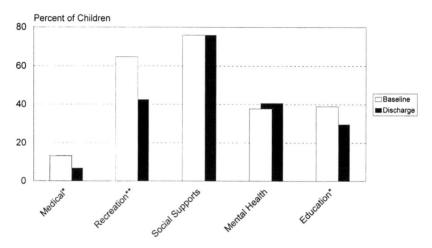

Figure 4.1. Unmet Needs at Baseline and Discharge
NOTE: N = 162. * $p < .05$. ** $p < .01$.

We therefore explored whether hospital and community tenure patterns observed in the postenrollment period differed significantly from the patterns expected in the absence of CYICM. This was studied for each child over a 4-year time frame, 2 years preenrollment and 2 years postenrollment (see Banks & Evans, 1994; Evans, Banks, et al., 1994).

Among the 166 children for whom we had complete data, there were 392 admissions to state hospitals in the pre-CYICM period and 69 in the post-CYICM period. The average time between admissions increased significantly, from 148 days in the preenrollment period to 621 days in the postenrollment period, an increase of 320%. Using a binomial (Wilcoxon Matched-Pairs Signed-Ranks) test, we found that this difference was significant at the .0001 level ($Z = -10.14$), indicating that enrollees were experiencing increased time in the community following enrollment in CYICM.

A second analysis was conducted to explore changes in the state hospital utilization pattern during the post-CYICM enrollment period, using a technique called regression discontinuity analysis (see Banks & Evans, 1994). Examined were differences in the intercept (level of utilization) and slope (trend in utilization) of the regression lines associated with the pre- and postenrollment periods. Figure 4.3 displays a graphic presentation of the findings. Based on the 917 children at risk for hos-

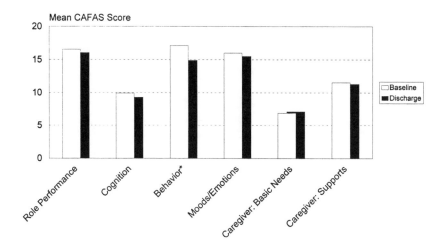

Figure 4.2. Mean CAFAS Scores at Baseline and Discharge
NOTE: $N = 162$. $* p < .05$.

pitalization, the analysis indicated a significant intervention effect. Following CYICM, the intercept shifts to a lower level, a reduction of 8.2 days (t [3, 42] = -40.15, $p < .0001$), representing a downward shift in average utilization. This analysis supports our notion that CYICM is effective in decreasing placement in the most restrictive setting for enrolled children.

Ultimately, a third analytic strategy was employed, involving a pre-post matched case analysis to examine hospital utilization of 392 CYICM enrollees compared to a comparison group of 392 matched case controls selected from the hospitalization database. This analysis confirmed the findings of the single-group pre-post analysis and demonstrated statistically significant reductions in hospital use for CYICM enrollees as compared with nonenrolled controls. For additional information on this analysis, see Evans et al. (in press).

Program and Policy Uses of
the Evaluation Results

Following the analyses discussed above, the data were used in several ways. First, researchers and program staff reviewed the data from the

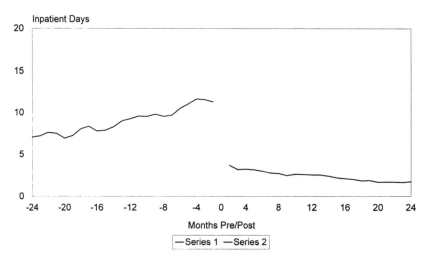

Figure 4.3. Pre-Post State Inpatient Utilization
NOTE: N = 917.

minimum data set and the evaluation to determine whether the target population was being served and whether the program seemed to be working to achieve its intended outcomes. Second, the findings were reviewed with the Division of the Budget, one of OMH's control agencies, and discussions focused on the issues of caseload size, use of flexible service dollars, and the determination of the intensity of the intervention through dosage studies. A cost analysis demonstrating cost savings realized by decreasing hospitalization was shared with budget staff. The analysis supported the agency's budget request for increasing the flow of money to the community rather than the inpatient side.

Third, the data were used in a presentation of findings at a joint Center for Mental Health Services (CMHS)/New York State legislative hearing. The commissioner of Mental Health requested that a presentation of findings be made to a panel of legislators, CMHS administrators, parents, and policy and program developers.

Finally, the data gathered in this evaluation and our experience with the program were used to shape a research agenda relevant to a complex and changing public policy environment. OMH's first research demonstration project, to be discussed shortly, created a new program model, Family-Centered Intensive Case Management (FCICM), to focus on increasing resources for families to provide care for their children with SED. This study was followed by another research demonstration designed to examine the differential outcomes associated with three intensive in-home crisis intervention programs, including a crisis case management option. Both of these grants were funded by the National Institute of Mental Health and are now funded by CMHS.

Project FIRST Research Demonstration Grant

The review of the outcome data on CYICM, which showed a discrepancy between child and parent improvements in functioning, led to the development of the new program model, FCICM, and the research demonstration called Project FIRST, which is comparing the outcomes of FCICM with those of FBT, New York's system of treatment foster care. In addition to the concerns raised by the data from CYICM, parents in New York State played a crucial role in the development of FCICM.

In 1988, the state introduced FBT, which is based on two principles. The first is that surrogate parents (known as professional parents) can form a cohesive support network in the development of problem-solving skills crucial to caring for children with SED. The second principle is that professional parents are the most important component of effective treatment. Given this key role, professional parents are offered a wide range of supports, including respite care, both planned and emergency; pre-service and in-service training opportunities; 24-hour crisis response services; and the support of an experienced child mental health specialist.

FBT offers many intensive supports to both the child and the professional parents. As natural parents in New York State gained a stronger voice, they said to policymakers, "Why can't we have those same supports and services? If we did, we could keep our kids at home."

FCICM, which was OMH's response to those parents, combines the strengths of both FBT and CYICM. FCICM acknowledges that natural families should be supported and empowered through concrete supports, including planned and emergency respite care, clinical consultation, mutual self-help groups with parent advocates, and training opportunities that emphasize building skills in caring for children with SED. In addition to providing intensive and individualized services to families and to the child with SED, FCICM also focuses on the development of the family's social network. Borrowing from the mutual support concept in FBT, FCICM brings together a family-centered intensive case manager and a parent advocate to work with two small clusters of families. Each cluster, composed of four families and a respite family, meets regularly. Transportation and child care are provided to facilitate parent participation, and parent education and training are offered also. Parent advocates, who are required to be parents of children with SED, facilitate cluster meetings, assist parents outside of meetings, and follow up with those parents who miss meetings. The cluster's respite family is available for planned and emergency out-of-home respite care. Additional respite services, including in-home respite care and after-school and weekend recreational events, are available as needed using flexible service dollars.

Project FIRST Research Design

The research uses a positive controlled experimental design with children referred to FBT for out-of-home placement being randomly assigned to either FBT or FCICM. We are examining the systems, child, and family outcomes of both interventions. Assessments are made at 6-month intervals, including 6 months postdischarge. Additional information describing this research demonstration and its implementation can be found in Evans, Armstrong, et al. (1994).

Characteristics of Children and Families

An initial sample of the 42 enrolled in the interventions thus far was examined. The mean age on admission was 8.7 years. Nearly all (82%) of the children were white and non-Hispanic, reflecting the nature of the rural areas in which they live. A surprising 90% were male. The majority (85%) were in the custody of a parent or other relative; 59% were in special education placements. The primary diagnosis was disruptive behavior disorders (69%). The children had experienced a mean of 1.6 family disruptions or placements out of home because of their mental health problems. On admission, they were impaired in a mean of 2.4 of 5 areas of functioning and had an average Child and Behavior Checklist (CBCL) (Achenbach, 1991) mean total problem score of 72, internalizing score of 67, and externalizing score of 74, all within the clinical range.

Case managers were asked to identify existing family situations that might interfere with the child's treatment. The following were identified: poverty (57%), unstable relationships (56%), adults abused as children (50%), mental illness of an adult family member (49%), chronic unemployment (36%), domestic violence (30%), and alcohol or substance abuse (17%).

Early Outcomes

On admission, the children were identified as having a mean of 6.7 problem symptoms or behaviors. There were no differences in symptom levels between the children in the two interventions. At 12 months, this had dropped to a mean of 3.5 symptoms or behaviors, a significant drop ($t = 5.85$, $p < .001$). This finding supports the hypothesis that if sufficient supports are given to families, children can be kept at home and not disadvantaged in regard to symptoms and functioning when compared with children receiving care from professional parents.

Regarding changes in functioning, Figure 4.4 shows significant ($p < .01$) improvements in Role Performance ($t = 3.10$), Behavior Toward Self/Others ($t = 4.28$), and Moods and Emotions ($t = 3.54$) between baseline and 12 months ($N = 31$). There were no significant differences between groups at either follow-up on measures of child functioning. There were significant between-group differences in the caregivers' basic needs at baseline, however, with families in FCICM displaying greater needs. Although neither group showed significant improvement over time regarding basic needs, the significant between-group difference at baseline diminished by 12 months, reflecting general improvement of families enrolled in FCICM vis-à-vis families enrolled in FBT—that is, the families in FCICM had "caught up" with families in FBT by 12 months.

The children and families will continue to be followed over at least an 18-month period to study the natural history of the interventions as well as to assess changes in child and family functioning and the system over time. In the meantime, on the basis of what has been learned in the

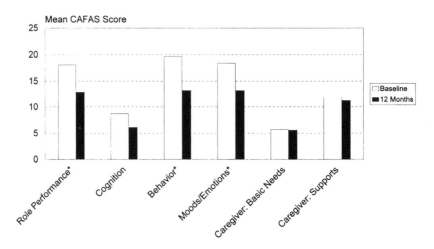

Figure 4.4. Mean CAFAS at Baseline and 12 Months, Project FIRST FCICM and FBT

NOTE: $N = 31$. * $p < .01$.

Project FIRST and the CYICM evaluation, researchers and policymakers have begun an effort called Project SEED (Services Evaluation and Dissemination), a study of the process by which recent research findings and innovative practice related to intensive case management services are disseminated. The goals of Project SEED include the following: (a) to summarize the outcomes and implementation experience of Project FIRST, the CYICM program, and New York's efforts to operationalize individualized care principles; (b) to work collaboratively with service providers and parents to integrate these research findings and to design a best practices model of case management; (c) to implement the best practices model in several sites; and (d) to describe the process of dissemination and implementation of the new model at these sites (Armstrong, Evans, Kuppinger, Huz, & Williams-Deane, 1996).

Discussion

Many potential strategies exist to redirect children's mental health services to a community-based and family-centered system of care. In this chapter, we describe how one state elected to use its formal authority to ensure that policy and operating practices conformed to its mission statement and values. In New York, the state mental health office operates, regulates, funds, and establishes rates for both inpatient and community-based services. The state office is a provider of services; a regulator of services (including state-operated services); and a funder of services through rate setting, grants to local governments, and contracts to private nonprofit agencies.

These seemingly disparate functions can create an appearance of conflict of interest. For example, the state mental health office provides children's inpatient services but also is responsible for the investigation of allegations of abuse and neglect in its programs, as well as in other programs it licenses. There are, however, definite advantages to this paradox. The potential exists to use the various functions and formal authority to shape policy for all children's mental health services (state operated, nonprofit, and for profit) and to create access to services, as well as to structure financing mechanisms that are policy driven.

New York and other state mental health officials are increasing their understanding of how to use their formal authority to forge relationships with local governments, providers, and families to encourage service accessibility for those children most in need. Of major importance in more effectively developing a child- and family-based mental health program and larger system of care is the consistent application of carefully considered policies in the operating and financing roles of government. Unless there is consistent analysis of programs and budgets against a future-oriented expectation of improved clinical outcomes for the child and family, it is unlikely that state officials will make sound policy decisions that result in the informed development of community-based systems of care. One challenge today is to use the state's authority to formulate a managed care strategy for children with SED that articulates the values of universal access, availability of an array of intensive community-based programs and services, and a parent-professional partnership.

The partnership of program and policy staff with researchers and program evaluators is key in facilitating consistent and ongoing analysis required for policy development. Thinking back over the collaboration discussed in the case management case study, we see several lessons that were learned that may be helpful to other policymakers and researchers seeking to establish effective working relationships.

1. It takes time to establish trusting, effective relationships. It is necessary, therefore, that time be allocated from busy schedules. In the case study, the policymaker and researcher both had schedules that extended well beyond the usual state work day. Time for meetings was generally scheduled at the beginning of the workday before others arrived to present their daily crises. Another very effective time to work together was while traveling together to visit program sites or attend meetings. During train and automobile rides, the policymaker and researcher had uninterrupted time to focus on the project of mutual interest and also learned to know each other as people, rather than as role incumbents.

2. Policymakers and researchers must share their paradigms and associated language and concepts with each other. For the researcher in the case study, this meant learning about the Child and Adolescent Service System Program principles, case management, serious emotional disturbance, financing of community-based mental health services, and treatment foster care, among other areas. Often, it was necessary for information, especially on financing mechanisms, to be repeated several times and discussions were supplemented by reading materials. For the policymaker, this project meant learning about minimum data sets, comparison groups, informed consent, random assignment to treatment conditions, and triangulation of methods and perspectives. The principal participants in the case study knew they had made progress when during the third site visit to engage provider agencies in Project FIRST, the policymaker could respond to the question about why random assignment to treatment condition was necessary and the researcher could discuss the features of family-centered intensive case management.

3. In addition to the exchange of written materials and to meeting times, it is very helpful in fostering working relationships for policymakers and researchers to make site visits. These visits expose researchers to how programs work in the real world, who the people providing services are, who is receiving services, what the setting is like, and other issues of importance in designing evaluative research studies. Visits expose policymakers to concerns that providers may have regarding a proposed demonstration and to issues related to referring prospective participants to a study, obtaining informed consent, and providing

clinical backup for persons in demonstrations as well as those choosing not to participate in the research. Site visits are necessary also to conduct an evaluability assessment, an analysis that helps policymakers and researchers determine whether the program has been implemented to such an extent that it can be credibly and reasonably evaluated.

4. At some point in the relationship between policymakers and researchers, it is generally both necessary and desirable to introduce other stakeholders into the project. Such stakeholders might include parents and children, service providers, control agency staff, and legislators. The introduction of a broad array of stakeholders is important because, as seems particularly common in government, key actors often change positions and the outcomes of the project may be more likely to be accepted by policymakers when the project has a broad base of support. In the case management case study, key stakeholders were known to the policymaker who then made the initial arrangements to introduce them to the researcher and to include them in the discussions and briefings. Moreover, parents have become actively involved in shaping evaluative research projects, assisting in the collection of data, in data interpretation, and in disseminating findings from the research.

5. Finally, it is helpful for policymakers and researchers to present their work jointly, both verbally and in writing. Working together to structure these presentations provides yet another opportunity for clarification and learning. In preparing presentations for control agencies and other policymakers, the policy person might take the primary role in structuring the presentations, whereas the researcher would do the same for research audiences. In the case management experience described above, one of the policymakers was the state's commissioner of mental health. Although he was very interested in preparing written presentations of the findings of the project, he had limited time to engage in writing. Having brief meetings, using outlined materials, and agreeing to assignments with reasonable time lines were helpful in maintaining his engagement.

It takes time to establish trust, collaborative working relationships, data sets, and programs of research, but this investment pays off as the partnership develops its own synergy and creativity. Legislators, budget makers, parents, and advocates become willing participants and partners as they recognize a policy framework that is informed by factual data on what works best for whom in what setting and at what cost.

References

Achenbach, T. M. (1991). *Manual for the child behavior checklist and 1991 profile*. Burlington: University of Vermont, Department of Psychiatry.

Armstrong, M. I., Evans, M. E., Kuppinger, A., Huz, S. & Williams-Deane, M. (1996). Project SEED: Services Evaluation and Dissemination. In C. Liberton, K. Kutash, & R. Friedman (Eds.), *The 8th Annual Research Conference Proceedings, A System of Care for Children's Mental Health: Expanding the Research Base* (March 6 to March 8, 1995) (pp. 251-255). Tampa: University of South Florida, Florida Mental Health Institute, Research and Training Center for Children's Mental Health.

Banks, S. M., & Evans, M. E. (1994). Initial outcomes of intensive case management for children with serious emotional disturbance. *1993 Proceedings of the Social Statistics Section of the American Statistical Association*, pp. 816-820.

Burns, B. J., & Friedman, R. M. (1990). Examining the research base for children's mental health services and policy. *Journal of Mental Health Administration, 17*(1), 87-98.

Evans, M. E., Armstrong, M. I., Dollard, N., Kuppinger, A. D., Huz, S., & Wood, V. (1994). Development and evaluation of treatment foster care and family-centered intensive case management. *Journal of Emotional and Behavioral Disorders, 2*(4), 228-238.

Evans, M. E., Banks, S. M., Huz, S., & McNulty, T. L. (1994). Initial hospitalization and community tenure outcomes of intensive case management for children and youth with serious emotional disorder. *Journal of Child and Family Studies, 3*(2), 225-234.

Evans, M. E., Huz, S., McNulty, T., & Banks, S. M. (in press). Child, family, and system outcomes of intensive case management. *Psychiatric Quarterly*.

Hodges, K. (1990). *Child and adolescent functional assessment scales*. Nashville, TN: Vanderbilt Child Mental Health Services Evaluation Project.

Leginski, W. A., Croze, C., Driggers, J., Dumpman, S., Geertsen, D., Kamis-Gould, E., Namerow, M. J., Patton, R. E., Wilson, N. Z., & Wuster, C. R. (1989). *Data standards for mental health decision support systems* (Publication No. ADM 89-1589). Rockville, MD: National Institute of Mental Health.

New York State Office of Mental Health. (1989). *Program guidelines—Intensive case management for children and youth*. Albany: Author, Bureau of Children and Families.

Robinson, G. (1991). Choices in case management. *Community Support Network News, 7*, 11-12.

5

State and Foundation Partnerships to Promote Mental Health Systems Reform for Children and Families

JUDITH C. MEYERS

KING E. DAVIS

In this chapter, we examine the nature and challenges of collaboration between private philanthropic foundations and states working together to reform mental health services and systems for children and their families. First, we explore the role of private foundations in stimulating and supporting major structural change to improve the quality of mental health services for children, adolescents, and their families at the state and local level. Next, we look at the role and importance of state government as a partner in this endeavor. Finally, drawing on our direct experience with the planning and early implementation phase of the Annie E. Casey Foundation's partnership with the commonwealth of

AUTHORS' NOTE: Judith Meyers was Senior Associate for Mental Health at the Annie E. Casey Foundation and managed the Mental Health Initiative for Urban Children from 1992 to 1994. King Davis was the Commissioner of the Virginia Department of Mental Health, Mental Retardation, and Substance Abuse during this same period. This chapter reflects the perspectives of the authors only and is not meant to represent the Annie E. Casey Foundation's point of view.

Virginia through the foundation's Mental Health Initiative for Urban Children, we present our observations about the factors that can contribute to an effective collaboration between foundations and state government.

The Role of Foundations in Supporting
and Sustaining Systems Reform

Private foundations have played a unique role as catalysts and supporters for state and local efforts to undertake reform in the delivery of services to children in need and their families (Annie E. Casey, Ford, and Rockefeller Foundations, 1992; Center for the Study of Social Policy, 1995; Cole & Poe, 1993; Edna McConnell Clark Foundation, 1993; Stephens, Leiderman, Wolf, & McCarthy, 1994). Such foundations are situated uniquely to foster collaboration in support of major change initiatives among the public, private, and nonprofit sectors; citizens; and government officials. Foundations can provide the developmental resources, flexibility in the use of funds, funding sustained for a longer period than by most government agencies, and the motivation to initiate and sustain the difficult and long-term work of reform.

The most obvious contribution of philanthropic foundations is their funding. They can provide risk capital to support activities for which public funds are often not available. Public dollars rarely can be used for the start-up activities involved in developing a vision; strategic planning; or support of the training, technical assistance, and evaluation activities that are critical to major system reform efforts. Funds provided by a foundation also can pay for additional staff time to work on such efforts, time that otherwise may not be available. Human service agency administrators and staff find it difficult enough to keep up with everyday demands without the added responsibility of planning and implementing a major reform effort. Thus, both the additional cash resources and the flexibility in its use are important contributions foundations can make.

Beyond the dollars, foundations have access to a network of resources, including their own staffs, national experts, and an array of research and training centers that can more easily be tapped for the most current information and thinking than can individual states and localities. These resources can be brought to bear on state and local reform initiatives.

A foundation's presence can provide the impetus and support for state or local policymakers to move forward with—and sustain—an ambitious reform agenda. The public sector is structured to maintain the status quo, providing few rewards for innovations that rapidly change structures, policies, direction, financing, or strategies. Immediate cost savings and crisis avoidance often take precedence over longer-term reform, as vividly demonstrated by the current drive to dismantle federal and state funding for many services and supports for children and families. Reforms that lead to better outcomes in the lives of children and families are usually not strongly supported when those outcomes will not be realized for several years or more or if the possibility of an increased commitment of state funding is involved. Foundations, by their very nature, invest in innovation and retain a long-term perspective: "The role of foundations in our society is to be on the cutting edge of progress, to support innovative activities and high risk endeavors, to enter fields of potential controversy where government agencies are reluctant to get involved. This social contribution is the justification for the special tax privileges that produce foundation funds" (Hallman, 1974, p. 291).

Foundations also provide other incentives for states to undertake a system reform effort. States are usually selected to receive foundation grants through some form of competition, whether in response to applications or by direct selection. To be chosen often brings prestige, along with a fairly rigorous set of expectations. If the state is among several that have been selected to participate in a national initiative, that involvement links the state's effort to a national agenda, bringing additional visibility, access to a broad base of expertise, and pressure to succeed. The opportunity to participate in a multistate initiative provides reassurance to state leaders, who often are encouraged by knowing that several other states are engaged in similar work, striving toward similar goals, and taking similar risks. Moreover, there is political cover for embarking on a potentially controversial reform agenda when the agenda is initiated by a nonpartisan organization outside the state.

In the past 6 years, three national philanthropic foundations have invested in partnerships with states to support the reform of mental health or health service systems for children. From 1989 to 1994, the Robert Wood Johnson Foundation funded the Mental Health Services Program for Youth (MHSPY) in eight sites to develop service reform strategies for youth with serious emotional disturbance (SED) and to stimulate innovations in the financing of services (England & Cole, 1992). The Annie E. Casey Foundation, through its Mental Health Initiative for Urban Children, began funding six states in 1992 to develop neighborhood-based, family-centered, prevention-oriented, comprehensive systems of care for children at risk or already identified as having some form of behavioral, cognitive, or emotional disorder. The foundation's intent was to reform policy and practice at the state and local level to support this approach. In 1992, the Pew Charitable Trusts funded five states for 2 years through the Children's Initiative to develop plans for an effective service strategy to improve child health and development through the design of a new system of services that was comprehensive, flexible, family centered, and focused on prevention (Stephens et al., 1994).

The emphasis in all three efforts was on reforming service systems for children rather than merely improving services and creating better linkages between children, families, and services. This direction was based on the belief that the underlying way that services are governed, organized, and financed has to be changed to sustain long-term improvements in outcomes for children. Successful models for serving families and children are fundamentally at odds with the attributes of mainstream service systems, which are usually categorical, crisis driven, fragmented, centralized, unresponsive to the needs of families, and insensitive to variations in culture.

No matter how good services are, they will not be able to keep pace with the increasing needs and demands resulting from the number of children who are born into poverty, exposed to drugs before birth, exposed to increasing levels of televised and actual violence, and suffering the other pressures that are increasingly common. Existing services address problems after the fact, rather than attempt to prevent or reduce the impact of the problems in the first place. If public policy is going to address the adverse conditions of children in any significant way, it must be at the level of organizations, communities, and society. Without changing the underlying structures that govern how services are conceptualized, organized, staffed, financed, and delivered, there will be only islands of excellent programs that cannot be replicated and nothing will have been done to change the conditions of the neighborhoods and communities where children live. Solutions that "fix problems" will continue to be devised as if the observed problems can be fixed without addressing the underlying conditions that led to their creation—"A system is reformed when the best practices known to improve outcomes for children and families have become standard operating procedure and when this reformed system becomes the child and family serving strategy for a community, a state or the nation" (Stephens et al., 1994, p. 6).

Although foundations have been the impetus behind reform efforts, they cannot be the sole actors in reforms that target mental health services for children—largely a responsibility of state government. A foundation can go only so far with its financial and technical resources. State and local governments need to be willing, available, and active partners. The resources provided by a foundation to support a reform initiative for children are relatively minimal when compared to federal, state, and local expenditures on services for children. Foundations can simply provide the seed money, the risk capital, or the impetus for trying, using private funds to leverage public action. Many of the problems, responsibilities, resources, and policies reside with state and local governments; thus, they must be active collaborators in any change effort.

The Role of State Government in Reforming the Children's Mental Health Paradigm

Historically, services for children and adolescents with mental illness have been conceptualized by law and precedent as under the aegis of state and, more recently, local governments. To operationalize their statutory responsibilities, states promulgated a series of policies and designed organizations and services based on the prevailing theoretical paradigms of mental illness and treatment and on the state's fiscal policies (Hudson & Cox, 1991; Mechanic, 1988).

Most of these organizations and their basic missions had their origins in the latter part of the 19th century when state and local governments saw only minimal differences between the mental health problems and needs of children and those of adults. From the late 1700s until recently, the primary method of treating major mental illness in adults was through placement and treatment in large state mental hospitals. Inpatient psychiatric care also became the major method of providing treatment to children and adolescents with SED (Omnibus Budget Reconciliation Act of 1993; Rothman, 1971; Weithorn, 1988). Minimal consideration was given to prevention, the need for structural change, or the creation of systems of care.

In addition, state governments tended to segment the needs of children and adolescents by establishing and financing categorical service approaches, policies, funding streams, and organizations. For many years, each service organization in a state's human service system was seen as disparate, rather than as part of an integrated system (Boyd, 1992; Macbeth, 1993). Consequently, children and adolescents with SED could be found in underfinanced and isolated child welfare systems, juvenile courts, special education, child guidance clinics, the general health care system, outpatient mental health systems, the state hospital system, or their own homes. Children and their families were required to meet different standards of eligibility and undergo numerous intakes. They were transferred from one system to another based on the mission, funding, policies, or auspices of the agency rather than on the needs of the child being served. The prevailing state paradigms of mental illness and treatment resulted in fragmented, inaccessible, complex, inefficient, duplicative, and competitive services driven by a complex array of regulations and policies, none of which adequately met the needs of children and adolescents with mental health problems or their families (Cole & Poe, 1993; Looney, 1988).

To address the problems in providing mental health services to children and families, the National Institute of Mental Health developed the Child and Adolescent Service System Program (CASSP) (Stroul & Friedman, 1986) to provide resources to states to improve their service systems at the state and local level. Within a few years of the implementation of CASSP in 1984, almost all states had availed themselves of the funding. The funding catalyzed the development and implementation of new programs and new service models and helped leverage additional funding to support a comprehensive, coordinated, community-based, family-centered system of care. The continued need for high-quality mental health services for children and adolescents with

SED and their families stimulated considerable interest in identifying and evaluating strategies and models for service system reform.

In the 10 years since the first CASSP grants were awarded, a great deal has been learned about the need for complete systems of care. There is also new understanding of collaborative relationships across child-serving systems, between levels of government, and between the public and private sectors. Most important, there is a greater understanding of the role of families as partners in treatment and of new models of intensive treatment that serve children in their own homes and communities rather than in residential placements. At the same time, much remains to be learned about how to develop a system that is more prevention oriented and targets children at risk, how to appropriately serve children and families from diverse cultural and socioeconomic groups, and how to sustain reform of state and local service systems (Knitzer, 1993). To this end, the Annie E. Casey Foundation designed the Mental Health Initiative for Urban Children.

The Annie E. Casey Foundation's Mental Health Initiative

The Annie E. Casey Foundation was founded in 1948 by Jim Casey, one of the founders of United Parcel Service, and his siblings. With assets of more than $1 billion, it is the nation's largest philanthropy dedicated exclusively to reforming public policies and improving the effectiveness of major institutions serving children and their families, with a particular emphasis on low-income children. The foundation supports efforts to transform community environments through comprehensive reform initiatives intended to create the fiscal, organizational, and policy environments in which effective programs that are more preventive, family focused, flexible, and community based can flourish at the state, local, and neighborhood levels (Annie E. Casey Foundation, 1994).

The Mental Health Initiative for Urban Children is one such effort of the foundation. Launched in 1992, the goal of this initiative is to improve outcomes for troubled children, adolescents, and their families in high-poverty urban neighborhoods. The initiative funds states to work in partnership with cities and neighborhoods to demonstrate new ways of establishing community-based approaches to mental health care that focus on prevention and early intervention, that deliver services in a culturally appropriate manner, that recognize the needs of family members and involve them in the design and delivery of services, and that improve state and local policies and practices to support this new approach to services (King & Meyers, 1996).

Systems change is to be achieved through three primary strategic interventions. State and local systems that serve children and families should (a) be neighborhood based, with more local control over the design, development, and implementation of services; (b) be integrated across all child-serving systems, including education, health, juvenile justice, child welfare, employment and training, and mental health; and (c) focus a greater proportion of resources on prevention and early intervention to keep problems from becoming so severe that out-of-home care or out-of-community placements are the only alternatives for children. Supports and services for children are to be expanded to include a full array of services that are more family centered, flexible, and culturally competent. Mental health services are to be integrated into existing community settings and activities that offer greater access for children and families and where the services are less stigmatizing, such as in schools, community health centers, churches, and recreation centers that are available to all children, not just those with special needs. Neighborhood development activities, including physical improvement and economic development, are to be increased.

In 1992, the Casey Foundation gave $150,000 planning grants to states selected for evidence of their commitment to, and demonstrated capacity for, reforming their mental health service systems for children. Beginning in 1994, four of these states—Florida, Massachusetts, Texas, and Virginia—each received additional funding of $3 million over 4 years to continue to develop and implement their strategies. Each state selected a neighborhood demonstration site. The neighborhood sites include the East Little Havana section of Miami, the Roxbury neighborhood of Boston, the Third Ward area of Houston, and the East End section of Richmond.

The foundation expects these states and localities to reform policies and practices to support the neighborhood-based approach through (a) integrating planning and programming across all child-serving systems, (b) restructuring financial practices and policies with necessary flexibility to provide for the development of a system of care at the neighborhood level, (c) developing new ways of delivering services, (d) developing the necessary management information systems to support an integrated approach, (e) involving families in a significant way, and (f) evaluating and tracking client and system outcomes. The Casey Foundation recognized that these goals may represent a significant shift in a state's prior or current approach to service delivery.

Here, we examine how this partnership between the foundation and one of the four states, Virginia, was forged, as well as what were the important elements of success during the first 2 years of the initiative, encompassing the planning year and first year of implementation funding. The foundation will continue funding the initiative and working in partnership with the states through 1997, so the present observations reflect only the first phase—getting started. Although only elements in the context of Virginia's experience are described here, the general conclusions are applicable to the other three sites as well.

The Climate for
Reform in Virginia

In 1989, the child-serving systems in Virginia exhibited many of the problems that the Casey Foundation's Urban Initiative sought to address. Leadership in the public and private sectors had recognized the need to bring about major reform in the way that services were conceptualized and implemented. The dilemma in Virginia was how to shift the historic costly overreliance on institutionalization and categorical thinking to a more collaborative and integrated system of services for children and families. Some previous efforts to effect reform had been limited by a lack of resources, as well as by a lack of supportive legislation and leadership.

Between 1987 and 1990, a number of modest reform efforts were implemented. These initial efforts created a service environment at the local and state levels that resulted in a significant decrease in the use of state hospitalization for children. The results demonstrated the importance of collaboration between agencies and organizations in the public and private sectors and the significant role that families and communities could assume with regard to services for children with SED.

In 1990, Governor L. Douglas Wilder focused his administration's leadership on modifying policies and resources to better serve the needs of children and families. Governor Wilder had an exceptionally good base of data on which to launch a legislative appeal for a major reform in services. A report by the Virginia Mental Health Association (1988) indicated that close to 50% of children in residential care were in placements outside the borders of Virginia. The overall rates of institutionalization for children and adolescents were among the highest in the country. These same children and their families also were receiving services from other agencies across a number of service systems, but care was not coordinated, let alone integrated, and there were no efforts to prevent hospitalization by providing more intensive home-based services. Moreover, legislative studies had clearly identified the extent to which children and adolescents with SED were extensive users of inpatient psychiatric care in state hospitals as well as in out-of-state placements.

On the basis of the findings of these studies, budget analysts in the governor's office sought to identify the costs for out-of-state placements and the potential savings if alternate models of care could be developed (McGaughey, 1990). They recommended major changes in policies and practice, allowing for more flexibility in planning, funding, and service delivery and for sharing information and data across state agencies and between state and local government and private agencies. Governor Wilder was able to use these studies to stimulate support for major legislative and fiscal initiatives that called for a comprehensive services system for children and their families—the Comprehensive Services Act for At-Risk Youth and Families of 1992. The services system for children in Virginia was totally redesigned, shifting the focus from the agency to the family, from treatment to prevention, from family separation to family preservation, from multiple funding streams to one consolidated funding stream, from residential care to community-based care, and from conflicting to cooperative policies. These core concepts clearly were consistent with the interests of the Casey Foundation and led to the foundation's selecting Virginia as a state with both the capacity and the commitment to engage with the foundation to further reform service delivery systems for children.

In 1993, Governor Wilder signed Virginia's application to participate in the Casey Foundation's Mental Health Initiative for Urban Children. In his letter to the foundation, Wilder strongly stated that revitalizing and reorganizing services for troubled youth and their families was his top priority. Virginia's interest in collaborating with the foundation was based on the desire to support and extend its existing reform efforts. The Mental Health Initiative was a means of bridging gaps between local and state government agencies, structuring services to meet the particular needs of urban youth, and gaining access to information and innovative models for financing service reform without using limited state general fund dollars.

Had Virginia not been in the midst of a major recession that threatened its ability to balance its budget and maintain services, state policymakers may not have been as ready to undertake such a significant reform effort. Although Virginians had sought to reform aspects of the child-serving system for over two decades, it seems likely that the effort would have followed a more traditional incremental approach rather than the major reform called for by the Casey Foundation. The Mental Health Initiative represented an opportunity to demonstrate the utility of collaboration beyond state and local government, expanding to include other stakeholders in the provision of services to children, adolescents, and their families. The Mental Health Initiative for Urban Children was a pioneering effort that was designed to learn as much as possible from the experience in the participating states, cities, and neighborhoods. Although the initiative is still in the early stages, the experiences of the first 2 years of the collaboration between the Casey Foundation and the commonwealth of Virginia—both the successes and the mistakes—are informative for others seeking to understand the nature of such a partnership and the important elements that potentially can contribute to its effectiveness.

Elements of Effective Partnerships
Between States and Foundations

The following nine factors were observed to be important ingredients for success in the collaboration between the Casey Foundation, the commonwealth of Virginia, and the city of Richmond.

1. *Compatible Vision and Goals.* The Casey Foundation's Mental Health Initiative was an ambitious reform effort that required states to reconsider the entire way in which they administered, financed, and governed children's service systems. The initiative was not likely to succeed in a state that did not share that broad vision or have the capacity to achieve it. For the foundation to use its resources to entice a state to adopt this reform agenda would likely have resulted in much time, energy, and resources being wasted, leading to disappointment for everyone involved. In Virginia, improving services for children and families was an instrumental goal of the Wilder administration. The foundation did not need to sell the governor on the efficacy of the Mental Health Initiative or the importance of reforming services for children.

2. *The Commitment and Involvement of Top Leadership.* For a reform of state policies and services to succeed, commitment from the top leadership is important. The state must have leadership that can articulate the vision, build the necessary consensus, manage the complex change process, weather the storms, and sustain commitment to ensure success over time. Structural changes of the magnitude contemplated by the foundation required that the governor or key cabinet members provide the leadership and impetus to support the desired changes, ultimately supporting the necessary legislative and fiscal initiatives to sustain the reform over time.

In Virginia, Governor Wilder's leadership and support guaranteed the participation of all key cabinet members and relevant local government officials. Meetings between the governor, his cabinet, and foundation staff helped to clarify the areas of commonality between the needs and plans of the state and the foundation and set the tone for successful collaboration.

3. *Attention to Other Needs of State Policymakers.* For foundations to engage the commitment of top leadership, it is helpful not only to form partnerships with governors who share the vision for reform but also to help state policymakers fulfill other concurrent obligations. Many components of the Mental Health Initiative have broader ramifications for the way states do business. The Casey Foundation could provide consultation on such concerns as refinancing, development of inte-

grated management information systems (MIS), fulfilling the planning requirements of the federal Family Preservation and Support Services Program under Title IV-B of the Social Security Act (Omnibus Budget Reconciliation Act of 1993), and preparing applications for the federal Empowerment Zone/Enterprise Community Program (EZ/EC). States could benefit in the short term while putting in place the mechanisms for long-term change. By being responsive to the complex and extensive needs of the state, a foundation can build and sustain commitment from a broad base of supporters at the state and local level.

In Virginia, consultants hired by the Casey Foundation assisted both the state and the city of Richmond with analyzing financing opportunities, furthering the development of the city's MIS system, and providing funds to assist with Richmond's EZ/EC application, all of which helped open minds as well as doors to the benefits of participating in the larger reform effort.

4. Broad-Based Commitment for the Vision and Strategies of the Reform Effort. Although congruence with the current administration's agenda is significant at the start, it does not guarantee sustained support. Since Virginia has one-term governors, the Mental Health Initiative became dependent on the extent to which the next governor made these same issues a priority. In 1994, Governor Wilder was replaced by Governor George Allen, a conservative Republican with a very different agenda from that of his Democratic predecessor. The Mental Health Initiative was identified as belonging to the former governor and his cabinet members. During the first 6 months of the new administration, the foundation staff had limited contact with the new Republican administration and state agencies were uncertain about continuation of support for the initiative. By the close of 1994, the initiative was still operative, but it was less of a priority in the Allen administration, and thus the continuation of the reform effort seemed uncertain.

As a result of the election, there also was a gradual turnover of staff at all levels in the office of the secretary of Health and Human Services and the Department of Mental Health, so that much of the initial groundwork for the reform initiative was in jeopardy. Bipartisan and legislative support may have helped circumvent some of the setbacks at the state level. Ownership by one individual, one party, one agency, or even one branch of government cannot sustain a reform agenda over time. Broadening the base of support at the earliest possible time with deliberate inclusion strategies is important.

Stephens et al. (1994) reported this same lesson in their experience with the Pew Charitable Trusts' Children's Initiative:

> To achieve maximum benefit, strategies to broaden commitment to the vision should be aimed at building support . . . among key legislators and private sector leaders, across multiple state agencies and among staff at many levels within state agencies. Private sector leaders at the state and community level and committed communities are essential; they become the force that moves system reform across administrative changes or changes in leadership in key state agency positions. Experience also shows that a broad base of support that includes these constituencies can keep system reform on the agenda through political and funding setbacks. (p. 17)

5. *Support From the "Bottom Up" as Well as the "Top Down."* The active participation by families, advocacy groups, local governments, and private providers in all phases of a restructuring effort is essential for building support for the change and also is key to sustaining support through changes in leadership at the top. Although leaders come and go, those at the community level, particularly families of children receiving services, local providers, and concerned community members, are there for the long haul and can be the most important force for sustaining the push for change. After all, they are the ultimate beneficiaries.

6. *Time to Forge State, City, and Neighborhood Partnerships for Reform.* The Mental Health Initiative was designed as a multilevel strategy. The Casey Foundation envisioned state government working in partnership with city government and one neighborhood within that city where a neighborhood governance group would be established. This arrangement would ensure that those most directly affected by the services would have a voice in services design and delivery. Stakeholders could bring the benefit of their experience, culture, and understanding of their needs to the table while also ensuring that those who currently had control of the policies, regulations, and resources would use their authority and power to make the necessary changes to support a more community-owned, community-driven system.

The development of this three-level partnership was much more difficult and took much longer than was originally anticipated. From the earliest stages of preparing a proposal to the foundation, the roles and relationships among the levels was a source of tension in Virginia. Each level of government saw itself as the rightful owner of the initiative. Neighborhood leaders in the East End believed that they should make decisions affecting their residents independent of the state, city, or foundation. Prior experience with city government had left them feeling that they would never be empowered unless they controlled all phases of the project. At the same time, unresolved tensions between local and state mental health authorities over ownership and management of resources were played out over this initiative. The local mental health agency in Richmond interpreted the state's more active fiscal role in the Mental Health Initiative as portending a major change in state policies in the direction of interfering with local autonomy. Local government and citizen groups are not accustomed to the level of shared authority and citizen empowerment envisioned by the foundation. The state, as the recipient of the grant from the foundation, believed it had ultimate responsibility and authority over the initiative. With the prior history of mistrust, tension rose and energy was diverted toward resolving these ownership issues rather than designing and developing a different approach to service delivery.

The foundation and state agency staff learned that this new way of working with states, cities, and neighborhoods requires a longer time than originally anticipated—perhaps 2 years or more—and benefits from the assistance of neutral external consultants to facilitate the process. Consultants proved to be very useful in resolving remnants of mistrust between neighborhood residents and city agencies in Richmond, as well as between the city and state. The negotiations about the balance of power and roles were, and are likely to be, an ongoing process. At the same time, the importance of this partnership became ever clearer, as commitment at the state level was wavering. The initiative's strong focus within the city of Richmond and the East End neighborhood has helped sustain the work.

7. *Building the Capacity of Participants.* Moving from a philosophical commitment to the actual implementation of system reform requires that the participants at the neighborhood, city, and state levels develop

new attitudes, beliefs, skills, and capabilities to alter what they can do and understand. Initially, this was most obvious in the participants at the neighborhood level. Although "empowerment" is much the buzzword these days, devolving authority without allowing for the development of skills and capacities to manage the responsibility can lead to chaos. There have been too many cases where locally driven efforts have had disappointing results because the community members engaged in the effort have not been given the tools to do the job well. Observations by Peter Senge and his colleagues (Senge, Kleiner, Roberts, Ross, & Smith, 1994) about the movement to empower workers in a private sector organization have relevance to community empowerment as well:

> Today, many executives are articulating a new philosophy revolving around "empowering people." But few organizations are working hard to introduce tools and methods to actually help people to make more intelligent decisions, especially decisions that improve systemwide performance. The result will likely be organizations that decentralize authority for a while, find that many poor and uncoordinated decisions result, and then abandon the "empowerment" fad and recentralize. The "empowered" soil will lie fallow, with no seeds to grow. This, of course, is precisely what many of the newly "empowered" workers, cynical from past management fads, fear. (p. 40)

Board members elected to the East End governing board grappled with these issues as they sought autonomy while recognizing the need for training in group decision making, needs assessment, program development, policy development, and financial oversight. It also became increasingly clear that staff in both city and state government needed training. If government was to fundamentally change the way it operated, workers, from managers to frontline staff, had to understand and act on this new approach in all aspects of their work so that the new beliefs, assumptions, attitudes, and sensibilities of systemic thinking permeated all they did. This would not happen without a strategic approach to training.

Because the initiative is a pioneering effort, it was difficult to anticipate in advance the training needs of participants at all levels. The experience of the Mental Health Initiative demonstrated that the provision of high-quality, targeted technical assistance can help build the capacity to manage and sustain the systems change effort and greatly add to future understanding of the capacities needed to succeed and the strategies for developing them.

8. *There Can Be Such a Thing as Too Much Money.* Although external funding can create excitement, focus attention, and provide an important incentive for participating in a reform effort, too much money can divert attention from the central purpose. The dollars may draw local agencies to the table to secure a piece of the pie. When they realize the money is not available to support existing services, they may withdraw or sabotage the effort if it is seen as critical of or competing with their own work. Misunderstandings potentially can occur—if they were doing a good job, why would there be a need for reform?

Also, when targeting change in poor urban neighborhoods with high and visible service needs, as in the East End of Richmond, it is difficult not to respond to pressing local needs for new programs, rather than fund longer-term reform. An initiative that brings extensive dollars with it may result in more motivation to secure the dollars to support current needs rather than to participate in efforts to reform the broader service system and improve outcomes for children in the future. The lesson learned is that too much money received too soon can divert attention from the central purposes of a reform initiative.

9. *The Importance of Evaluation.* A critical role for foundations is to evaluate and disseminate the impact of reform efforts on children, communities, and public policy. To contribute to more informed public policy for disadvantaged children, the Casey Foundation conducts rigorous outcome and process evaluations of its major demonstrations. The goal is to provide policymakers, administrators, and direct service providers with well-documented examples of what works, what does not, and why.

To document and describe the benefits of the reform and to maximize learning from the process, the evaluation has to measure outcomes for the children and families in the neighborhood site as well as the changes in policy and practice at the state and local levels. The evaluation also has to provide the participants with timely information that assists them with their work.

The Florida Mental Health Institute of the University of South Florida, in collaboration with the Casey Foundation and with input and participation from each demonstration site, is conducting a comprehensive, independent evaluation of the Mental Health Initiative. The evaluation will describe the fundamental processes by which system changes occur in the different sites and measure the ultimate outcomes for children and families touched by the intervention. To do this across four states, the evaluation team is using the case study approach as a framework for data collection as well as a combination of longitudinal and cross-sectional research designs for data analysis and interpretation. Under this approach, each site is considered a "case" and studied independently with a variety of methodologies, including focus groups, individual case studies, key informant interviews, surveys, and quantitative data on service arrays and capacity. In addition, a qualitative ethnographic study is intended to provide a baseline description of social and cultural characteristics of two project sites, Richmond and Houston. Because of the long-term nature of the initiative, the evaluation will follow each site's progress over time to document system change. Finally, findings from the individual sites will be compared and general conclusions drawn regarding the effectiveness of the initiative as a whole (Hernandez, 1994).

The evaluation is an important component of the partnership between states and the foundation. The expectation that a state will participate in an evaluation is stated up front and is a condition for the receipt of grant funds. But the collaboration still is not easy. The perception that evaluation is synonymous with criticism can create an atmosphere in which sharing information involves risks that many prefer not to take. To establish baseline information about services in a neighborhood required the cooperation of a great many people from a multitude of public and not-for-profit agencies with varying degrees of sophistication with regard to their data. The commitment to produce the data was made at the top and did not necessarily carry over to agencies and staff down the line. The evaluation team offered extensive technical assistance to help retrieve and analyze the data, but in environments where the threat of the budget ax is ever present, agencies are not eager to share detailed information to outsiders about whom they serve and at what cost. This, and the lack of technology in many public agencies, makes evaluation of this type of initiative a particular challenge.

The state of the art in developing methodologies to measure outcomes in a multidimensional intervention such as this initiative is still in its developmental stage. Foundation support for this type of evaluation, which often fails to meet the more rigorous requirements of federal funding agencies, has been significant in helping to accumulate an experience base on which to build better tools.

The Challenges of Foundation-State Collaboration

Foundations can serve as catalysts for change, but ultimately they cannot make specific changes happen. Comprehensive reform is complex, time consuming, and politically difficult. It requires people in state government to think and act broadly and deeply, challenges the status quo on a wide number of issues, and asks for simultaneous action across the whole spectrum of social policy. It takes a long time to do, yet people expect fast results and can easily become discouraged. Politicians who face reelection every few years are particularly eager to see demonstrable results quickly but become anxious if the pace of change is too rapid and the extent of reform too substantive. Gradualism often is politically more acceptable.

States may not always welcome outside funders with open arms. Although a funder may use the rhetoric of promoting an equal partnership, a certain degree of power comes with control of funding. The funder determines whether or not to continue funding and always has the option of walking away from the grantee or the initiative, leaving the state in an awkward position. On the other hand, the funder has few controls over how the state keeps to the terms of the partnership. Once the grant funds are accepted, there are many ways for the state to fail to fulfill its obligations, not the least of which is to pull out altogether when an election leads to a change in administration. As in any partnership, the commitment to the task has to be reevaluated and renewed periodically.

Foundation funding ultimately ends. It is often referred to as "glue," "bridge," or "seed" money, to help a state effort get started, to pay for planning activities that are harder to fund with state general funds, or to provide a bridge to pay for new services while a system undergoes reform. The state and federal expenditures on services for children far exceed the amount any foundation can supply. Ultimately, if any reform effort is to be sustained, a state has to reform the way in which it uses its resources to support a new direction in service delivery. States often fear that they will be unable to keep the work going after a foundation's grant of limited duration ends. The concern of foundations is that the state will not have committed to or achieved substantial reform in its financing of services to make enough of a difference in the long term.

Conclusion

Over the past several decades, considerable progress has been made in some states in changing the direction of services for children and their families. But close examination of these efforts shows that services for children remain underdeveloped and too dependent on inpatient hospitalization. For many reasons, services for children and their families remain low in priority for state and local governments.

Part of the impediment to change in services has been the inability of state governments to invest the requisite financial, political, and human capital to plan and implement new initiatives. In too many instances, fundamental change is thought of as involving greater risk than state governments are willing to assume alone. Foundations offer state and local governments the opportunity to modify their systems of care for children and families by participating in collaborative efforts in which costs, risks, and benefits are shared. In return for their investment of risk capital and expertise, foundations have asked state and local governments to stretch their vision of how services for children are to be conceptualized, structured, financed, implemented, coordinated, and evaluated. A number of states have entered these collaborative relationships with the Casey Foundation, among others.

The Casey Foundation was able to build a collaborative relationship with state and local government in Virginia. The factors that supported this collaboration are multiple. Perhaps most important in understanding why this collaboration occurred is to recognize the importance of thinking in systems terms. The Casey Foundation based its initiative on the idea that the approaches to serving children form interlocking systems. Where services are provided in isolated and disjointed ways, children and their families suffer. In Virginia, the Casey Foundation found its conceptual perspective was congruent with that held by Governor Wilder, key legislators, and organizations. This compatibility of perspectives about caring for children helped stimulate and sustain the collaboration. The absence of this congruency in the new administration threatens the continuation of collaboration.

It is clear that foundations cannot take on the task of comprehensive reform without this sense of a shared vision for children. Successful collaboration is built on government and foundations joining forces and committing resources to this vision. Because foundation investments and political positions are by definition time limited, the desire for change in services must be embedded deeply in the ethos of the state. In the final analysis, the foundation's presence simply provides the reinforcement, the opportunity, and the encouragement for states to pursue an agenda to which they already are committed.

References

Annie E. Casey, Ford, and Rockefeller Foundations. (1992). *Building strong communities: Strategies for urban change* [Conference report].

Annie E. Casey Foundation. (1994). *Annual report*. Baltimore, MD: Author.

Boyd, L. (1992). *Integrating systems of care for children and families*. Tampa: University of South Florida.

Center for the Study of Social Policy. (1995). *Building new futures for at-risk youth: Findings from a five-year, multi-site evaluation*. Washington, DC: Author.

Cole, R., & Poe, S. (1993). *Partnerships for care: Systems of care for children with serious emotional disturbances and their families*. Washington, DC: Washington Business Group on Health.

Comprehensive Services Act for At-Risk Youth and Families of 1992, Code of Virginia, Ch. 46, §§ 2.1-745-2.1-759.

Edna McConnell Clark Foundation. (1993). *Annual report*. New York: Author.

England, M., & Cole, R. (1992). Building systems of care for youth with serious mental illness. *Hospital & Community Psychiatry, 43*, 630-633.

Hallman, H. (1974). *Neighborhood government in a metropolitan setting*. Beverly Hills, CA: Sage.

Hernandez, M. (1994). *Evaluation of the Mental Health Initiative for Urban Children*. Tampa: Florida Mental Health Institute.

Hudson, C., & Cox, A. (1991). *Dimensions of state mental health policy*. New York: Praeger.

King, B., & Meyers, J. (1996). The Annie E. Casey Foundation's Mental Health Initiative for Urban Children. In B. Stroul (Ed.), *Children's mental health: Creating systems of care in a changing society* (pp. 249-261). Baltimore, MD: Paul H. Brookes.

Knitzer, J. (1993). Children's mental health policy: Challenging the future. *Journal of Emotional and Behavioral Disorders, 1*, 8-16.

Looney, J. (1988). The struggles for a strategy. In J. Looney (Ed.), *Chronic mental illness in children and adolescents* (pp. 237-259). Washington, DC: American Psychiatric Association.

Macbeth, G. (1993). Collaboration can be elusive: Virginia's experience in developing an interagency system of care. *Administration and Policy in Mental Health, 20,* 259-282.

McGaughey, K. (1990). *Study of children's residential services in Virginia.* Richmond: Department of Planning and Budget, Office of the Governor, Commonwealth of Virginia.

Mechanic, D. (1988). *Mental health and social policy* (3rd ed.). Englewood Cliffs, NJ: Prentice Hall.

Omnibus Budget Reconciliation Act of 1993 (P.L. 103-66, § 13711. Codified as Subpart 2 of Title IV-B of the Social Security Act) 42 U.S.C. §§ 430, et seq.

Rothman, D. (1971). *The discovery of the asylum: Social order and disorder in the new republic.* Boston: Little, Brown.

Senge, P., Kleiner, A., Roberts, C., Ross, R., & Smith, B. (1994). *The fifth discipline fieldbook: Strategies and tools for building a learning organization.* New York: Doubleday.

Stephens, S., Leiderman, S., Wolf, W., & McCarthy, P. (1994). *Building capacity for system reform.* Bala Cynwyd, PA: Center for Assessment and Policy Development.

Stroul, B. A., & Friedman, R. M. (1986). *A system of care for severely disturbed children and youth.* Washington, DC: Georgetown University, Child Development Center, CASSP Technical Assistance Center.

Virginia Mental Health Association. (1988). *The invisible children's report.* Richmond: Author.

Weithorn, L. (1988). Mental hospitalization for troublesome youth: An analysis of skyrocketing admission rates. *Stanford Law Review, 40,* 773-838.

The Tennessee Children's Plan

How Do We Get There?

KATHLEEN A. MALOY

Everyone agreed about the goals of the Children's Plan . . . but no one agreed about how to get there.

—A Tennessee State Official

The Need to Study Reform Efforts of Individual States

The time is long overdue to begin addressing the compelling needs of children and families (National Commission on Children, 1991). There is considerable agreement among policymakers about the necessity for services that are family focused, community based, culturally competent, and linked to other systems such as education and social welfare (Duchnowski & Friedman, 1990; Knitzer, 1993; Stroul & Friedman, 1986). These policymakers assert a concomitant belief that

AUTHOR'S NOTE: This research was conducted while the author was a research associate at the Center for Mental Health Policy, Vanderbilt Institute for Public Policy Studies, Vanderbilt University, Nashville, TN. The research was funded primarily by the Annie E. Casey Foundation and the state of Tennessee and was supported by Vanderbilt University.

117

the availability and effectiveness of community-based interventions to address these critical needs are often compromised by disorganized and fragmented systems of care. Consequently, efforts are under way in many states and communities to reform the delivery of health and mental health services by creating coordinated and integrated systems of care that encompass a full range of community-based options (Stroul, 1993; Stroul & Friedman, 1994).

There is no exemplary way, however, to go about making these kinds of broad-based, community-oriented system changes. In fact, researchers and advocates agree that although much knowledge is available about what should be done for children and families in need there seems to be much less knowledge about how to move forward with needed reforms (Saxe, Cross, & Silverman, 1988; Schorr, 1988). Moreover, there is a significant lack of knowledge about whether large-scale system reform efforts make the most sense in terms of achieving the policy goals of serving children and their families in need (Maloy, 1991). Serious concerns are expressed that the political, financial, and organizational changes necessary to implement such broad and comprehensive system reforms may be too difficult to achieve in states and communities (General Accounting Office, 1992). This gap between knowing what ought to be done and knowing how to do it is well known in the public policy arena. The research literature documents the significant lack of empirically based knowledge about effective processes for translating policy goals into concrete actions amenable to the capacities of state and local governments (Ethridge & Percy, 1993).

In light of the severity and complexity of the problems facing children and families, the crisis conditions in many service systems intended to address these problems, and the lack of knowledge about how to successfully implement reform efforts, there is an urgent need to examine and assess current reform efforts (Friedman, 1993; Rog, 1992). The dynamics involved in establishing such broad-based reforms at the state and local levels are necessarily complex and involve the interests of multiple stakeholders. There are, however, valuable lessons to be learned from careful examinations of individual reform efforts (Saxe, Cross, Lovas, & Gardner, 1993). Although there are always unique aspects associated with the circumstances of any single endeavor, there is much constructive and generally applicable knowledge to be gained from informed and structured inquiry into individual cases (Paul-

Shaheen, 1990). The Tennessee Children's Plan presents just such an opportunity for studying a significant statewide reform effort.

Unveiled in early 1991, the Tennessee Children's Plan signaled the advent of fundamental changes in the philosophy and operation of the service delivery system for children in Tennessee. The policies underlying the Children's Plan envisioned a system designed to expand and improve children's services so that fewer children would have to be removed from their homes and placed in state custody to obtain needed services. When completely implemented, the Children's Plan would establish a delivery system with an innovative approach to financing that (a) provides uniform assessment of all children in state custody or referred to precustodial assessment; (b) develops a comprehensive array of treatment, prevention, and reunification services; (c) provides treatment for children in the least restrictive alternative possible; and (d) utilizes state and community resources in an efficient, well-managed care coordination network.

The Children's Plan was, and continues to be, the product of an intensive effort involving numerous state departments, the executive and legislative branches, and various organizations with long-standing concerns about children's issues. As in most states, in Tennessee there was a long-standing awareness of the problems and deficits in services for children (Edwards, 1992; Maloy, 1994). The policymaking and implementation process was a complex one that drew on significant resources outside the state, the commitment of key individuals in state government, years of activism by child advocates, and the cumulative effects of various state initiatives.

Consequently, the Tennessee Children's Plan provided an important opportunity to examine the process of how the public policies underlying the Children's Plan were initially established and operationalized. In this chapter, I present the results of a case study that examined the decision-making and implementation activities associated with the Children's Plan during the first 2 years of implementation, 1991-1992. The broad goal of this study was to generate knowledge about *how* and *how well* reformed and coordinated systems for service delivery to children *can actually be put in place* at the state and local levels.

This single-case study approach provides an effective vehicle for creating a richly descriptive, empirically based assessment of the initial efforts at implementation and of the nitty-gritty aspects of making the changes envisioned by public policies. Although the data are drawn from one state's efforts at reform, a properly contextualized and carefully framed case study can provide instructive insights that are applicable to situations in other states and local communities. To facilitate informative comparisons with efforts in other venues, I describe the historical context for addressing children's issues in Tennessee as well as an overview of the origins of the Tennessee Children's Plan and its activities during 1991-1992 are described below. I then review the study methods, present the results of the data analysis, and discuss the results and their implications.

Historical Context for the Tennessee Children's Plan

The Tennessee Children's Plan, although heralded as a new approach to families and children in crisis, did not come out of the blue. Preceding the introduction of the Children's Plan was a more-than-decade-long period of concerted activity addressing children's issues in Tennessee. There have been task forces, commissions, committees, lawsuits, cabinet councils, and advocacy organizations addressing the problems and issues associated with various aspects of children's services in Tennessee (Maloy, 1994).[1]

As in most states, the initial focus was on services for delinquents and juvenile offenders, driven largely by the federal focus on deinstitutionalization pursuant to the Juvenile Justice and Delinquency Prevention Act of 1974. In the late 1970s and early 1980s, the Tennessee Law Enforcement Planning Agency and the Tennessee-based Institute for Children's Resources—a federally funded youth advocacy initiative— focused their reform efforts on the juvenile justice system. Although the primary vehicle for these efforts was the enactment and enforcement of a jail removal bill, the reforms always included an emphasis on improving and expanding the delivery of services to juvenile offenders. In 1985, an extraordinary session of the state legislature on corrections, although primarily focused on adult corrections, generated a set of mandates and recommendations addressing the need for central intake, uniform assessment, community-based alternatives, computerized record keeping, and interagency coordination and suggested the desirability of a more comprehensive approach to serving delinquent youth. The successful efforts to revise the 1988 Youth Corrections Plan and to create the Department of Youth Development in 1989 continued a broadened emphasis on community-based services and the need for a more coordinated approach.

Notwithstanding the compelling demands of reforming the juvenile justice system, efforts and attention also were gradually focused on other populations of children in need. The 1980 *Report of the Select Committee for the Study of Children's Services* focused on the need for a continuum of care, community-based service delivery, and coordinated communication between the custodial departments. In 1983, the Task Force on Mental Health Services for Children and Youth reiterated these objectives and identified the need for more creative financing to support service development. In 1985, the governor's Cabinet Council on Social Services assessed the condition of children's services and identified the need for improved planning and increased resources, more flexibility in accessing programs, and standardized record keeping. In 1989, another task force, the Children's Mental Health Task Force Report Committee, produced yet another lengthy report with numerous recommendations. These recommendations revisited and expanded on the importance of community-based principles in service delivery and the need for innovative financing strategies. This report also emphasized the necessity of a family-focused approach to serving children.

In the late 1980s, the state took steps to address these reports and recommendations. Two initiatives, the Interdepartmental Case Assessment and Management (ICAM) and the Assessment Intake and Management System (AIMS), represented efforts to implement mechanisms for central intake, uniform assessment, and interdepartmental cooperation. The Department of Mental Health and Mental Retardation pursued the development of community-based child mental health services through efforts such as the federal Child and Adolescent Service System Program (CASSP). The three custodial departments—the Departments of Mental Health and Mental Retardation, Human Services, and Youth Development—collaborated in developing family preservation services and in pursuing additional funds for these programs. The Department of Youth Development took steps to meet its statutory mandate to reduce the number of youth in institutional placements by developing community-based programs. The latter part of the 1980s seemed to bring more progress on children's services issues in Tennessee, although the focus of attention and resources continued to be primarily on children in state custody.

In pursuit of further information about placements and services for these children, David Manning, commissioner of the Department of Finance and Administration (DF&A), ordered a one-day case review of all children in state custody on May 1, 1989. This study, drawing on a sample of children in custody and relying on the efforts of all child-serving departments, was intended to assess the type and appropriateness of services being received by these children. A report, *Assessment of Children and Youth Committed to State Care on May 1st, 1989* (Tennessee Department of Finance and Administration, Division of Budget), was published in April 1990. The results indicated that although approximately 60% of children were appropriately placed, 10% of the children needed more intensive placements and 30% of the children needed less intensive placements. The report concluded that well over half of the children in the most intensive and expensive placements did not need to be there; too many dollars were being spent in unnecessarily restrictive placements. This report provided both the catalyst for the introduction of the Children's Plan in early 1991 and the basis for the leadership of Manning and the DF&A.

Overview of the
Tennessee Children's Plan

In early February 1991, Manning's presentation to the Tennessee Select Committee on Children and Youth (SCCY) on the Children's Plan articulated the following philosophies and policies concerning children and families in crisis and the need for change:

- The services provided by the state should be based on need.
- The system should be family focused and grounded in the belief that families, not governmental agencies, are the most ideal custodians for children.
- Funding of services should be noncategorical, that is, resources should be flexible enough to follow the needs of individual children and families.

- Services to families should not only be crisis driven but also be available to families at risk before the health, safety, or removal of the child is threatened.

- The system should produce the information necessary to effectively serve and be managed.

- Parents, local communities, and the state should share both fiscal and programmatic responsibility whenever a decision is made to commit a child to the state's care.

Manning concluded by noting that Tennessee was moving from a system of forcing children into programs that happened to be available to a system of providing services according to an individual assessment of the needs of individual children and families.

Numerous specific goals associated with these broad philosophies and policies also were identified during early 1991. Most notably, these goals or aims were to (a) carry out a strategic refinancing of children's services; (b) establish statewide family preservation, family support, and community services; (c) implement a statewide uniform assessment and individual case planning process built around case management services; (d) create special budget accounts and a centralized billing and payment system for children and family services to allow funds to follow the needs of children and families; (e) develop a child management information and quality control system; and (f) establish regional and local planning with incentives and accountability for developing more appropriate family and community services.

Twelve committees of primarily state officials were established in spring 1991 to address operational and implementation issues associated with these sweeping and numerous changes. The committee names suggest their diverse foci: Community Health Agencies, Regional Assessment, Intake and Management Team, State Department Services, Contracts for Services, Licensing/Program Monitoring, Target Population/Education Issues, State and Federal Laws and Regulations, Public Awareness and Relations, System Evaluation and Reporting, Accounting Procedures, Systems Development, and Maximize Medicaid Reimbursement. The broad philosophies and initial financing goals of the Children's Plan forecast a significant redesign of the children's services delivery system. The redesign would involve moving from a collection of numerous parallel, and sometimes competing, programs and services administered by four state departments to a unified system of services and providers. The dimensions of these proposed changes would involve myriad diverse players and entities, clearly requiring numerous adjustments and realignments in complex relationships.

By fall 1991, these broad philosophies and goals for change had become four specific goals for the Children's Plan with identified strategies:

1. *Reduce number of children in state custody* by (a) expanding family preservation and support services, and (b) getting children in state custody into permanent situations expeditiously through reunification, adoption, and so forth.

2. *Provide more appropriate placements and services* by (a) providing comprehensive assessments and case management, (b) providing services based on needs, (c) allowing dollars to follow the child, and (d) focusing services on the family.

3. *Improve management of the children's services delivery system* by (a) revising the state accounting system to report placement and treatment expenditures for children, and (b) developing a computerized management information system to record core information and track children for all departments.

4. *Maximize the collection of federal funds through refinancing* by (a) reviewing the eligibility of all children in care or custody, (b) identifying reimbursable programs and program components, and (c) utilizing the potential of federal entitlement programs such as the IV-E Child Welfare program and the Medicaid program.

In February 1992, more formal and centralized structures were established for the Children's Plan. The Office of Children's Services Administration (OCSA) was created as a division within the D&FA. The new director of OCSA, Dr. Nancye Thomas, immediately established an Interdepartmental Children's Services Committee (ICSC). This committee was composed of leaders from the Departments of Mental Health and Mental Retardation (DMHMR), Human Services (DHS), Youth Development (DYD), Finance and Administration (DF&A), Health (DoH), and Education (DoE); the Tennessee Commission on Children and Youth (TCCY); and the Tennessee Council of Juvenile and Family Court Judges (TCJFCJ). The ICSC was given a charge by the department commissioners to address developing program and administrative issues as well as emerging problems associated with the Children's Plan implementation.

The central event of 1992 for the Children's Plan development and implementation was the establishment of the uniform assessment (central intake) mechanism using the community health agencies (CHAs). The CHAs, established by legislation in October 1989, are regional, independent, and quasi-governmental agencies with the primary responsibility to improve access to health care services for low-income persons and develop community-based resources. By contract with the DF&A, the 8 rural and 4 urban CHAs would employ and supervise 14 assessment and care coordination teams (ACCTs). These teams would have assessment, case planning, and case management responsibilities for all children in their region committed to state custody. The reasons for using the CHAs and creating the ACCTs were twofold: (a) the statutory responsibility of the CHAs to develop community-based resources was consistent with the community-based focus of the Children's Plan, and (b) removing the assessment function to a "neutral" agency from the departments whose assessment could be influenced by services available from the department was seen as desirable. It also was anticipated that the ACCTs would address the second goal of the Children's Plan, the provision of more appropriate services. The initial plan was for all fourteen ACCTs to be in operation by the middle of 1992.

The intensive efforts to consolidate and centralize the financing of children's services continued in 1992. Work largely completed during the year included (a) adoption of a single contract and standardized rates for all providers of children's services, allowing cross-department access to services; (b) introduction of open-ended, fee-for-service contracts that allowed for flexible, as-needed use of services; and (c) development of specialized requests for proposals (RFPs) that would stimulate the targeted development of needed, community-based services. The complex work associated with the refinancing strategies also continued through identifying various ways to increase the ability to claim federal reimbursement for children's services and finalizing the centralized accounting system.

By the end of 1992, state officials could point to several important accomplishments. In addition to those described in the previous paragraph, the efforts to consolidate and centralize the financing of children's services included the ongoing development of a comprehensive financial information system. In concrete terms, these efforts resulted in (a) an increase of approximately 40% in the amount of federal dollars received for children's services in Tennessee by the end of fiscal year 1992, (b) an increase of approximately 220% in the number of children and their families receiving family preservation services between fiscal year 1990 and fiscal year 1992, and (c) the establishment of statewide capacity to provide access to family preservation services for families and children in need. The development and introduction of the ACCTs created the vehicle for implementation of the statewide system for uniform assessment and case management.

Study Methods

The foregoing review indicates that significant work was done during 1991 and 1992 in articulating broad philosophies and goals for the Children's Plan and establishing strategic plans for action to achieve concrete objectives. This change effort also relied on numerous work groups and established a high-level interdepartmental committee to address development and implementation issues. Missing from this review, however, is detailed information about the actual processes and decision making associated with moving from the broad philosophies and goals to the nitty-gritty aspects of making the changes in the service delivery system envisioned in these philosophies and goals. The study methods were designed to develop this information.

Achieving System Reform—Conceptual Basis for Research Questions. The conceptual approach of this study is illustrated in part in Figure 6.1. This logic model displays in a flow chart format the major conceptual and programmatic assumptions about how the Children's Plan is supposed to work as a vehicle for reform. Consequently, the model suggests a progression from policy statement to broad goals to system change goals to system intervention strategies to system intervention goals and so forth. Such a model can provide a useful method for identifying the necessary intermediate steps between broad policy goals and the desired outcomes of these goals. Investigators examined the critical points of decision making and implementation depicted in the top half of Figure 6.1, that is, the processes and activities that served to move the

Children's Plan from the system change goals to the system intervention to the goals of the intervention and ultimately to the intervention effects.

The research approach was premised on the desire for a close and detailed examination of the decision making and implementation activities at the initial stages of the system change effort as shown in Figure 6.1. The specific focus on these initial efforts to establish the Children's Plan in 1991-1992 provided the structure for research questions intended to assess the progress and problems in establishing the Children's Plan in the context of the real-world exigencies and constraints associated with implementing public policy. For example, what were the political and practical aspects of initiating such fundamental changes in children's services from the DF&A? What initial decision-making procedures were utilized to mandate cooperation and shared responsibility for services delivery between five state departments? What strategies were used to promote change while addressing the various interests and competing goals of the key players? What significant problems occurred early in the implementation process and how did these problems affect implementation and the shape of the Children's Plan?

Case Study Approach and Data Collection. The research utilized a single-case study approach. In general, case studies are the preferred strategy when "how" or "why" questions are being posed, when the investigator has little control over events, and when the focus is on contemporary phenomena in a real-life context (Yin, 1993, 1994). This study can be seen as both descriptive and explanatory in terms of the dual purposes to document the initial decision making and implementation of the Children's Plan and to examine how this process worked and what the effects were. The primary sources for data collection included interviews with 21 key players associated with the implementation of the Children's Plan (most of these individuals also were associated with children's issues during the past 20 years in Tennessee) and a review of a variety of documents, including archival records and other materials directly associated with the Children's Plan.

The interviews were primarily open ended, although informed by an initial set of questions focused on decision-making and implementation activities in 1991-1992. All interviews were confidential. The interview-

128

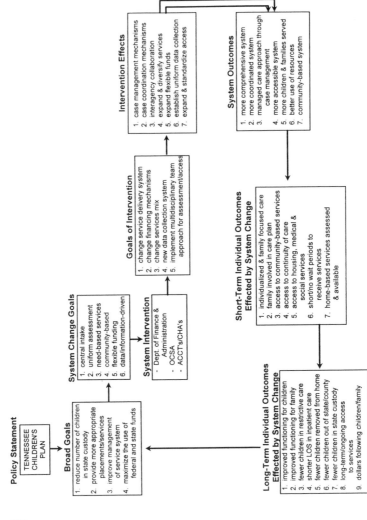

Figure 6.1. Preliminary Conceptual/Logic Model for the Tennessee Children's Plan

ees were, and continue to be, public officials, for the most part still charged with the responsibility for the ongoing implementation of the Children's Plan. Confidentiality served the important purpose of allowing the interviewees to be candid with their responses. As noted above, the primary goal of this study was to examine the *actual* processes of decision making and implementation; the ability to collect data that candidly reflected the interviewees' personal experiences and perspectives was essential. Consequently, in the discussion below, the interview data are reported in summary fashion with explanation of source(s). When appropriate, more specific presentation of the data utilizes the following protocols: (a) in general, opinions or statements are paraphrased or summarized and presented in italics; (b) recitations of individual data are rarely used and to the extent possible are accompanied by anonymous identifiers; and (c) groups of interviewees may be given a general identifier, such as department staff, committee member, or outside advocate.

For several participants, two or three interviews were conducted and these follow-up interviews were somewhat more focused and structured. It is important to note, however, that the interview process was designed primarily to encourage participants to identify what they thought was important to talk about vis-à-vis the Children's Plan and the change process. It was felt that the documentation of the individual perspectives of such high-level participants would be particularly valuable data to capture. The interview process resulted in approximately 32 interviews and 150 pages of transcribed interview notes.

Planned Change and Public Policy Implementation Literature: Theoretical Approach to Data Analysis. The analyses of this rich qualitative database were guided by principles from areas of the research literature on planned change for organizations and on public policy implementation. This theoretical approach is based on the assumption that to reform systems and implement policy goals the organizations that operate these systems must change. The goals underlying the Children's Plan exemplify this dynamic—changing the organizations that constitute the children's services delivery system to improve children's services in Tennessee.

In his classic work on organizational behavior, Schein (1980) discussed both organizational effectiveness and planned change. Because organizations change only through the people within them, establishing both the motivation to change and the appropriate vehicle for change is very important. In Schein's words, the change process must "unfreeze" old values and perceptions; develop new values and understandings as well as concomitant skills and procedures; and, finally, "refreeze" the environment to ensure the integration of change. The organization and individuals should emerge with manageable and effective structures for forward-looking action. In the introduction to their classic textbook on the planning of change, Bennis, Benne, and Chin (1985) described planned change as the conscious, deliberate, and collaborative effort to improve the operations of a human system through the utilization of knowledge. Because change is painful and threatening, and people and organizations resist change, change should be planned and managed as an interactive and multistage process.

The organizational behavior literature is frequently addressed in the public policy implementation literature (Hasenfeld & Brock, 1991). In an article exploring this relationship, Elmore (1978) asserted that understanding organizations is necessary to the analysis of implementation. Organizations are an essential aspect of undertaking implementation, and organizational capacities must be assessed and understood (Calista, 1986). The implementation of policy goals in the human services arena presents particularly difficult challenges (Lipsky, 1980), and collaboration based upon trust and respect has been identified to be essential to strategies for change in human services systems (Bruner, 1991; Kimmich, 1994).

To summarize very briefly, when making change and implementing new policy, the research literature indicates that it is very important to (a) begin the change process with clearly communicated philosophies and values (Elmore, 1978; Kennedy, 1985); (b) clarify goals and objectives as the implementation or change proceeds to ensure cohesion and unanimity (Klein, 1985; Schein, 1980); (c) recognize and enable the important role and responsibility of leaders to navigate organizations and people through the demanding process of change—designated leaders should focus on creating stability, knowledge, ownership, and excitement (Elmore, 1978; Mason & Mitroff, 1985); (d) ensure that there is ongoing clarity of development and direction based on shared leadership and decision making (Kennedy, 1985); (e) recognize that careful, detailed, and comprehensive planning is essential to a successful implementation process—comprehensive planning encompasses a complete and concrete articulation of the actual steps necessary to achieve the ultimate outcomes of change (Chase, 1979; Ethridge & Percy, 1993); and (f) appreciate that change is a multistage process and that strategies for rapid change must pay special attention to this reality (Schein, 1980). Although the foregoing recommendations concerning change strategies are not necessarily sufficient for success, compelling empirical evidence indicates they are essential for success.

Results of the
Data Analysis

Guided and informed by the foregoing principles and existing research, the goal of the data analysis was to create a more complete and "real" picture of what actually happened during 1991-1992. The rich qualitative database supported the development of a detailed description and critical assessment of the players, problems, and progress associated with establishing the broad changes envisioned by the Children's Plan.

The Early Challenges in 1991. The complexities of the issues to be addressed as the implementation of the Children's Plan began in 1991 are illustrated in part by the 12 committees created to address these issues. State department officials recalled the almost overwhelming list of issues requiring attention to translate the broad philosophies and goals of the Children's Plan into concrete strategies and implementation activities. A review of minutes from these committee meetings shows the depth and breadth of the issues and the seemingly endless questions about all aspects of the Children's Plan. As noted above, the plan's broad philosophies and initial financing objectives seemed to forecast a significant redesign of the children's services delivery system. Although not entirely clear at the outset, the changes would involve moving from a collection of numerous parallel programs and services administered by four state departments to a unified system of services and providers, requiring the cooperation of myriad diverse players and entities. With the benefit of hindsight, a state department official intimately involved with the Children's Plan observed, *in January 1991 we had no idea about the changes that would be made or how different the departments' roles would become.*

Comments from most interviewees suggest that the challenges and constant demands of the early months of 1991 cannot be overstated. The interviewees generally agreed that there were too many meetings and many of them were not well managed—*things felt very chaotic.* In the urgency to address all the issues raised by the Children's Plan, there was very little planning or management of the committee meetings. *People individually understood some of the issues . . . but no one had the overall picture of where we were going. There was a lot going on but with little coordination or integration.* Interviewees recalled trying to figure out their role in a changing system with little concrete guidance or consistency in leadership. Another very time-consuming aspect of this period for everyone leading this effort was dealing constantly with calls from field staff, providers, and clients anxious to know what the as-yet undefined changes would mean.

Lack of Operational Clarity Persists in Late 1991 and Takes a Toll. By fall, the articulated focus of the Children's Plan involved four goals: (a) reduce the number of children in state care or custody, (b) provide more appropriate placements and services, (c) improve the management of the children's services delivery system, and (d) maximize the collection of federal funds through refinancing. There also was an intensified internal focus on developing and implementing the uniform assessment and central intake mechanism. Few operational details, however, had been put in writing or clearly articulated concerning how the Children's Plan would work, particularly in terms of specific departmental roles. A slide presentation, which was used for the initial presentation in February, continued to be the only "written" form of the Children's Plan during this period. Although this slide presentation included updated information about the funding gains achieved through the refinancing strategies, there were few specifics about the structural system changes and no indication of who or what was "in charge" of the Children's Plan.

The fact that little was written down or formalized during 1991 created ongoing difficulties for those charged with implementation. State department officials recalled, *things kept changing so you couldn't write things down. The number and pace of the changes and revisions created an atmosphere of uncertainty and, frankly, of fatigue. It was difficult to sustain the confidence of staff.* There continued to be much confusion and misinformation and many questions about the Children's Plan. Important stakeholders in children's services issues, such as the juvenile court judges, seemed to be out of the information loop.

The frequency of the committee meetings slowed toward the end of 1991, and most of the 12 committees stopped meeting. *People were worn out with so many meetings and discouraged by a sense that nothing was being accomplished by the meetings.* Some interviewees recalled frustration and impatience with the committee process—so many meetings and never any closure on subjects. Others commented that the committees suffered from the lack of a formal decision-making process to address the issues being raised and the solutions being proposed. *No consensus-building process that state department officials could understand or identify from previous experience had surfaced from the work of these committees, for example, a cabinet council or single interdepartmental committee.*

There were significant differences in opinion among the interviewees about the reasons for these committee dynamics during this period. Interviewees primarily outside the state departments observed that the committees' slow progress demonstrated that it was still difficult for different departments to work together effectively and that perhaps there was not competent leadership within the departments. They also pointed to the committee process as a clear opportunity for the departments to contribute to the development of the Children's Plan. Instead, *the departments dragged their feet, raised problems, and offered few solutions.* Interviewees primarily in state departments felt that many of the 12 committees produced work important to the Children's Plan, for example, a report on field staff needs and recommended case-to-staff ratios, delineation of a continuum of care for children with specific services described, and a document costing out all services being provided to children. As 1991 drew to a close, however, it was not clear what would be done with this work. *This contributed to a sense that the committee efforts were not viewed as important to the decision-making and implementation process.*

No Clear Process for Shared Planning and Decision Making. What were decision-making and implementation dynamics in 1991? This year was clearly a time for tackling numerous complex issues as state officials and other leaders responded both to Manning's announcement of a new way to serve children and to a fast track for implementation. At the end of 1991, various department officials were moving forward with changes in contracting for services and refinancing strategies. Additional services for children had been established, the CHAs had been brought on board, and planning for the start-up of the first assessment teams had begun. By the end of the year, however, many of the key players were weary from the demands of constant change and concerned about the continuing lack of clarity in direction for the Children's Plan. Broad issues concerning how the service system would be changed, how people's roles would be affected, how services would be delivered differently, and how all this change would work had still not been addressed in much detail. The Children's Plan was more of a concept than a plan in the early spring, and it remained so at the end of 1991.

These continuing uncertainties and ambiguities about program direction, created by the particular circumstances during 1991, had implications for establishing shared planning and decision making. Essentially, people were charged with immediately implementing a plan that had not been developed beyond broad statements of philosophies and goals. The demands of this fast-paced approach to implementation left little time for planning and clarifying with regard to roles, goals, and direction. Moreover, Manning's bold unilateral approach to addressing children's issues, although applauded by all, also meant that he seized the initiative in terms of leadership. Without a clearly identified and inclusive decision-making process, there was no meaningful vehicle for department officials to assume leadership and responsibility for implementation issues. It is likely that the fast-paced and demanding approach undertaken in 1991 precluded consideration of the need for, and value of, a structure and process for shared planning, decision making, and authority.

Efforts at Building a Structure in Early 1992. The creation of the OCSA in February 1992, with Thomas as the director, and of the ICSC, with its interdepartmental staffing, was an encouraging development for department officials and others involved in the implementation of the Children's Plan. There was anticipation that OCSA and ICSC would provide the much-needed structures for shared decision making and clarifying direction for the ongoing implementation of the Children's

Plan. *The ICSC was seen as a way to facilitate the interdepartmental role in the Children's Plan in a more efficient and effective manner than the twelve committees had provided.* Department officials recalled approaching this new committee with a renewed *commitment to working together and eager for a fresh start from the lack of structure in 1991.*

Minutes from the first two meetings of the ICSC show once again the lengthy list of issues requiring attention to move forward with the implementation of the Children's Plan. *There seemed to be little time, however, to assess or incorporate the work of the 1991 subcommittees—the ongoing pace of implementation required the ICSC to hit the ground running.* The most immediate challenge facing the ICSC was the establishment of 14 ACCTs in the 12 CHAs across the state. Although the ICSC almost immediately requested an extension of the schedule for the establishing ACCTs, July 1, 1992, remained the deadline for setting up 14 teams with approximately 500 new employees.

Although the ICSC ostensibly presented a structure for shared decision making and leadership as well as a vehicle for providing more direction on the Children's Plan, in the view of many interviewees who served on the ICSC, the inability to obtain this extension on the ACCTs was the first of many experiences indicating that shared decision making and leadership did not actually develop. *It appeared that many decisions about important issues were made without real consultation with ICSC.* Moreover, these decisions would frequently be made public before ICSC members were aware of them. Committee members recalled that ICSC decisions or recommendations would be overturned or ignored with no explanation. There seemed to be little consistency regarding the scope of the committee's decision-making authority; for example, *the process for reviewing and approving contracts would sometimes include the ICSC and sometimes not.*

Clear Delineation of Authority and Accountability Was Never Established. Although there were differences about how much actual decision-making authority the ICSC had, there was unanimity among the interviewees that the ICSC was not established as the place where important decisions could consistently be made about the development and implementation of the Children's Plan. The issue of broad-based leadership—or the lack of thereof—was troubling to all of the interviewees, even though they had widely varying perspectives about the dimensions of this issue. Everyone agreed that Manning was providing leadership, but with an initiative involving so many departments, *there needed to be a visible sharing of leadership and decision making among all the commissioners.* This approach might have created *a much-needed delineation of authority and accountability among the departments* concerning the implementation of the Children's Plan. Most interviewees agreed that whatever their feelings about the ICSC the other department commissioners took few steps to assert their leadership and to empower the ICSC to act in their stead.

The uncertainties associated with leadership and decision making created many difficult challenges for implementation activities in 1992. Department officials felt undermined by a process in which contradictory and confusing messages were often received by field staff, frequently without the knowledge of these officials. *Our* [department officials'] *credibility with the field staff was damaged by our inability to assure them that we knew what was going on and could help them understand the changes. Ironically, this made it very difficult for us to lead the field staff effectively in terms of ensuring support and cooperation in the Children's Plan.* Although some interviewees believed that department officials did not really try to lead, those officials felt that their ability to do so was seriously compromised.

Limited Resources and Excessive Demands Slowed Progress in 1992. Given the limited resources and excessive demands, it is not surprising that little progress was made in 1991-1992 in two areas critical to the success of implementation efforts: (a) the development of intensive, interdisciplinary, and ongoing training for the ACCTs and department field staff around the Children's Plan; and (b) the development of the comprehensive management information system (MIS) for children designed to create a standardized database and financial accounting system across all departments. The undisputed (among the interviewees) lack of training in particular continued to create significant problems for the implementation process.

The implementation activities during 1992 did address many of the substantial changes and deadlines proposed by the Children's Plan: Considerable progress was made on the start-up of the ACCTs, additional federal funds had been generated and used to establish new programs and services, and the process of instituting the redesigned contracting and accounting system was almost complete. There continued to be a need, however, to lessen the uncertainties and lack of structure associated with rapid change. For example, rapid implementation of the ACCTs did not allow time for careful role clarification. Most of the interviewees agreed that *the ACCTs began operating with very little training and were completely overwhelmed by the enormity of their responsibilities.* Department officials were constantly intervening to resolve crises related to ill-defined relationships between the ACCTs, the field staff, and the juvenile judges.

Developments during 1992 did not appear to provide additional resources or create new capacities with which leaders and department officials could grapple successfully with the challenges of making such fundamental system changes. A leading child advocate outside the departments observed that *everyone* [leaders] *was already overloaded with too much on their plates. The Children's Plan created additional full-time jobs for these people and provided no relief from existing duties.* Given that the implementation of an initiative as ambitious as the Children's Plan was just 2 years old, however, the fact that these dynamics existed at the end of 1992 is probably not surprising and even to be expected.

Most of the key leaders and state officials interviewed agreed that the major problems encountered with the implementation of the Children's Plan in 1991-1992 can be attributed to a lack of shared and broad-based leadership, a failure to clarify roles, and the almost complete lack of adequate training. The rapid implementation of a barely conceptualized Children's Plan with limited shared decision making meant that little room was allowed for planning with regard to translating philosophies and goals into concrete strategies for change. The lack of clarity about goals and strategies made it particularly difficult for department officials to lead their field staff in making organizational changes. Although there was disagreement about the need for planning and the concomitant importance of rapid implementation among the interviewees, many interviewees did agree that a planning process could have provided the vehicle to clarify and define concretely the vision associated with the Children's Plan, to assess the organizational capacities and needs and allocate resources accordingly, to anticipate and address proactively substantial challenges in the implementation process, and to reallocate additional resources for addressing unexpected but inevitable problems.

Discouragement and Mixed Results at the End of 1992. The demanding circumstances created by the rapid implementation of such an ambitious initiative probably took its greatest toll on those responsible for implementation. By the end of 1992, many members of the ICSC reported that they were discouraged and *no longer saw the value of committing time and energy to this committee.* The events of the year had convinced them that *they had no meaningful decision-making role to play and that they were primarily a conduit for information about the Children's Plan.* The DoH officials felt that *their role in the Children's Plan had made them a focus of frustration for the other departments.* Many interviewees recalled being deeply discouraged by the demands of continuing uncertainty, the lack of consistent structure and process, and the continual changes in policy and direction. There seemed to be little tolerance for the desire to plan or to slow down or any appreciation of the demands posed by implementing the Children's Plan. Department officials and others increasingly had come to feel that *if they expressed concerns about the speed of implementation and related problems they were labeled as obstructionist and not supportive of the Children's Plan.* Agreeing about the goals was plainly not sufficient—the lack of a satisfactory structure and process for agreeing about how to achieve the goals created demanding and daunting challenges for those responsible for implementing the Children's Plan.

Certainly much was accomplished in Tennessee by virtue of the introduction and initial implementation of the Children's Plan in 1991 and 1992. Significant progress was made toward creating a unified system of care for troubled children and their families, a system that would assess the service needs of children and families appropriately and uniformly, provide a broad array of community-based services, and expand available resources through innovative refinancing strategies. It also is fair to say that by the end of 1992 many of the structures necessary for effectively implementing and institutionalizing change were not adequately in place in Tennessee. The consequences of this lack of structure are most evident in the problems associated with the establishment of the ACCTs, the lack of resources devoted to essential training programs, and the failure to make substantial progress in creating an adequate management information system.

Discussion: Lessons Learned

The Children's Plan represents an initiative of ambitious and impressive proportions. The system intervention goals included fundamental change in the way services are delivered, consolidating financing mechanisms and generating new funds, and improving and expanding the availability of services and programs. In this study of the Children's Plan, I examined what happened between the articulation of policy goals and the achievement of system change during the first 2 years of implementation. The data indicate that a viable process for translating these broad goals into concrete and feasible strategies for change was not created. The structures for shared decision making and broad-based responsibility necessary to implement and sustain the desired reforms were not firmly established.

The successes and frustrations and the gains and setbacks experienced by those leading the efforts to implement the Children's Plan in 1991-1992 are not unique or, for that matter, surprising. The research literature on planned change and public policy implementation provides numerous examinations and illustrations of exemplary and nonexemplary strategies for making change. Drawing upon this accumulated knowledge and the reported experiences from Tennessee, the following lessons are proposed for future efforts concerned with how to agree about, as well as accomplish, getting there with respect to the goals of the Children's Plan.

1. *Vision must support long-term change efforts.*
   - Recognize that change is not a short-term process; the complexities of this kind of change cannot be overestimated and are frequently underestimated; be patient, the vision should not override the process— vision is necessary but not sufficient.
   - Articulate the vision again and again in a manner ensuring that people understand the scope and direction of change as well as their roles; ensure that consensus is created concerning conceptual issues as well as practical steps with all constituencies.

2. *Clear authority and shared decision making must be established.*
   - Put someone with the background, knowledge, and skills sufficient to establish credibility and confidence clearly in charge; don't underestimate the value of establishing formal authority in terms of legislation or regulation. Create meaningful structures for shared leadership,

decision making, and authority. Build a leadership coalition with both old and new faces.

- Establish effective mechanisms and stable structures for communication, shared decision making and authority, and mutual support between local and state levels and between public and private agencies; goals of local responsibility and community-based services cannot be achieved unless these mechanisms and structures are established and adequate resources are allocated.

3. *Comprehensive and informed planning must be an early priority.*

- Address as many aspects of change as possible and promote an awareness that all efforts at reform must be coordinated at all times to move the agenda for change forward; if only the first few steps can be mapped out, take them and then consciously stop, assess, and plan the next steps. Implementation of initiatives such as the Children's Plan requires purposely building in sufficient time for planning and developing cohesion and consensus at all levels of participation; structures should be in place to support and promote planning processes that incorporate a bottom-up approach, for example, meaningful involvement of field staff. Lay the necessary groundwork for organizational and programmatic infrastructures that incorporate fiscal policies. Financing strategies should not be allowed to determine program and system decisions, but decisions about program and system issues must incorporate a complete understanding of financing strategies.

4. *Adequate resources and support must be allocated.*

- Promote stability and ongoing functioning of organizations and systems as part of establishing new roles for participants and new structures for services and programs; sufficient time must be allocated for training, building teams, creating group cohesion, and establishing new structures.

- Recognize the work of developing true collaborative relationships as a critical and time-consuming task that cannot simply be added on to existing jobs; it is critical to allocate sufficient time and resources for this work.

- Enhance capacities of leadership, technical assistance, resources, and staff to provide the requisite support for dealing with such ambitious change; comprehensive written materials must be an integral part of such support and capacity building.

The foregoing is not, of course, intended to be an exhaustive list. Feasible efforts to reform children's service delivery systems must be responsive to the needs of children, respectful of the complexities associated with serving children and families, and cognizant of the capacities of those charged with running these systems. Although financing strategies are essential, these efforts must employ multi-faceted strategies with broad programmatic underpinnings. The difficulty *and* the importance of understanding how or whether implementation can be achieved underscore the necessity for the ongoing accumulation through research of knowledge about making fundamental change in children's services.

The advent of the Children's Plan was intended to begin the process of reforming the service delivery system for children and families in Tennessee. Despite the difficult circumstances for implementation, the interviewees described several areas of progress toward the goals of reform during 1991 and 1992. As an adjunct to the lessons learned format and the foregoing analysis examining barriers, it also is useful to summarize interviewees' reported experiences in terms of the facilitating factors associated with these initial efforts to implement the Children's Plan to extend further this development of knowledge about how to define, establish, and maintain change in service delivery systems for children and their families at the state and local levels.

A number of important factors facilitated these gains: (a) the leadership and commitment of David Manning, (b) the presence and participation of many department officials and other leaders with a long history of working on children's issues, (c) the commitment of these experienced, top-level officials and leaders to the philosophies and goals of the Children's Plan, (d) the technical assistance made available from outside consultants and foundations, (e) the support from the legislature by way of the Select Committee on Children and Youth, (f) the recent history of departments already taking some steps to work together on children's issues, and (g) the dedication and energy of particular state officials in the Office of Children's Services Administration.

Conclusions and Recommendations

This case study of the Children's Plan created important information about how the process of decision making and implementation actually worked in Tennessee. The public policy implementation and planned change literature provided a useful framework for analyzing these data. Informed conclusions, instructive insights, and forward-looking recommendations were drawn from this examination of the nitty-gritty aspects of making the system change goals proposed by the Children's Plan. These results contribute to a better understanding about how things really work and what processes, structures, and strategies are required to make and sustain broad-based change at the state and community levels. This study also underscores the importance of determining whether, how, and in what form reform has actually been achieved before beginning the assessment of impacts and measurement of outcomes attributable to reform.

These results also are consistent with or complementary to findings from other implementation studies of existing system reform efforts in children's services. An assessment of the first 5 years of state activity under the NIMH-funded CASSP found that strong political leadership at the state and local levels was necessary for securing program resources and that institutionalizing structural linkages and resource-based supports was essential for sustaining interagency services (Schlenger, Etheridge, Hansen, Fairbank, & Onken, 1992). A review of the early efforts at implementing reform in child mental health services in Minnesota confirmed the need for solid interagency linkages and supports and indicated that choices for organizational structures and financing strategies have specific implications for successful implementation strategies (Petr & Pierpont, 1992). Studies examining the implementation of service system reforms in Ventura County, California, and Fort Bragg, North Carolina, concluded that the clear articulation of well-conceived implementation plans provided the necessary starting point for developing meaningful plans for evaluation (Heflinger, 1993; Jordan & Hernandez, 1990). Finally, a case study evaluation of Michigan's approach to promoting new programs for health services delivery at the state and local levels illustrated that the ongoing implementation of system-level reform efforts was affected in fundamental ways by the continuously evolving political and public policy landscape (Paul-Shaheen, 1990).

In light of both the lessons learned and the facilitating factors and barriers described above, the following recommendations are offered to state officials responsible for implementing large scale reform efforts such as the Children's Plan:

1. Create adequate statutory or regulatory authority and structure for reform efforts.

2. Establish substantial and meaningful structures for shared decision making and authority sufficient to ensure the responsible participation of all parties necessary for institutionalizing the changes and reforms that are articulated.
3. Provide for and implement comprehensive and ongoing training for all participants at all levels in public and private agencies.
4. Commit adequate resources to the development of a comprehensive management information system for children's services.
5. Slow the process of implementation and allow sufficient time for stabilization of the initial changes and for careful assessment and planning of next steps in light of the changes achieved.

How can community-based, family-focused, flexibly funded service systems be established, and what difference will these service systems make for children in need and their families? The Tennessee Children's Plan provided an opportunity to expand knowledge about how to establish such systems. Many questions continue to remain unanswered about whether state and local communities have the expertise, capacities, and resources to implement successfully these strategies to improve the lives of children and families. Case studies offer a particularly effective approach to examining and understanding the real-world constraints involved in implementing complex and multifaceted strategies for system change. The results of such research can make an important contribution to the collaborative efforts of advocates, policymakers, service providers, public and private officials, and families to improve the future for children.

Note

1. For a more lengthy and detailed review of the historical background with extensive documentation of sources, please see Maloy (1994, chap. 2).

References

Bennis, W. G., Benne, K. D., & Chin, R. (Eds.). (1985). *The planning of change: Readings in the applied social sciences* (4th ed.). New York: Holt, Rinehart & Winston, CBS College Publishing.

Bruner, C. (1991). *Thinking collaboratively: Ten questions and answers to help policy makers improve children's services.* Washington, DC: Education and Human Services Consortium.

Cabinet Council on Social Services. (1985). [Working papers on the recommendations to address the service needs of Tennessee children from birth to age 10 and Tennessee adolescents.] Nashville: State of Tennessee, Governor's Policy Office.

Calista, D. (1986). Linking policy intention and policy implementation. *Administration & Society, 18*(2), 263-286.

Chase, G. (1979). Implementing a human services program: How hard will it be? *Public Policy, 27*(4), 387-435.

Children's Mental Health Task Force Report Committee. (1989). *Draft recommendations for review and comment by the Children's Mental Health Task Force, revised 10/12/89.* Nashville: State of Tennessee, Department of Mental Health and Mental Retardation.

Duchnowski, A. J., & Friedman, R. M. (1990). Children's mental health: Challenges for the '90s. *Journal of Mental Health Administration, 17*(1), 3-12.

Edwards, K. (1992). *The Tennessee Children's Plan: Family preservation and broader systems reform.* Unpublished manuscript.

Elmore, R. F. (1978). Organizational models of social program implementation. *Public Policy, 26*(3), 185-228.

Ethridge, M. E., & Percy, S. L. (1993). A new kind of public policy encounters disappointing results: Implementing Learnfare in Wisconsin. *Public Administration Review, 53*(4), 340-347.

Friedman, R. M. (1993). *Restructuring of systems to emphasize prevention and family support.* Tampa: Research and Training Center for Children's Mental Health, Department of Child and Family Studies, Florida Mental Health Institute.

General Accounting Office. (1992). *Integrating human services: Linking at-risk families with services more successful than system reform efforts.* Washington, DC: Author.

Hasenfeld, Y., & Brock, T. (1991). Implementation of social policy revisited. *Administration and Society, 22*(4), 451-479.

Heflinger, C. A. (1993). *Final report of the implementation study of the Fort Bragg evaluation project.* Nashville, TN: Vanderbilt University, Center for Mental Health Policy.

Jordan, D. D., & Hernandez, M. (1990). The Ventura Planning Model: A proposal for mental health reform. *Journal of Mental Health Administration, 17*(1), 26-47.

Juvenile Justice and Delinquency Prevention Act of 1974, 42 U.S.C.A. §§ 5601 et seq.

Kennedy, A. A. (1985). Ruminations on change: The incredible value of human beings in getting things done. In W. Bennis, K. Benne, & R. Chin (Eds.), *The planning of change: Readings in the applied social sciences* (4th ed., pp. 325-334). New York: Holt, Rinehart & Winston, CBS College Publishing.

Kimmich, M. (1994). Collaborative action. In V. J. Bradley, J. W. Asbaugh, & B. C. Blaney (Eds.), *Creating individual support for people with developmental disabilities.* Baltimore, MD: Paul H. Brookes.

Klein, D. (1985). Some notes on the dynamics of resistance to change: The defender role. In W. Bennis, K. Benne, & R. Chin (Eds.), *The planning of change: Readings in the applied social sciences* (4th ed., pp. 98-105). New York: Holt, Rinehart & Winston, CBS College Publishing.

Knitzer, J. (1993). Children's mental health policy: Challenging the future. *Journal of Emotional and Behavioral Disorders, 1,* 8-16.

Lipsky, M. (1980). *Street-level bureaucracy: Dilemmas of the individual in public services.* New York: Russell Sage Foundation.

Maloy, K. A. (1991). *Mental health for children: Can we get there from here?* Washington, DC: Mental Health Policy Resource Center.

Maloy, K. A. (1994). *Report to the Annie E. Casey Foundation and the state of Tennessee: The Children's Plan.* Nashville, TN: Vanderbilt University, Center for Mental Health Policy.

Mason, R. O., & Mitroff, I. I. (1985). A teleological power-oriented theory of strategy. In W. Bennis, K. Benne, & R. Chin (Eds.), *The planning of change: Readings in the applied social sciences* (4th ed., pp. 215-222). New York: Holt, Rinehart & Winston, CBS College Publishing.

National Commission on Children. (1991). *Beyond rhetoric: A new American agenda for children and families: Final report of the National Commission on Children.* Washington, DC: Government Printing Office.

Paul-Shaheen, P. A. (1990). Overlooked connections: Policy development and implementation in state-local relations. *Journal of Health Politics, Policy and Law, 15,* 833-856.

Petr, C. G., & Pierpont, J. (1992). Early implementation of legislative children's mental health reform: The Minnesota/Hennepin County experience. *Journal of Mental Health Administration, 19*(2), 195-206.

Report of the Select Committee for the Study of Children's Services. (1980). Prepared by the Office of Legal Services, Tennessee State Legislature, Nashville.

Rog, D. J. (1992). Child and adolescent mental health services: Evaluation challenges. *New Directions for Program Evaluation, 54,* 5-16.

Saxe, L., Cross, T., Lovas, G. S., & Gardner, J. (1993). Evaluation of the mental health services for youth demonstration: Examining rhetoric in action. In L. Bickman & D. J. Rog (Eds.), *Creating a children's mental health services system: Policy, research, and evaluation* (pp. 206-235). Newbury Park, CA: Sage.

Saxe, L., Cross, T., & Silverman, N. (1988). Children's mental health: The gap between what we know and what we do. *American Psychologist, 43,* 800-807.

Schein, E. H. (1980). *Organizational psychology* (3rd ed.). Englewood Cliffs, NJ: Prentice Hall.

Schlenger, W. E., Etheridge, R. M., Hansen, D. J., Fairbank, D. W., & Onken, J. (1992). Evaluation of state efforts to improve systems of care for children and adolescents with severe emotional disturbances: The CASSP initial cohort study. *Journal of Mental Health Administration, 19*(2), 131-142.

Schorr, L. B. (1988). *Within our reach: Breaking the cycle of disadvantage.* New York: Doubleday.

Stroul, B. A. (1993). *Systems of care for children and adolescents with severe emotional disturbances: What are the results?* Washington, DC: Georgetown University Child Development Center, CASSP Technical Assistance Center.

Stroul, B. A., & Friedman, R. (1986). *A system of care for severely emotionally disturbed youth.* Washington, DC: Georgetown University Child Development Center, CASSP Technical Assistance Center at Georgetown University.

Stroul, B. A., & Friedman, R. (1994). *A system of care for severely emotionally disturbed youth* (Rev. ed.). Washington, DC: Georgetown University Child Development Center, CASSP Technical Assistance Center.

Task Force on Mental Health Services for Children and Youth. (1983). *A report to the Commissioners of the Tennessee Department of Mental Health and Mental Retardation.* Nashville: State of Tennessee, Department of Mental Health and Mental Retardation.

Tennessee Department of Finance and Administration, Division of Budget. (1990, April). *Assessment of Children and Youth Committed to State Care on May 1st, 1989.* Nashville, TN: Author.

Yin, R. (1993). *Applications of case study research.* Newbury Park, CA: Sage.

Yin, R. (1994). *Case study research.* Thousand Oaks, CA: Sage.

7

Effectiveness of the California System of Care Model for Children and Youth with Severe Emotional Disorder

C. CLIFFORD ATTKISSON

ABRAM B. ROSENBLATT

KARYN L. DRESSER

HAROLD R. BAIZE

JUNE MADSEN CLAUSEN

SAMUEL L. LIND

In this chapter, we present findings from three service system research projects designed by the University of California, San Francisco, Child Services Research Group (UCSF CSRG) to investigate the ongoing implementation and the effectiveness of the California System of Care

AUTHORS' NOTE: The Child Services Research Group (CSRG) conducts services research on systems of care for children and adolescents suffering from severe emotional disorder. The CSRG is funded, in part, by a Services Research Center Grant from the National Institute for Mental Health, Division of Epidemiology and Services Research. Research data presented in this paper reflect information available on or before January 1, 1996. Research activities were supported by research and training grants from NIMH (MH46122, MH43694, and MH18261) and evaluation research contracts from the Califor-

Model for Children and Youth with Severe Emotional Disorder (SED) (Attkisson, Dresser, & Rosenblatt, 1991, 1995; Attkisson, Rosenblatt, & Dresser, 1990; Children's Mental Health Services Act of 1987; Children's Mental Health Services Act of 1992; Public Health Services Act, 1992). For each line of investigation, we describe important aspects of the study design, including the services research methods used; overview measures employed in data collection; and present methods of data analysis. Empirical findings then are reviewed for each investigation and the direction of future research is discussed.

The California System of Care Model

Inception and History

The California System of Care Model is an integrated service system strategy developed to promote access to high-quality, least restrictive possible, home-based or close-to-home services for children and adolescents with SED. The model, which is cost *and* results focused, was derived from pioneering efforts in Ventura County, California. The system of care model is designed to integrate four service sectors that are critical to youth with severe emotional disorder: mental health care, social services, educational programs, and juvenile justice programs.

The service system innovations in Ventura County resulted in legislative action and policy changes in California state government. Following the compelling demonstrations in Ventura County, legislative action resulted in state grants that enabled county-level alternatives to fragmented, discontinuous, and uncoordinated care for children suffering from SED. Initially, these grants were awarded to three additional California counties: Santa Cruz, San Mateo, and Riverside.

nia State Department of Mental Health (89-70225, 90-70195, 91-71106, 92-72090, 92-72347, 93-73346, 94-74252, 94-74285, and 95-75217). The authors gratefully acknowledge the many contributions of our colleagues and associates Lasse Bergman, Ralph Catalano, Donna Dahl, Justine Desmarais, Susan De Magri, Albert Fernandez, Rachel Guerrero, Luz-Mary Harris, Teh-wei Hu, Jennifer Hui, Patricia Jordan, Karla Kruse, Nancy Mills, Lonnie Snowden, Sue Tico, and Norm Wyman. The views expressed in this chapter represent those of the authors only.

In 1987, Assembly Bill 377 (AB377) became legislation enabling the replication and expansion of the California System of Care Model for Children and Youth (Children's Mental Health Services Act of 1987). It stipulates that (a) public sector resources are to be expended *on behalf of youth with the most severe disorder who are at risk of out-of-home placement* (estimated to average 1% to 2% of the total child population in the demonstration counties, with variation dependent on population demography and associated risk factors), and (b) that services for youth are to be integrated across component agencies through joint service plans and continuous case management. The fundamental goal of the System of Care Model is to provide comprehensive, coordinated, and integrated care to each child and adolescent. Resource conservation, reliance on least restrictive possible levels of care, ongoing program evaluation, and a focus on outcomes further characterize the model. Subsequent state and federal legislation (Children's Mental Health Services Act of 1992 [Assembly Bill 3015, or AB3015]; Public Health Services Act of 1992) provided additional grant funds for expansion of the System of Care Model to a broader range of California counties. Currently, 14 counties are implementing the model; of these, 7 have received federal service system development grant funds from the U.S. Substance Abuse and Mental Health Services Administration, Division of Community Mental Health Services (SAMHSA/CMHS), to increase the scope and impact of the service system. At this time, additional counties in California are poised to begin implementation of the model.

Content of the System of Care Model

A description of the System of Care Model and results from the original Ventura County demonstration are presented in Jordan and Hernandez (1990). In the model, a series of planning steps are followed to create individualized plans of care and case management procedures (Feltman & Essex, 1989; Ventura County Children's Mental Health Services Demonstration Project, 1988). Administrative structures also are created to allow coordination and monitoring of services provided to children and adolescents in the target population. In the integrated care system, an emphasis is placed on reducing reliance on restrictive levels of care through effective and coordinated community- and home-based care. The desired system and client outcomes are achieved through emphasis on prevention of out-of-home placement in restrictive care settings such as state psychiatric hospitals, local acute care hospitals, and group homes; maintenance of progressive educational achievement; and reduction of recidivism in the juvenile justice system. Cost containment and cost avoidance also are primary goals of the integrated approach to delivery of services to this most-in-need population of youth. Members of the UCSF Child Services Research Group currently are conducting a systematic analysis of the content of the model for future publication.

The System of Care Model is constructed by following five planning steps designed to guide implementation of an effective multiagency system. The steps include (a) *Defining the Target Population* (in this case, youth with SED who are most in need of public services); (b) *Establishing the System of Care Goals* (in this case, higher benefits for youth, families, and the community as well as judicious use of tax dollars reflected in cost offsets and avoidance); (c) *Building Interagency Coalitions* (in this case, between the different sectors such as juvenile justice, social services, mental health, and education programs); (d) *Designing Services and Building Standards for Quality, Continuity, and Client Centeredness*; and (e) *Monitoring the System for Client Benefits and Public Agency Costs*. Recently, the model also emphasizes *Cultural Competence* within the system of care as a sixth primary planning goal.

The general principles of the planning model lead to a convergence on a common set of characteristics for systems of care at both service program and service system levels. Service program level characteristics include (a) broad-based screening via a common screening protocol used by all agencies who refer youth to system of care services; (b) a multidisciplinary assessment of youth who are referred to determine needs and establish service plans; (c) family-centered case management designed to coordinate and integrate care across agencies, including case management by multiagency teams for those youth most in need; and (d) the careful and strategic use of out-of-home placements as a last resort with extensive use of wraparound services, therapeutic foster care, in-home counseling, and day treatment to avoid more restrictive levels of care. Service system characteristics include (a) clearly articulated target populations as specified in the original Ventura County innovations, (b) clear and measurable outcome objectives, (c) interagency collaboration at all levels of care, (d) cultural competence at all levels of care, (e) ongoing and constant evaluation for program administration and feedback regarding goal attainments, and (f) recapturing of cost savings from system improvements and reductions in expensive placements to further enhance the care system.

Although specific program interventions implemented in the counties vary, each county has programs falling in the following general areas: (a) emergency care and crisis intervention available 24 hours per day, 7 days per week; (b) home-based services such as family preservation teams that rapidly respond to family needs in the field; (c) respite care for caregivers, including foster parents; (d) enriched foster care to help youth remain in high-quality foster home settings; (e) school-based programs that are conjointly run between education and mental health (these programs offer counseling as well as creative arts, occupational therapy, and parental and group counseling); (f) juvenile justice programs that provide on-site crisis intervention and counseling, screening, and follow-up; (g) wraparound services backed by a flexible funding pool (Burchard & Clarke, 1990; Katz-Leavy, Lourie, Stroul, & Zeigler-Dendy, 1992; VanDenBerg & Grealish, 1996); (h) a range of family involvement services such as parenting workshops, support groups and peer mentoring, peer counseling, caregiver training, and involvement of parents in policy setting; (i) minority outreach and recruitment to churches, businesses, and other neighborhood community organizations to recruit volunteers and secure institutional commitments of time and money; (j) resource development to obtain private sector support for public services; and (k) transitional services to work with older adolescents as they make the transition to adulthood.

Empirical Studies of the
Child Services Research Group

Several longitudinal system of care research projects have been implemented by the UCSF Child Services Research Group (CSRG) since its inception 7 years ago. Three of these projects have reached maturity and various publications report information about study designs and findings (Attkisson & Rosenblatt, 1996). Viewed together, the three projects form a cluster of complementary investigations. In aggregate, the

CSRG services research activities constitute a multifaceted study of the implementation of the California System of Care Model for Children and Youth. Data collected and analyzed include (a) secondary analyses of statewide and county-level mental health and social services information; (b) collection of primary data from four California counties; and (c) collection of questionnaire and interview data from staff, consumers, and family members in various other California counties.

The three major research endeavors of the CSRG that are discussed in depth in this chapter include the California CASSP Evaluation Research Project, the California System of Care Model Evaluation Research Project, and the Clinical Epidemiology in Three Systems of Care for Youth Research Project. Following the discussion of each, we summarize our findings to date as well as the implications that derive from these results.

California CASSP Evaluation Research Project

The Child and Adolescent Service System Program (CASSP) was funded in California in 1989 by the National Institute of Mental Health (NIMH). In 1993, CASSP was moved within the federal government from NIMH to the Center for Mental Health Services in SAMHSA. CASSP was established to assist states and communities in their efforts to improve child and adolescent service systems (Day & Roberts, 1991; NIMH, 1983). CASSP has several special areas of emphasis, including the development of (a) systems of care for children and their families, (b) community-based service approaches, (c) cultural competence, (d) services for special populations of high-risk youth, and (e) strategies for financing services.

CASSP Mission and Objectives

CASSP promotes the development of systems of care that are child centered and family focused, with the needs of the child and family dictating the types and mix of services provided (Stroul & Friedman, 1986). Accordingly, systems of care also should be community based, maximizing the use of services that are in or close to a child's community. As outlined by the CASSP service system model, systems of care are best characterized as

- Comprehensive services to address the child's physical, emotional, social, and educational needs
- Individualized services in accordance with the unique needs and potential of each child
- Services provided in the least restrictive, most normal environment possible
- Full participation of families
- Integration with other child-caring agencies and programs
- Coordination through case management mechanisms
- Early identification and intervention
- Smooth transitions to the adult service system
- Protection of children's rights and effective advocacy
- Cultural sensitivity and nondiscrimination

In addition, the system of care promoted by CASSP includes a range of nonresidential services (such as outpatient, day treatment, home-based, and crisis services) and a range of residential services (such as therapeutic foster care, group homes, residential treatment, and inpatient services).

Description of the California CASSP Evaluation Project

In California, CASSP is administered by the California Department of Mental Health (Cal-DMH). In 1994, a retrospective evaluation of the California implementation of CASSP was conducted by our research team (Madsen, Dresser, Rosenblatt, & Attkisson, 1994). The major objectives of this CSRG research project included evaluation of CASSP efforts

- To develop interagency and interdepartmental coordination and collaboration
- To develop family participation and advocacy related to services for children and adolescents with emotional disorder
- To promulgate cultural competency in systems of care for children and adolescents
- To enhance allocation of resources to children's services and systems statewide

• To develop more effective data collection and research related to services and systems of care for children and youth with emotional disorder

These objectives were accomplished through a variety of research methodologies. A representative sample of the 58 urban, suburban, and rural counties in California was selected for the conduct of face-to-face interviews with management and program staff in state and county departments of mental health, social services, juvenile justice, and education, as well as with state legislators, state and local parent leaders, and mental health advocates. Second, telephone interviews were conducted employing a random sample of members of a statewide network of parents of children with SED. Third, a review of relevant documents, including recent state legislation, departmental and organizational policy statements, and minutes of various state and local councils and committees, was undertaken (Dresser, Clausen, Rosenblatt, & Attkisson, 1995).

California CASSP Evaluation
Project Findings

The implementation of CASSP in California was constrained by the scope of the national goals established for CASSP and the size and complexity of the state of California. CASSP in California was underfunded, understaffed, and insufficiently supported at the executive levels of state government and in Cal-DMH. Despite these limitations, CASSP had a modest, positive impact in the state of California. Specifically, results indicate that CASSP

• Demonstrated high visibility and impact in urban and suburban counties that had previously existing system of care movements in place—although CASSP leadership efforts were appreciated and well respected by county administrators and parents of children with SED throughout the state
• Legitimized and stabilized the California System of Care Model throughout the state
• Increased interagency collaboration in human service planning and delivery for youth with SED in most areas of the state;
• Increased family participation in all aspects of human service delivery to children with SED, especially with respect to training agency staff and

parents, empowering individual parents, and organizing local parent organizations

- Inspired county mental health administrators to be leaders in the effort to establish culturally competent systems of care for children and adolescents
- Aided Cal-DMH efforts to implement a system for performance monitoring, including modifying existing state management information systems and implementing new data collection strategies
- Contributed to the development of strategies that are enabling counties to cope creatively and innovatively with budget reductions

Apart from information about the impact of CASSP in California, results provided additional insight into California's mental health service system for children and youth with SED:

- Public service agencies throughout the state collaborate and coordinate services for children and adolescents with SED better than they did 4 years earlier.
- According to agency staff and parents, mental health providers are more aware and supportive of parents and families than they were 4 years earlier.
- Many parents encounter significant difficulties negotiating their way through the multiple agencies that provide services to their children; most feel unempowered and isolated in these efforts.
- Although human service agency staff believe that services have become more culturally competent, parents of children with SED do not perceive this change, indicating that this shift has not yet translated into concrete changes in service delivery.
- With a few notable exceptions, counties do not systematically monitor outcomes of services delivered to children and youth.
- Most public agency staff are convinced that county and state resources are inadequate to address the needs of youth with SED.

Summary and Implications

With modest federal funding, CASSP in California had some positive impact on interagency collaboration, parent involvement in mental health services, and awareness of the importance of cultural competence in mental health service delivery. Generally, parents of youth with SED do not perceive positive changes to the extent reported by human service agency staff. Parents and agency staff agree that the needs of children with SED in California are not being addressed adequately.

Although agencies throughout California have implemented structural and organizational changes designed to increase interagency collaboration, parents and families still receive services in a categorical fashion. Thus, for the most part, parents remain burdened with navigating a difficult and complex myriad of agencies to obtain the optimal blend of care for their children with SED. Such findings indicate that local, state, and federal governments must work together to make major reforms in the way in which services for children and youth with SED are funded and implemented. With such reforms, consumers of services will not have to spend precious time, energy, and emotional resources attempting to obtain services from the agencies mandated to provide them.

Although agencies report they have taken steps to involve parents at all levels of service planning, delivery, and evaluation, parents report that only a small number of outspoken parent leaders are involved in human service agencies beyond the care of their own child. Indeed, parents noted that providers of mental health services were more receptive to them and generally involved them to a greater extent in the care of their child, but reported that they were not given the opportunity and means to become involved in system reform efforts. If human service agencies truly desire to increase family participation in services, they must move beyond involving parents in treatment planning for their individual child and make it possible for these parents to join committees, councils, and advisory boards responsible for overall program development, implementation, and evaluation.

Due largely to the efforts of CASSP, human service agencies in California have become aware of the importance of cultural competence in human service delivery. Most county agencies have taken steps to move their systems of care toward the ideal of cultural competence. But for the most part, parents of children with SED report that services still fail to address cultural factors in the treatment of their children and families. Thus, agencies' increasing awareness of the importance of cultural competence has not yet translated into sufficient changes at the direct service level and has therefore not been perceived by service consumers and their families. Agencies must move beyond rhetoric to make treatment more accessible and more effective for all cultural groups.

Although the majority of counties in California do not systematically monitor outcomes of services for children and youth, CASSP has played an important role in developing strategies for useful and efficient data collection and information management. Agencies must give priority attention to such strategies if services to children and youth are to become optimally effective. Yet, in conclusion, despite time and funding constraints, results indicate that CASSP in California contributed to moving the state's professional caregivers toward a philosophy of providing coordinated multiagency care for children in a culturally competent manner in the least restrictive environment possible and with the involvement of family and parents.

The California System of Care
Model Evaluation Research Project

The California System of Care Model Evaluation Research Project (formerly called the California AB377 Evaluation Project) is a multiyear, collaborative mental health services research effort between the University of California, San Francisco, and Cal-DMH. Funded by a Cal-DMH contract, the study was initiated in October 1989 and is now in its seventh year of operation; it currently encompasses 11 participating counties. Work with a new set of counties began over the last year, but this chapter presents results from the original three counties encompassed in the AB377 Evaluation Project (see also Attkisson et al., 1995; Attkisson & Rosenblatt, 1993; Rosenblatt & Attkisson, 1992, 1993b, in press; Rosenblatt, Attkisson, & Fernandez, 1992). It is anticipated that this research may extend to a 10-year time frame with ongoing inclusion of additional California counties; increased scope focusing on statewide data analyses; and use of the findings in mental health policy development, state legislation, and service system change. The California System of Care Model Evaluation Research Project is best conceived as formative evaluation research designed to document, assess, and stimulate constructive modification of the California Integrated System of Care for children and youth suffering with severe mental disorder.

The original AB377 Evaluation Project followed legislative mandates to collect and analyze data regarding four important system of care performance criteria: (a) to ensure that the target population is being served as intended; (b) to reduce reliance on restrictive levels of care, especially reliance on state hospital and group home admissions; (c) to reduce the likelihood of rearrests and recidivism for youth in the target population who also are involved with the juvenile justice system; and (d) to improve the school attendance, educational performance, and academic achievement of target population youth in school settings. When the expansion of system of care efforts was enabled through new legislation (AB3015), new data collection elements were added to the original AB377 evaluation research protocol. As a result, the California System of Care Model Evaluation Project now collects data on child and family functioning across all counties.

The long-term, central goal of the California System of Care Model Evaluation Project is to determine the costs and effectiveness of the systems of care in counties adopting the California model. Ongoing project objectives include assisting Cal-DMH in determining and disseminating system of care performance criteria, assisting the counties in their data collection efforts, monitoring program performance through analysis of data related to the performance criteria, and collecting and integrating data from multiple state and county sources. During the study, we have collected and analyzed secondary data provided by the counties and several state agencies. The available data sets contain individual level service recipient data; diagnostic and demographic data; fiscal data; and service utilization variables, including placement data. Individual-level clinical or service outcome data were not available from these sources. (The collection of outcome data is discussed in the next major section of this chapter, "Clinical Epidemiology in Three Systems of Care for Youth.")

The California AB377 Demonstration Counties. In 1989, three counties were awarded Cal-DMH contracts. Funding made possible by the AB377 legislation was provided to enable implementation of the System of Care Model. Three counties, Riverside, San Mateo, and Santa Cruz, were selected through a multicounty competitive application process. The three counties differ substantially in population size and composition. Descriptive characteristics of these counties and information about the initial implementation process have been reported previously (see Attkisson et al., 1995; Rosenblatt & Attkisson, 1992).

AB377 Evaluation Project Findings

Characteristics of Youth Served. Data are continuously collected to determine if the system of care demonstration counties are serving the designated child and adolescent target population. These populations include children and youth with SED who are either in out-of-home placement or assessed to be at risk for out-of-home placement. In prior research conducted on a San Francisco population, risk for out-of-home placement was associated with several other factors, including ethnic minority status; history of abuse and neglect; having a primary language other than English; and having a clinical diagnosis of Affective Disorder, Conduct Disorder, or Attention Deficit Disorder (Barber, Rosenblatt, Harris, & Attkisson, 1992). It is important that the county care systems enroll all youth known to have severe disorders; youth in or at risk for out-of-home placement; and youth, as appropriate, from all ethnic, cultural, and racial origins.

Ethnicity. In Santa Cruz County, 70% of the youth caseload is Anglo American, compared to 74% of the county's total population under age 18. Another 22% of the youth caseload is Latino American, close to the 17% of the population under age 18. An additional 3% of the youth caseload is African American, matching the 3% of the total population under age 18 that is African American. In short, the ethnic breakdowns of the youth served in Santa Cruz are virtually identical to the ethnic breakdowns of the general population under 18.

In San Mateo County, the youth served by the AB377 programs are less reflective of the total population characteristics. The proportion of Anglo Americans served by the programs and of Anglo Americans in the population under 18 in the county are roughly equivalent (45% of the youth served; 48% of the population under 18). African Americans are overrepresented in the target population, however, representing 20% of those being served but only 6% of the general population under 18. Asian Americans, on the other hand, are underrepresented in the target population, representing only 4% of the target population but 20% of the population under 18. Finally, Latino Americans are slightly underrepresented in the target population (20% of the youth served; 25% of the population under 18).

Finally, 61% of the youth caseload in Riverside is Anglo American, compared to 54% of the general population under age 18. Latino American youth constitute the second-largest proportion at 24% (less than the 36% found in the general population under 18). Conversely, the African American caseload is overrepresented at 11%, compared to the 6% of the population under age 18 that is African American. Only 2% of the youth caseload is of Asian American or Pacific Islander descent and only .25% of the youth caseload served is of American Indian descent (compared to 4% and .3%, respectively, of the Asian American and Pacific Islander population under age 18).

In Santa Cruz, the service population closely mirrors the population as a whole. This is probably because the population is mostly Latino American and Anglo American, two groups that usually receive mental health services in proportion to their numbers in the general population. In San Mateo, the service population is characterized by an underrepresentation of Asian Americans and an overrepresentation of African Americans, a trend commonly found in studies of mental health services utilization (e.g., Snowden, 1987; Sue, 1977). African Americans are similarly overrepresented in Riverside, although Latino Americans are underrepresented. In general, the youth in the services program in San Mateo are the most ethnically diverse, with over half being of ethnic minority origin.

These findings indicate that the ethnocultural profile of the caseloads in all three counties fit what would be expected given prior studies of mental health service utilization. In the absence of population epidemiologic information for mental disorder, we cannot assume that this is optimal vis-à-vis the actual community prevalence of disorder. We can only speculate that there are few major barriers to access that pertain to ethnic, cultural, or racial origin. If distributions of disorder are not the same across ethnocultural groups, however, when socioeconomic status is controlled, then the lack of apparent differences in our data could mask problems of access to care and masked ethnic, cultural, or racial barriers.

Clinical Diagnoses. In all the system of care counties, the treating clinician or caseworker reports *DSM-III-R* (American Psychiatric Association, 1987) diagnoses on admission to programs in the county. These clinical diagnoses are made "in the field" or in service agencies by service providers. Clinical personnel do not utilize standardized or structured clinical diagnostic interviews. Clinicians in the study counties are diverse in disciplinary background, amount and kind of formal clinical training, and years of experience. They also have varying views with regard to the use of diagnostic systems, the value of diagnosis in clinical work, and the level of specific training required for psychodiagnostic procedures. Thus, diagnoses are subject to a variety of biases, administrative contexts, and systemic pressures. Nonetheless, these clinician-generated diagnoses provide important information regarding how clinicians view and assess the at-risk youth in their counties. The limitations of clinical diagnoses, however, were a primary factor in our plan to collect research diagnostic data on a random sample of the county system of care enrollees. This plan, a clinical epidemiology and service system outcome study funded by a research project grant from NIMH and now being concluded, is described in the next major section of this chapter, "Clinical Epidemiology in Three Systems of Care for Youth."

Distributions of Clinical Diagnoses. In the three AB377 system of care counties, the distributions of clinical diagnoses on enrollment in the systems of care were generally similar. Disruptive behavior disorders were the most prevalent diagnoses in all three counties (29% of the youth served in San Mateo; 48% of the youth served in Santa Cruz; and 34% of the youth served in Riverside). The second most prevalent diagnoses in all three counties were the affective disorders (16% in San Mateo; 24% in Santa Cruz; 26% in Riverside). Adjustment disorders were the third most prevalent in Riverside (17%) and San Mateo (14%) but not in Santa Cruz (only 5%). Anxiety disorders were the third most prevalent group in Santa Cruz (7%) but the fourth most prevalent in San Mateo (10%) and Riverside (10%). Frequencies of severe diagnoses for major mental disorders such as schizophrenia and other psychotic disorders in the study counties ranged from 1.6 % to 2.3%.

In summary, most youth were assigned clinical diagnoses of behavior disorders, affective disorders, or adjustment disorders. These findings are consistent with those reported by Brandenburg, Friedman, and Silver (1990) and suggest that the severity and persistence of disorder among youth enrolled in the systems of care may be strongly related to factors such as level of family disruption, various forms of abuse, or historical adequacy and integrity of the total system of care.

Reliance on Restrictive Levels of Care

The goal of reducing inappropriate out-of-home placements through integrated, coordinated, and effective community care is a key part of the innovative system of care service demonstrations for youth now being replicated in California (for descriptions, see Attkisson et al., 1991; Attkisson et al., 1995; Feltman & Essex, 1989; Jordan & Hernandez, 1990; Rosenblatt & Attkisson, 1992).

In California, the most important publicly funded out-of-home placements for youth with SED include state hospitals, group homes, foster family homes, special education residential placements, probation camps, and California youth authority incarceration. Group homes, special education residential facilities, and state hospital placements were targeted for reductions in placements because they represent the most restrictive out-of-home placement options that are amenable to mental health intervention. Juvenile justice incarceration is subject largely to sentencing decisions made by judges. Such decisions are difficult to impact through mental health intervention once a crime is committed. Therefore, the focus in the juvenile justice setting is on preventing rearrests once youth are released from incarceration. In fiscal year 1988-1989, group home, AB3632 special education residential, state hospital, and foster home placements amounted to $598 million in expenditures, reflecting 82% of the state of California's public out-of-home care expenditures for youth (County Welfare Directors Association, Chief Probation Officers Association of California, & the California Mental Health Directors Association, 1990). Here we focus on an evaluation of the efforts in the System of Care Demonstration Counties to reduce and avoid unnecessary placements of children and youth in group homes, state hospitals, foster family homes, and special education residential placements.

Group Homes. Group homes, as they exist in California, are unusual both in size and in capacity to provide mental health services. In many other states, residential treatment centers (RTCs) provide the types of services found in the higher-level California group homes. Typically, RTCs are considered larger and more "medically" oriented than group homes. They also are funded through different mechanisms (the availability of Civilian Health and Medical Program of the Uniformed Services [CHAMPUS] funds has made RTCs a more popular treatment option in recent years). In California, however the higher-level group homes provide many of the same medical and psychiatric services as RTCs. Unlike RTCs, group homes are funded largely by Aid for Families and Dependent Children—Foster Care (AFDC-FC) program. They are administered by departments of social services and serve only youth who are abused, neglected, or wards of the court. In the public sector in California, group homes far exceed RTCs in popularity. In large part, this is due to the relative accessibility of AFDC-FC funds.

Surprisingly little is known about the youth who reside in these group homes. The vast majority (approximately 70%) of youth are placed because of parental neglect, incapacity, or absence. The remainder are placed because of sexual or physical abuse. The underlying reasons for these placements or the proportions of youth who have diagnosable psychological or psychiatric disorders are not known. In 1987, 70% of the children placed in group homes resided in either the "psychiatric" or the "psychological" homes, which are designed to provide some type of mental health services. Psychiatric and psychological homes constituted 89% of the newly licensed programs in 1987. Yet it was estimated that *only* 10% of all children in group homes receive services from local departments of mental health. In essence, the group home program in California represents a de facto mental health system, outside of the formal mental health apparatus, for youth who primarily suffer from parental absence, abuse, or neglect.

In fiscal year 1988-1989, $347 million was spent on group home placements, more than any other out-of-home placement option (County Welfare Directors Association et al., 1990). These expenditures comprised almost half of the $728 million total dollars spent on out-of-home placements for children and youth in California in 1988-1989. Group home placements alone in 1994-1995 accounted for $576 million in California expenditures for out-of-home expenditures for children and youth.

As shown by Attkisson et al. (1995), California's group home costs have continued to rise at an alarming rate when viewed at the statewide aggregate expenditure level. From 1984 to 1990, the average annual rate of growth in group home expenditures for California was approximately 20%. Although leveling off to about 6% per year in 1994, the rate of increase remains substantial at about two to three times the current rate of inflation. Given the current growth rate, expenditures for group home placements will exceed $600 million in fiscal year 1995-1996. Group home placement is second only to state hospital admission as the most costly alternative (per child) when children are placed out-of-home. The average annual group home cost per child *per year* in 1988-1989 was $31,100 compared with $106,200 per child *per year* in the state psychiatric hospital. State hospital costs are roughly 10% of the total amount expended on group homes. These costs are much higher today.

Group home facilities vary tremendously, from those relatively small in size (4-10 beds) to structures with more than 100 beds that physically resemble psychiatric hospitals. The group home system in California is composed of 14 rate classification levels; group homes are assigned to these levels by a system in which points are calculated by a formula that includes the hours of services provided per child weighted by the training or professional level of the individual providing the service and incorporating the licensed bed capacity of the home. The highest-level group homes (levels 13 and 14) provide full-time psychiatric services and extensive mental health care and may exceed 100 beds.

State Hospitals, Foster Family Homes, and Special Education Residential Placements. The state hospitals represent a highly restrictive and institutional level of care, whereas foster family homes represent a substantially less traditional and restrictive level of care. Group homes fall between these two extremes and may range from facilities quite similar to foster homes to facilities quite similar to the state hospital. The two California State hospital facilities, administered by Cal-DMH, are large, institutional settings designed to treat youth suffering from the most severe and disruptive disorders (Madsen, Rosenblatt, & Attkisson, 1994). Although one facility is located in northern California and the other in southern California, youth often have to travel significant distances from their natural home to be placed in these facilities. Foster family homes, on the other hand, are administered through the California Department of Social Services. Unlike the state hospital placements, youth do not need to be suffering from a clinically diagnosed mental disorder to be eligible for placement in foster homes. Typically, children are placed in foster homes after being removed from the original home for reasons of abuse and neglect. Foster homes are located throughout the state and are quite small in size.

A fourth residential placement option discussed in this chapter represents a blending of the different administrative and funding mechanisms that serve youth suffering from SED. California Assembly Bill 3632 (AB3632) mandates that mental health and social services be provided to youth in special education programs who are designated by the schools as suffering from SED. Such services may include residential placement. As a result, many local mental health departments place youth who are designated to have SED by the schools into residential settings that are most often administered through the Department of Social Services (e.g., group homes and foster family homes). In short, these youth are identified and referred by departments of education and are placed with Cal-DMH funds and resources into social services-administered facilities. Such placements are commonly referred to as "AB3632 residential placements."

A brief set of statistics illustrates the differences between the latter three types of treatment options (County Welfare Directors Association et al., 1990). In fiscal year 1988-1989, 38,600 children were placed in foster family homes, 500 children were placed through AB3632, and 300 children were placed in the state hospitals. The average cost per child per year was only $5,300 for a youth in foster family homes compared with $31,800 for a youth placed through AB3632 and $106,200 for a child per year in the state hospital. There are two state hospital facilities for youth in California. In 1989, there were 18,019 licensed foster family homes (we do not have data on the number of foster care settings serving youth placed through AB3632). In fiscal year 1994-1995, $339 million was spent on foster family homes, $47 million was spent on AB3632 residential placements, and $29 million was spent on state hospital placements for youth.

In sum, group homes, state hospitals, foster family homes, and AB3632 residential placements illustrate the wide range of placement settings and funding mechanisms that characterize the current state of residential care for youth suffering from SED in California. Data on the utilization of these services are of interest in their own right, but they are of specific import to the System of Care Model implementation in California counties. If reductions in group home expenditures and placements occur, it could merely be because utilization is shifted to other restrictive residential services, such as state hospitals or AB3632 special education residential placements.

Analysis of Group Home Expenditures and Placements. The analysis of group home expenditures was the primary initial task of the evaluation research (Rosenblatt et al., 1992). Two primary reasons for this continuing focus include the alarming rise of costs associated with group home placements of youth in California and the emphasis of the initial Ventura County demonstration and the System of Care Model Demonstration Counties on reducing group home placements and costs as a central element of cost containment, cost avoidance, and service system redirection.

The expenditure data we have analyzed represent dollars expended for group home placements through the AFDC-FC program. The data are provided by the California Department of Social Services. The data currently available for analysis reflect only these expenditures and therefore are not inclusive of total group home costs. We estimate, however, that approximately 90% of total public expenditures for group home placements are now captured by our analyses. The largest proportion of noncaptured costs are expenditures in the mental health sector whereby approximately 7% of the children in group homes receive supplemental funding through a mental health "patch"—supplemental funding from Cal-DMH.

In our analyses, the AFDC-FC costs for the System of Care Demonstration Counties were compared with the aggregate AFDC-FC costs for the state of California. The use of total California group home expenditures as a comparison provides a fiscal baseline against which to judge progress of the System of Care Demonstration Counties in achieving service system goals that include county-level cost savings and cost avoidance. To compare counties with each other and with the state, the county costs and the state costs are adjusted to reflect cost per number of youth residing in the appropriate geographic areas. Thus, the comparison data are expressed as county or statewide per capita amounts. The per capita costs were calculated by dividing the group home costs in each county by the number of youth in each county (defined as persons under 18 years of age). The same calculation was performed for the state of California as a whole by dividing the total costs for California by the number of youth in the state. When these comparisons are made, the System of Care Demonstration Counties, taken together, have progressively achieved lower per capita expenditures and a lower rate of increase in per capita cost over time than the state aggregate per capita costs.

Figure 7.1 illustrates these trends in expenditures (inflation-adjusted per capita dollars) and placements into group homes (per 10,000 population age 18 or younger) and displays expenditures and placements for both California and the model demonstration counties (AB377 expenditures) across a 13-year period beginning with 1982. Figure 7.1 illustrates that the annualized combined expenditures per capita, for children and youth in the System of Care Demonstration Counties (at $22.22 per capita inflation adjusted in 1994), are lower than the combined expenditures per capita for the total state of California (at $41.62 per capita in 1994). Figure 7.1 further illustrates that the group home per capita expenditures for the System of Care Demonstration Counties and the state were comparable until the middle of 1986. July 1986 is approximately one year after the Ventura County demonstration project began. On a county-by-county basis, there is substantial external evidence demonstrating that the System of Care Demonstration Counties already had begun to implement the system of care modeled in Ventura County by the middle of 1986 (Rosenblatt et al., 1992). This shift undoubtedly made these counties highly competitive in the state competition for the System of Care Model demonstration funding awards.

In addition to group home expenditures, Figure 7.1 also depicts group home placements of children and youth from among the system of Care Model Study Counties and the state of California. The number of group home placements for children and youth in each county reflects only the number of placements in group homes, not unduplicated counts of youth. So, for example, a youth who has two group home placements in the course of a reporting period would be counted twice. These data can be used to help understand whether the lower per capita expenditures in the System of Care Model Demonstration Counties, relative to the statewide expenditure level, reflect a reduction of the

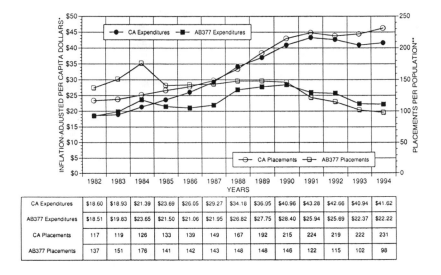

	1982	1983	1984	1985	1986	1987	1988	1989	1990	1991	1992	1993	1994
CA Expenditures	$18.60	$18.93	$21.39	$23.69	$26.05	$29.27	$34.18	$36.95	$40.96	$43.28	$42.66	$40.94	$41.62
AB377 Expenditures	$18.51	$19.83	$23.65	$21.50	$21.06	$21.95	$26.82	$27.75	$28.40	$25.94	$25.69	$22.37	$22.22
CA Placements	117	119	126	133	139	149	167	192	215	224	219	222	231
AB377 Placements	137	151	176	141	142	143	148	148	146	122	115	102	98

Figure 7.1. Annual AFDC-FC Group Home Expenditures and Placements, State of California and Combined AB377 Counties

NOTE: * Based on the CPI, populations under 18; ** per 10,000 population under 18.

aggregate number of placements or, alternatively, a reduction in the aggregate expenditure per placement. This analysis helps in specifying whether the System of Care Model Demonstration Counties are controlling the number of placement episodes or, alternatively, the expenditures per placement episode.

Figure 7.1 further illustrates that the pattern of group home placements is virtually identical to the per capita expenditure pattern. This finding is what would be expected if the number of placements drives expenditures. Although the cost per placement for the state as a whole has steadily increased from 1980 to 1995, the study counties were able to decrease their total expenditures by reducing the frequency of placements. Of course, this may not account completely for total expenditures, but it is apparent that a significant portion of the capacity of the System of Care Model Demonstration Counties to reduce expenditures on group homes is due to their ability to reduce the number of placements. This is an important finding because placement frequencies are a controllable element in county service systems.

Time-Series Analysis of the California System of Care Model. Understanding these temporal variations in the associated placements and costs of system of care policies for youth can contribute to both theory and practice of mental health services. Time-series methods are helpful in explaining more explicitly the illustrated longitudinal divergence in the rates of group home placements and expenditures between the intervention counties and the state of California. Our comparisons of placement and cost data for the intervention counties indicate that the reductions in both placements and costs are significant with respect to the historical trend in aggregate data for California. Time-series models of data for the three study counties analyzed individually and collectively display real cost savings over aggregate state expenditures. Results from our time-series analyses are based on the totality of expenditures and placements and not on sampling estimates. Although subject to minimal survey measurement errors, the results reflect a significant effect for the intervention.

Time-series analyses of data for the three demonstration counties (San Mateo, Santa Cruz, and Riverside) were designed to test the hypothesis that their observed relative differences in placements and expenditures comparative to state aggregate levels are the result of the implementation of the System of Care Model. Specifically, interventions for the system of care associated with reductions were tested for statistical significance at appropriate time intervals for each county. Although the time spans of the tests are imprecise due to complex and irregular funding and general program readiness, the interventions were tested as series interruptions beginning July 1986 for San Mateo, January 1989 for Santa Cruz, and July 1991 for Riverside. These dates correspond approximately to the actual implementation dates for the respective counties' system of care program.

Precisely defining a date at which the interventions began is difficult given the breadth and complexity of the interventions. Care systems are implemented over a relatively long period and take time to reach maturity. Nonetheless, our method does require that a point be selected to designate the beginning of system implementation. San Mateo had a relatively well funded program already in place before the other counties, deriving from its early involvement with the demonstrations of the model in Ventura County. Santa Cruz had an extremely limited care system before receiving funding from Cal-DMH through AB377. Consequently, Santa Cruz required more time to develop a system of care, experiencing about a 2-year lag after San Mateo in its implementation. Finally, an even later date was selected for Riverside because although a large county with some programs in place, the county did not receive full funding for system of care implementation until approximately 2 years after the other counties were funded. Graphic plotting of the data confirmed that these respective dates were appropriate intervention points for the three counties in our analysis. Accordingly, we tested our hypothesis, choosing the dates as specified above for the series interventions. To smooth the monthly trends, data sets for the individual counties collected between July 1981 and June 1995 were aggregated into quarterly data, resulting in 56 cases for analysis.

The time-series method attributed to Box and Jenkins (Box, Jenkins, & Reinsel, 1994) was selected to measure the association between the system of care intervention points and the series declining trends. Using the Statistical System software available from Scientific Computing Associates (SCA, 1994), the best-fitting model of the dependent series (county expenditures) was identified with autoregressive, integrated, moving average (ARIMA) procedures. ARIMA models, which empirically apply any of a large family of possible models to a time series, are mathematical expressions that impose particular patterns of regular behavior observed in a series such that only temporal, nonpatterned (random) noise is allowed to pass through a filter. The Box-Jenkins approach is an iterative model-building process by which the researcher infers the appropriate filters to identify the variables interacting in the series. The modeling technique is conceptually equivalent to reducing the flow of a series to random noise with the objective of specifying the parameters responsible for the series' behavior (Catalano & McConnell, 1993).

Generally, modeling the three individual series followed several steps. Each independent series was differentiated to remove trends or cycles. Independent variables (cyclically adjusted if necessary) for the state of California as a control and the county intervention points were specified in the equations. The coefficients of the full model were estimated to test for significance. Finally, residuals (presumably random noise) of the model were reviewed for autocorrelation (correlation between members of the series) and appropriate ARIMA parameters were specified to remove any remaining serial correlation.

The time-series equations for the three demonstration counties explain a significant portion of the variation in the data (San Mateo R^2 = 79.1%, Santa Cruz R^2 = 90.7%, Riverside R^2 = 99.4%), reflecting the quality of the modeling process. The high R^2 values indicate that the time-series models have captured nearly all of the variance in the data and therefore account for most events that could explain the temporal fluctuations in the data.

The best-fitting models for the three series among the demonstration counties provided statistically significant relationships for the system of care interventions as specified. The estimated coefficients for the effect of the interventions were significant for San Mateo (*coef* = − 114,600; *S.E.* = 55,500; *t* value = −2.07; *p* < 0.025; one-tailed test), Santa Cruz (*coef* = −62,500; *S.E.* = 18,100; *t* value = −3.46; *p* < 0.01; one-tailed test), and Riverside (*coef* = −312,400; *S.E.* = 44,600; *t* value = −7.01; *p* < 0.01; one-tailed test). The finding of a significant inverse relationship between the system of care intervention (binary or dummy independent variable) for each of the three counties and their respective group home expenditures (dependent variable) is consistent with the research hypotheses and expectations described above. These findings support the hypothesis that in the targeted counties the reduction in expenditures is attributable to the system of care implementation. The economic implications of these results for each county are as follows: On average, the effect of the system of care implementation on a quarterly basis is a savings of $114,600 for San Mateo, $62,500 for Santa Cruz, and $312,400 for Riverside for each quarter that the intervention is included in the time-series equation.

Time-series correlation supporting the observed relationships is subject to rival hypotheses or plausible explanations of the effects other than the cited hypothesis for the systems of care (Catalano & Serxner, 1987). For example, separate impinging events (seasonal factors) or shared developmental patterns (growth, recession, etc.) may cause spurious correlation of characteristics across phenomena leading to erroneous conclusions. A third confounding variable interacting between two observed variables may cause both variables of interest to move similarly over time. Statistical control of these third variables as classified by Catalano (1981) may be offered to discredit alternative explanations in time-series analysis of the systems of care data.

Our methods control for many of the factors that could confound the effects of the intervention on observed placement and cost outcomes. For example, potential confounding variables that exhibit trends, cycles, or other patterns are detectable with the Box-Jenkins time-series methods. In addition, replication of the intervention in three counties discredits the opportunity for claiming that other locally occurring third variables caused the cost outcomes. Moreover, by including data for the state of California as a whole in the time-series equations, we have controlled for most other external events that were occurring throughout the state that could also impact the demonstration counties.

Estimated Cost Avoidance. Over a 6-year period, the System of Care Demonstration Counties have experienced lower per capita group home expenditure and placement rates than the state of California as a whole. A general estimate of the cost avoidance represented by these lower per capita expenditure rates can be provided given the following assumptions: (a) California per capita rates represent an accurate standard against which to judge the performance of the counties, (b) changes in per capita rates of group home expenditures in the System of Care Demonstration Counties are due to the innovative interventions and began in February 1989, (c) all other counties in California can realize similar decreases in group home expenditures if they implement the innovative system of care, and (d) costs of the interventions are *not* included in the analysis.

Given these assumptions, the System of Care Demonstration Counties collectively expended a total of $213.76 per capita less than the state of California over the 6 years from February 1989 to January 1995. The expenditure rate differences between the System of Care Demonstration Counties and the state of California can be converted to overall cost differences by extending per capita amounts to the state population. This calculation shows the amount of expected cost avoidance for California if state expenditures were reduced to the per capita rate demonstrated by the AB377 study counties.

For the 6 years from February 1989 to January 1995 the state of California could have avoided a total (in nominal, non-inflation-adjusted dollars) of $1.1 billion in group home costs *if the state of California had followed the trend of the System of Care Demonstration Counties instead of the existing trend in the state.* These estimated reductions do not reflect the costs of providing alternative forms of care for the youth. Given that group home placements are second only to hospitalizations in costs per placement, however it is assumed that other forms of community- and home-based care provided to the youth would not completely offset the magnitude of the group home cost avoidance. Moreover, since the expenditure data are per capita and inflation adjusted, these results are probably not related to changes in population or relative price increases. Finally, it is important to note that this estimated cost avoidance is not the consequence of actual cost measurements but reflects theoretically achievable results based on the assumptions outlined above.

Foster Family Homes Expenditures and Placements. In general, the System of Care Demonstration Counties have not focused on reducing foster family home expenditures or placements. These placements are considered preferable to those made in group homes because of the less restrictive, more family-like environment. In fact, the System of Care Demonstration Counties are attempting to enrich and bolster existing foster family homes so that youth can be maintained in these homelike settings rather than moving to group homes. Therefore, we began our analysis of foster family home expenditures expecting to find increases in foster family home utilization and expenditures. This was not the case in any of the three counties (Rosenblatt & Attkisson, 1993b).

The analysis of foster home expenditures is being conducted as a multiple time-series design (Cook & Campbell, 1979) in a manner identical to those for group home analyses. A comparison of the per capita, inflation-adjusted foster home expenditures for all three counties combined and each county separately to those for the State of California reveals that the rates are not increasing in any of the counties. Taken together, the aggregate foster home placement and expenditure data for all three System of Care Demonstration Counties (Figure 7.2) indicate a relatively level pattern of expenditures since the first several months of 1989.

In fact, until approximately August 1988, foster home expenditures for all three counties, in aggregate, mirrored the expenditures for the state of California. At that point, the expenditures for the System of Care Demonstration Counties began to deviate to a lower level than the state rate of expenditures. In January 1995, the inflation-adjusted rate was

$2.02 per capita for the state of California and $1.44 (in 1983 dollars) per capita for the System of Care Demonstration Counties in aggregate. Thus, it appears that youth are not being shifted in large numbers from group home to foster home settings. This would have been the most likely place for youth to be placed who might have otherwise been placed in group home settings. Two other likely possibilities, special education residential placements and state hospitalization, are presented below.

Special Education Residential Expenditures. The overall amounts of special education residential expenditures are small relative to AFDC-FC group home or foster home expenditures (amounting to approximately 10% of the group home expenditures in each county) but do represent significant sums over the course of time. For example, the amount spent in the state of California on this type of placement in fiscal year 1994-1995 was $47 million and has increased steadily year by year. The AB3632 programs did not begin until late 1986 and the expenditure data from these programs were collected soon thereafter.

The special education residential expenditure data are presented graphically in Figure 7.3. These expenditures were obtained from records of the California Department of Social Services in reports made monthly at an aggregate level from individual counties to the state. The between-county comparisons were analyzed with statewide trends as previously performed for the group home data. Like the AFDC-FC foster home data, these expenditures also were adjusted for population growth, although a cost per 10,000 population was used to permit a more clear presentation of the data. Although the state level of expenditures has increased steadily, the level of expenditures for the System of Care Demonstration Counties together has not increased significantly since the beginning of 1991.

State Hospital Charges and Utilization. Relatively few youth in the System of Care Demonstration Counties are hospitalized in the state facilities at Napa or Camarillo. The charges for each utilization can be extremely high, however. Furthermore, hospitalization in these facilities represents the most restrictive placement alternative for youth with SED. The data we have collected indicate that $31 million in charges for bed and

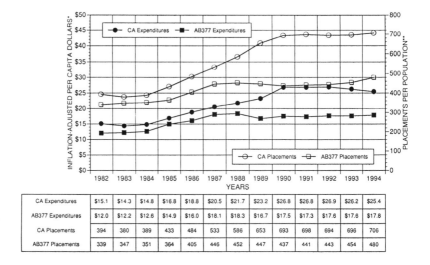

Figure 7.2. Annual AFDC-FC Foster Home Expenditures and Placements, State of California and Combined AB377 Counties

NOTE: * Based on the CPI, populations under 18; ** per 10,000 population under 18.

ancillary state hospital placements for persons under 18 years of age were accrued during the 1990 calendar year.

We collected data from the California Department of Developmental Services. Analyses of billing data document the total charges and payments case by case. Because of changes in the information system at the state agency, we currently are able to analyze only the charges for youth residing in a state hospital during the period from January 1990 to July 1992. Thus, the available data reflect all youth during this 30-month time period who were under age 18 on admission to Napa or Camarillo Hospitals.

Data demonstrate that overall the System of Care Demonstration Counties have been utilizing state hospitals at a lower per capita rate than in the state of California as a whole. One county (Santa Cruz) did not use the state hospital at all from January 1990 to July 1992, one county (Riverside) used the state hospital at a lower per capita rate than would be expected, and one county (San Mateo) utilized the state hospital at a slightly higher per capita rate than would be expected.

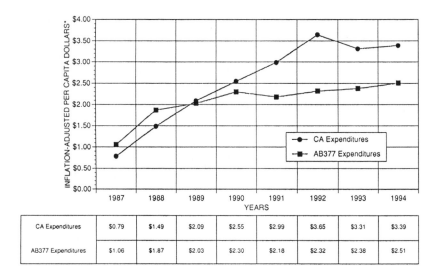

Figure 7.3. Annual AB3632 Special Education Residential Expenditures, State of California and Combined AB377 Counties
NOTE: * Based on the CPI, populations under 18.

During the 30-month period, San Mateo placed 16 youth, and Riverside placed 11 youth in a state hospital. Importantly, although the numbers of youth placed in both San Mateo and Riverside were low, the charges per youth were in some cases extremely high. For example, in Riverside, over the course of the 1990 calendar year, the bed charges alone for the most expensive youth were $142,665. When the $5,330 in ancillary charges are added, the total charges for this one youth amounted to $147,995. Similarly, in San Mateo the bed charges for the most costly youth were $125,995, with ancillary charges of $1,634, for a total of $127,629. The range in Riverside for state hospital charges was $2,437 to $142,665, with a mean of $45,282. The range in San Mateo for state hospital charges was $3,314 to $125,995, with a mean of $69,239.

Clearly, avoiding the placement of even one youth in a state hospital can save substantial sums of money. We attempt to reflect state hospital utilization over the defined 30-month period by comparing the per capita charges in the System of Care Demonstration Counties with the per capita charges throughout the state of California. According to the 1990 census, 6.8% of the youth in California reside in the three System of Care Demonstration Counties. Consequently, we would expect 6.8% ($4,781,559) of the $70,317,042 in total California charges to be reflected in these three counties. In this 30-month period, however, the total charges for the System of Care Demonstration Counties is about three-quarters of this amount ($3,108,739). Using similar logic, the charges in Riverside would be expected to amount to $3,062,352 but actually to-taled about half that amount ($1,523,190). In Santa Cruz, the expected amount would be $502,675 rather than the total of zero. Unlike the other two counties, San Mateo accrued charges at a higher rate than the state as a whole, with actual charges of $1,585,549 as compared with expected charges of $1,309,311.

Impact on Juvenile Justice
Recidivism and Rearrests

To assess the impact of the systems of care on AB377 target population youth who have contact with the juvenile justice system, the rate of rearrests for these youth is being measured, as is the severity of the crime in the instance of a rearrest. These variables are being monitored for the year preceding and the year following admission to joint juvenile justice/mental health programs. Preliminary results indicate that for 28 youth in Santa Cruz County, the mean number of arrests in the year prior to admission for treatment was 4.4, the mode was 1.0, and the median was 4.0. The number of arrests ranged from 0 to 10. The number of arrests in the year following admission ranged from 0 (13 youth) to 11 (one case). Exactly half of the youth were not arrested in the year following system of care enrollment. The mean was 1.9, the mode was 0.0, and the median was 1.0. Similar results were found for 104 youth in San Mateo. Across all programs, the mean number of arrests before admission to the programs was 2.5, with a mode of 1.0, and a median of 2.0. Slightly less than half (48%) of the youth were arrested in the subsequent year. Two youth however, had eight arrests. As a result, the postadmission mean was 1.0, although both the mode and median were 0. Data from Riverside County have still not been made available for analysis.

Regardless of how the data are analyzed, there is a reduction across the two counties in the number of charges filed and charges sustained from the year preceding treatment to the year following treatment. At least half the youth in both San Mateo and Santa Cruz were not arrested in the year following enrollment in the system of care. These data are preliminary and suffer from methodological problems deriving largely from the lack of control or comparison groups. Such evaluation research problems are being addressed as the research effort continues.

Nonetheless, the systems of care programs are predicating their success on the nesting of juvenile justice treatment programs within the broader system of care. The care systems are designed on the principle that for youth who suffer from serious emotional disorder and who commit crimes, the cessation of the program and the ending of the incarceration period rarely signals the end of the emotional difficulties that may have contributed to the delinquent behavior. Once released from these programs, youth still require ongoing effective intervention to avoid rearrest. In short, after the programs in juvenile probation end, in many cases, effective treatments for the underlying emotional disorder must continue, or in some cases, begin. The findings indicate that such an approach is promising and merits further study and understanding.

Impact on School Attendance
and Achievement

Data on school attendance and academic achievement test scores are being collected to assess the impact of the system of care on the academic performance of youth in the target population who are being served in school-based programs. Preliminary results (Attkisson & Rosenblatt, 1993; Rosenblatt & Attkisson, in press) are briefly summarized here.

Attendance was defined as physical presence in the classroom; therefore, credit was not given for "excused" absences. Even so, attendance levels across all programs were high. The average attendance across programs in San Mateo was 87%. Attendance in the programs in Santa Cruz was similar, at 88%. The average attendance in Riverside was only slightly lower, at 83% across programs. Attendance was reported for four programs in Riverside and varied considerably by program.

Standardized achievement tests were given at program entry and exit to measure academic achievement. In Santa Cruz, youth were on average one to two grade levels in achievement behind their expected grade level upon enrollment in the system of care. The differences between the test scores at enrollment and at follow-up ranged from .88 for the writing subscale of the Woodcock-Johnson Psych-Educational Battery (Woodcock, 1977) to 1.02 for the reading subscale. The average length of time between the pretest and the posttest (and hence the average length of time in the school program) was 333 days, and so the youth were on average one year older than when pretested. These figures demonstrate that on average the youth increased approximately one grade level on each subtest for each year spent in the special school. This represents a level of attainment that was not being reached by the students before entry into the program.

In Riverside, achievement data were collected from a total of 158 youth across four separate programs, including three community schools (Indio, Perris, and 12th Street) and a juvenile justice residential facility for wards of the court that includes an on-site school. As was the case in Santa Cruz, achievement was lower than the actual grade levels of the children. Across the three programs where actual grade level information was available, the mean reading, spelling, and math achievement scores were at least one year below the mean actual grade level. Across all programs, mean posttest scores for Riverside County youth are on average at least one grade level higher than the pretest scores. Some programs demonstrated greater amounts of change from the pre- to the posttest periods than other programs (see Rosenblatt & Attkisson, in press).

Finally, in San Mateo County, scores across programs on the Wide Range Achievement Test-Revised (WRAT-R) (Jastak & Wilkinson, 1984) increased approximately one grade level from the pretest to the posttest on math and reading subscales (mean pretest scores of 7.0 for math and 7.2 for reading; mean posttest scores of 8.0 for math and 8.7 for reading). An increase of approximately one-half grade level was evident on the spelling subscale (mean pretest score of 6.8; mean posttest score of 7.2). The data from a second test (the Woodcock Johnson), given in some programs in the county, were less encouraging. The math and spelling subscales did show increases of three-quarters to one-half grade level, respectively. There was, however, a slight, but not statistically significant, decrease on the word subscale.

When the school performance and achievement results are examined at a county level, the results are positive. Whereas on average, across all programs, the youth in these three counties were well below their expected grade level at pretest, Riverside and Santa Cruz counties demonstrated grade level increases of one year or more for all subscales of either the WRAT-R (Riverside) or the Woodcock-Johnson (Santa Cruz). Across all programs and two different achievement tests, San Mateo County demonstrated increases of slightly less than one year on two of the three subscales of either the WRAT-R or the Woodcock-Johnson.

The findings on educational achievement and attendance add depth to the results presented in this chapter and our prior research reports. The systems of care have demonstrated an impressive capacity to control placements and expenditures in specifically targeted restrictive levels of care (Rosenblatt et al., 1992; Rosenblatt & Attkisson, 1993a). Interestingly, the county that demonstrated the most drastic reductions in out-of-home placements made through special education programs also demonstrated the most consistent level of improvement in educational achievement (Santa Cruz). The data indicate that a majority of the youth enrolled in programs specifically designed to control out-of home placements are showing gains in academic achievement.

This study is important in two key regards: (a) it is the first published study, to our knowledge, in a scientific journal that reports details on educational attendance and achievement in an integrated system of care; and (b) the results offer hope for positive educational achievements in a population that fares extremely poorly in regular special education programs. Cast in the most positive light, the results presented in this chapter, combined with our prior publications, illustrate that it is possible to reduce and control placements in restrictive levels of care while improving the academic performance of a vast majority of the youth served in these care systems. Results from Santa Cruz are marked in this regard, and results from the other two counties range from highly promising (Riverside) to more mixed but still positive (San Mateo). Because of problems with sample size, results from San Mateo must be considered less rigorous than results from Santa Cruz and Riverside. Given the documented lack of the positive effects of special education programs with these youth, we view these results as encouraging.

The California System of Care Model evaluation research study relies primarily on secondary data to achieve study goals. For several of the minor variables of interest, we do collect individual-level data: educational achievement, school attendance, and juvenile justice recidivism. For group home, state hospital, special education residential, and foster care placements and expenditures, we analyze aggregate county-level data gathered from secondary sources. Although such data are invaluable for purposes of the evaluation research activities, dependence on secondary and aggregate data precludes many important individual-level data analyses that address research questions related to prevalence of disorder, social functioning status, and satisfaction with services. In addition, questions about cost-effectiveness of services, service use, and the relationship of psychiatric diagnosis and functional status to service use and cost outcome cannot be addressed without collection of original, individual-level data. To pursue our research objectives to this level of analysis, we sought extramural research support from NIMH. This study, "Clinical Epidemiology in Three Systems of Care for Youth," is presented in the next major section.

Clinical Epidemiology in Three Systems of Care for Youth Research Project

Once the California System of Care Model Evaluation Project contract with Cal-DMH was implemented, we sought NIMH support for a longitudinal study of clinical incidence and prevalence of mental disorder, service utilization, service outcomes, and cost outcomes in three California counties. Two of the demonstration counties and a control county were selected for study. The control county, San Francisco, was selected because it is geographically contiguous to two of the demonstration counties, Santa Cruz and San Mateo.

The NIMH-funded clinical epidemiology project directly studied individual children, youth, and their families enrolled in the organized systems of care in the study counties. The protocol encompasses original collection of individual-level data on demographic and family status, psychiatric diagnosis, functional status, utilization of services, cost of care, and service outcomes. In contrast, the state-funded evaluation research project encompasses system-level data with particular attention to outcomes of greatest currency to a community, managing costs associated with hospital care and out-of-home placements, tracking school attendance and performance, and decreasing juvenile justice recidivism. This focus complements the clinical epidemiology emphasis on the sociodemographic and clinical profiles of at-risk youth identified by and enrolled in the system of care counties employing a repeated measures research design.

Pilot Research Findings

In preliminary investigations, we studied at-risk youth in San Francisco who had multiple residential changes over time coupled with a high rate of out-of-home placement and frequent use of restrictive levels of mental health care. Findings indicate that multiple placement youth in San Francisco frequently have ethnic minority backgrounds, are non-English-speaking, are male, have experienced early separation from their parents, have experienced physical abuse as well as sexual abuse and neglect, have lower language achievement scores, and frequently have a clinical diagnosis of Personality Disorder or Pervasive Developmental Disorder (Barber et al., 1992). Similar results were found when predicting number of inpatient admissions, except that clinical diagnoses tended to be more severe, including, most frequently, psychotic disorders and major affective disorders. When inpatient psychiatric admissions are excluded from the number of total placement changes, several variables assumed special prominence in predicting a high rate of out-of-home placement, including the presence of physical abuse, a clinical diagnosis of affective disorder, early separation from a caretaker, a high overall symptom count, and male gender status.

Research Goals and Design

The clinical epidemiology study is a comparative analysis of mental health and related services for youth with SED and their families in the three county systems, San Mateo and Santa Cruz, both original California System of Care Model demonstration counties, with San Francisco, which was selected as a comparison. The pilot research findings of Barber et al. (1992), based on data abstracted from service program records and databases, inspired the development of a prospective design that allows control of a number of additional variables and more precise measurement of variables of interest. We included multiple county sites, a representative sample of youth from all sectors of the total system of services, research diagnostic interviews, assessment of socioeconomic status, assessment of clinical status and functional and social adaptation, documentation of history of abuse and neglect, and recording of service use history across the spectrum of services.

Subject Eligibility Criteria and Research Design

Samples were drawn randomly from those children and adolescents with serious emotional and behavioral problems (including children and youth in an out-of-home placement or at risk of being placed in an out-of-home setting) enrolled in the county service systems. The children and youth in the research samples are representative of those receiving care in the county systems at the time the investigation was implemented. The original research goal was to collect data from 250 subjects and their families in each county and to reinterview 100 randomly selected subjects in each county after one year. The follow-up data, when analyzed, will allow a comparative assessment of effects of system change on outcomes for the children and youth being served. The sampling goals were exceeded in all three counties, both for the initial wave of data collection and at follow-up. In addition to reinterviewing at least 100 subjects from each county sample, the total sample in each county is currently being assessed for service utilization and cost variables over time. If currently available resources are sufficient, we plan to collect lifetime service use and to calculate service use costs over the service use career.

The clinical epidemiology study is currently in the sixth year of implementation. Collection of Wave 1 and follow-up data have been completed in all three study counties, and 840 children and youth have been enrolled in the research. In addition, we have enrolled a larger number of family members, family surrogates, service providers, and teachers as research participants. Because separate interviews are carried out with the child and the family members or surrogates, we have performed over 1,600 interviews using structured diagnostic and social-functioning measures. Extensive demographic, family structure, and family history data also were collected on each child or youth participating in the study.

The Data Collection Protocol

The study was focused on the collection of diagnostic and social-functioning information using structured diagnostic interviews and standardized functional assessment instruments. Information was gathered in separate interviews with youth and their parents or parental surrogates. These interviews were conducted by master's-level trained interviewers. All participants, except service providers, teachers, and program administrators, were reimbursed for their time. Supplementary clinical and social-functioning information was gathered from human service professionals most involved with the child's care at the time. Altogether, total subject time, summed across the several sessions constituting a complete data collection cycle, required an average of 8 hours for an experienced interviewer. Sessions of approximately 3 to 4 hours each were spent with the parent and the child in direct contact.

The data collection protocol includes the following four modules that are discussed below: I. Background Module; II. Behavior and Symptom Checklists; III. Psychiatric Diagnostic Assessment; and IV. Supplementary Measures.

Module I. The Background Module was developed and piloted by the CSRG. It includes a brief time line (life event history) and documents the child's demographic and family (parental) background, current family composition and structure, residential history, education, health, global ratings of health and happiness, immigration status, use and satisfaction with services, and self-reports about the child's relationships with parent figures. Additional information on service use, contemporaneous and historical clinical diagnoses, and family background are currently being gathered through chart reviews. Surveys of service use, cost of care, and other variables abstracted from service agency and system of care records are scheduled for completion by fall 1996.

Module II. Behavior and symptom rating scales are completed by both the parent and child. Parents complete the Child Behavior Checklist (CBCL); youth age 11 and older complete the complementary Youth Self Report (YSR) (Achenbach & Edelbrock, 1983, 1986; Achenbach, Edelbrock, & Howell, 1987; Achenbach, McConaughy, & Howell, 1987). In addition, younger children (age 10 and younger) complete the

Children's Depression Inventory (CDI) (Kovacs, 1991) with assistance from the interviewer, and youth age 11 and above complete the Beck Depression Inventory (BDI) (Beck, Ward, Mendelsohn, Mock, & Erbaugh, 1961).

Module III. The diagnostic assessment is a thorough survey of the presence of childhood psychiatric symptomatology over the past 6 months. The older age group (age 11 and older) is administered the Diagnostic Interview Schedule for Children (DISC) Version 2.1 (Shaffer, Fisher, Piacentini, Schwab-Stone, & Wicks, 1989) and the younger children (age 10 and younger) are given the Kiddies Schedule for Affective Disorders and Schizophrenia (K-SADS) (Cohen, O'Conner, Lewis, Velez, & Malachowski, 1987; Costello, 1989; Costello, Edelbrock, & Costello, 1985; Costello, Edelbrock, Dulcan, & Kalas, 1984). These standardized instruments yield *DSM-III-R* Axis I psychiatric diagnoses, encompassing Anxiety and Affective Disorders, Psychotic Disorders, and Disruptive Behavior Disorders (American Psychiatric Association, 1987). Additional modules were developed by our research team and piloted as part of our research efforts. These include additional modules on Posttraumatic Stress Disorder (Fisher, 1991), Pervasive Developmental Disorder, and Alcohol and Substance Abuse. Children are assessed for their level of cognitive abilities using the Kaufman Brief Intelligence Test (K-BIT) (Kaufman & Kaufman, 1990).

Module IV. Additional ratings were made by the clinical interviewers upon completion of the parent and child structured interviews. Data also were collected from human service professionals involved with the child's treatment, case management, or education. The clinical interviewers completed a brief questionnaire in which they rated the interviews and documented substantive and procedural topics to be discussed with supervising staff. They also completed a Children's Global Assessment of Functioning (C-GAS) rating (Shaffer et al., 1983), provided their own summary diagnoses, and made assessments or diagnostic comments on all five *DSM-III-R* diagnostic and assessment axes, drawing on information gathered throughout the entire data collection cycle. Social workers, mental health workers, and probation officers completed functional ratings (C-GAS). The Teacher's Report

Form (TRF) (Achenbach & Edelbrock, 1986) was completed by the child's most recent teacher.

Each completed protocol offers a rich survey of the child's history, service use, and clinical profile. When information about service use and cost are integrated with the information collected in the four data collection modules, the total data set will represent a major resource for the development of quantitative analyses and qualitative narratives about children and youth served in public systems, as well as analyses of the risk factors, protective factors, and vulnerabilities of children and youth with SED.

The completed data set also will allow analyses of methodological problems in the field of child mental health and epidemiology. One set of problems involves the reliability of clinical and research diagnoses. Comparisons can be made between the various sources of diagnostic information, including (a) practitioners working directly with children over time, (b) computer-generated algorithms from a standardized structured interview, (c) structured interview diagnoses (DISC or K-SADS) derived from the parent versus the child, and (d) research diagnoses of interviewers following completion of the data collection cycle.

Creation of the Sampling Frame

The sampling frame for subject selection into the clinical prevalence study was generated from county management information systems where numerical client identifiers and additional demographic and service information are electronically stored for each child or youth. At the time of the sample construction (December 31, 1991), these databases included information on 562 youth in San Mateo and 516 youth in Santa Cruz, or respectively, clinical populations representing .39% and .94% of the total population of children and youth in these two counties. (For comparison purposes, the percentage in Riverside County is 1.4%.) A sampling pool of children and youth meeting study inclusion criteria was created by the research team for San Francisco. Eligibility criteria employed in San Francisco were identical to the California System of Care Model criteria: youth having SED and currently in out-of-home placement or at risk for out-of-home placement. The resulting clinical roster made possible a comparable sampling frame for San Francisco.

Prior to enrolling subjects in the clinical prevalence study, a random list was generated from the clinical rosters for the three counties. Random lists were generated for each of four subpopulation groupings: ethnic minority males, ethnic minority females, Anglo males, and Anglo females. This strategy of stratified random sampling was designed to maximize the likelihood of enrolling adequate numbers of youth in each grouping to ensure the feasibility of cross-group comparisons. As recruiting of study participants proceeded from the randomly generated lists, additional efforts were made to oversample, including all females and all youth younger than age 11, due to the relatively low numbers of these youth in the client populations. Oversampling of ethnic youth in some counties also was undertaken to create an opportunity for comparisons between ethnic subgroups. With the completion of the data set, prevalence estimates are being generated with the assignment of numerical weights for each subgroup in proportion to the numbers of like youth in the respective study populations.

In general, the samples closely mirror the clinical pool in all three counties. In addition, our oversampling did provide slight but statistically significant higher proportions of minorities and younger children. Our attempt to increase the proportion of females did not result in a distribution that differed significantly from the clinical pool in any of the three counties. The counties compared well with the clinical population on the distribution of ethnicity, revealing some effect of oversampling efforts. In Santa Cruz, there was no significant ethnicity difference between the clinical population pool and our sample; in San Mateo and San Francisco, we were able to produce modest increases in targeted minorities. The San Mateo and San Francisco samples were significantly different from the clinical pool in the distribution across the six ethnicities (San Mateo, $\chi^2 = 19.91$, $df = 5$, $p < .001$; San Francisco, $\chi^2 = 14.15$, $df = 5$, $p < .01$). This difference is evident in a successful effort in both counties to oversample Hispanic Americans. In San Mateo, we obtained a sample with 23.8% Hispanic Americans versus 16.1% in the clinical pool. In San Francisco, we obtained 19.6% Hispanic Americans, compared to a clinical population of 11.8%. This oversampling provides sufficient power to perform analyses comparing the three most prevalent ethnic groups: Caucasians, African Americans, and Hispanic Americans (see Table 7.1).

Table 7.1 Ethnicity, Gender, and Age by County and Total Sample, Wave 1 Samples

	Santa Cruz		San Mateo		San Francisco		Total	
	n	%	n	%	n	%	n	%
Ethnicity								
Caucasian	203	67.7	114	39.3	41	16.4	358	42.0
African American	12	4.0	58	20.0	131	52.4	201	24.3
Hispanic American	53	17.7	69	23.8	49	19.6	171	17.6
Mixed/Other	17	5.7	27	9.3	19	7.6	63	11.5
Asian/Islander	8	2.7	20	6.9	8	3.2	36	4.1
American Indian	7	2.3	2	0.7	2	0.8	11	1.1
Gender								
Male	206	68.7	178	61.4	167	66.8	551	65.6
Female	94	31.3	112	38.6	83	33.2	289	34.4

	M	Mdn	SD	M	Mdn	SD	M	Mdn	SD	M	Mdn	SD
Age	13.17	13.75	3.44	14.86	15.35	3.36	12.31	12.46	3.14	13.50	13.93	3.48
N		300			290			250			840	

The Study Sample

Ethnic, gender, and age characteristics of study samples from each county are presented in Table 7.1. Sampling goals were met or exceeded in all three counties. We planned for at least 250 Wave 1 subjects in each county. Sample sizes in excess of this goal strengthened the power of subgroup analyses. Overall, 850 subjects were enrolled, with recruitment efforts generating 300 subjects in Santa Cruz County, 290 in San Mateo County, and 250 in San Francisco.

Overall average age was 13.50 years with a large standard deviation (3.48). The age range across all subjects was 17.40 years (4.1 to 21.5); the total sample median age was 13.93. Oldest average age was observed in San Mateo (mean = 14.86, median age = 15.35); lowest average age was observed in San Francisco (mean = 12.31, median age = 12.46); and for Santa Cruz, the average age was 13.17 with a median age of 13.75. These differences in average age across the three study counties were statistically significant (F [2, 837] = 41.85, $p < .0001$) and reflected the average age differences in the county service populations from which the research samples were drawn. The median differences in the distribution of age between the three counties revealed a statistically significant difference. The proportion of children older than the overall sample median was highest in San Mateo (65.6%) and lower in Santa Cruz and San Francisco (48.6% and 33.2%, respectively; $\chi^2 = 57.62$, $df = 2$, $p < .0001$).

In all three study counties, approximately one-third of the sample is female (34.4%) and two-thirds male (65.6%). The predominance of males to females in the sample was greatest in Santa Cruz County (68.7%) and least in San Mateo County (61.4%), with the gender split in San Francisco (66.8%) similar to that in Santa Cruz. These findings show that the distribution of gender for children receiving services is very similar for the counties ($\chi^2 = 3.70$, $df = 2$, $p = .157$, ns). The findings also mirror the clinical pools in the three counties and indicate that the study samples are similar to the clinically enrolled populations in the three counties. These results parallel the findings of other published studies and indicate that at-risk youth enrolled in systems of care for individuals suffering from SED are predominantly boys and adolescent males (Bickman et al., 1994; Brandenburg et al., 1990; Burns et al., 1995). Girls and female adolescents are generally less prevalent in systems of care. Future research must address the questions related to this frequently documented difference. Does the difference occur because of cultural factors, differential access, different forms that disorder takes in gender groups, or differences in community prevalence of disorder or in need?

Overall, the study sample is ethnically diverse. Across all counties, subjects are 42% Caucasian, 24.3% African American, 17.6% Hispanic American, 11.5% of mixed ethnic heritage, 4.1% Asian and Pacific Islander, and 1.1% American Indian. Although the individual counties are diverse with regard to ethnic composition, there is considerable difference between the counties in regard to subgroup proportions in the research samples ($\chi^2 = 237.18$, $df = 10$, $p < .00001$). In each county, the ethnic composition reflects the comparative differences in county population demography, and as detailed in the prior section, the observed ethnic group proportions reflect the county clinical subpopulations.

In summary, we were successful in recruiting a large random sample of subjects in each county that is representative of children and youth being served by the county care systems. The sample is ethnically diverse in aggregate. By county, the ethnic compositions reflect subpopulations from which referrals for care are most frequent. The samples also reflect the broad age range of children and youth in the county care systems, thereby ensuring generalizability of study findings to the clinical populations of interest.

Prevalence of Psychiatric Disorders in the Study Sample

Table 7.2 presents the distribution of psychiatric diagnoses derived from systematic structured diagnostic interviews as discussed previously. Out of the total research sample of 840, we obtained completed parent diagnostic interviews for 838 subjects (two emancipated minors had no available parent to interview). Of these, 300 subjects were in Santa Cruz County, 288 were in San Mateo County, and 250 were in San Francisco. Raw totals and percentages for each research diagnostic category are included in Table 7.2. Results indicate that the most prevalent single disorder is Oppositional Defiant Disorder (35.32%), closely followed in prevalence by Attention Deficit/Hyperactivity Disorder (31.50%) and Conduct Disorder (22.08%). These data reflect the frequent occurrence of multiple diagnoses in individuals. Also of high frequency are Depression and Affective Disorders, Anxiety and Panic Disorders, and Phobic and Avoidant Disorders. In the composite of depressive disorders, Major Depression has a clinical prevalence of 15.75%, making this disorder the most prevalent of the major debilitating psychiatric disorders. Schizophrenia, another of the most debilitating psychiatric disorders, with a frequency of 5.96% in the research sample, has a clinical prevalence consistent with its expected population prevalence of less than 1% in the general population of children and youth.

These findings are similar to other studies of the distribution of diagnoses for youth in treatment. A recent national study of youth in a range of treatment settings found a similar diagnostic distribution using the same research diagnostic tools (Greenbaum et al., in press). As in our study, Conduct Disorders were the most prevalent diagnostic category. The prevalence of depression, however, was about half that found in our sample. The youth in our sample also had a much higher prevalence

Table 7.2 Prevalence of Psychiatric Disorders From Parent Report (DISC & K-SADS)

	Santa Cruz	San Mateo	San Francisco	Total	Percentage Reaching Diagnostic Criteria
Disorder					
Simple Phobia	15	15	19	49	5.85
Agoraphobia	15	15	17	47	5.61
Panic Disorder	4	2	1	7	0.84
Social Phobia	22	9	14	45	5.37
Separation Anxiety	25	26	25	76	9.07
Avoidant Disorder	8	7	10	25	2.98
Overanxious Disorder	36	33	33	102	12.17
Generalized Anxiety*	25	19	19	63	7.52
Obsessive Compulsive	3	5	9	17	2.03
Anorexia Nervosa	1	0	0	1	0.12
Bulimia Nervosa	2	2	4	8	0.95
Major Depression	58	38	36	132	15.75
Dysthymia	52	40	39	131	15.63
Mania	7	10	11	28	3.34
Hypomania	3	3	1	7	0.84
Schizophrenia	16	19	10	45	5.96
Attent/Hyper (ADHD)	106	63	95	249	31.50
Oppositional Defiant	121	98	77	282	35.32
Conduct Disorder	78	60	47	185	22.08
Post-Traumatic Stress	14	9	11	34	4.06
Cyclothymia**	1	0	1	2	0.24
Other Affective Dis.**	9	1	3	13	1.55
Total Diagnoses	621	474	482	1577	
N of subjects	300	288	250	838	

NOTES: * Diagnosis available from DISC only.
       ** Diagnosis available from K-SADS only.

of Attention Deficit Disorder. The prevalence of Anxiety and Schizophrenia was virtually identical. Bickman et al. (1994), in a study of a continuum of care in Fort Bragg, North Carolina, found slightly lower frequencies of Oppositional Defiant Disorder, Attention Deficit Disorder, and Major Depression. The frequency rate of Conduct Disorder reported by Bickman et al., however, was approximately half that found in our sample. Frequencies of Schizophrenia and Mania were even lower than those found in our sample (1% for each diagnosis in the Fort Bragg demonstration compared to 6% and 3%, respectively, in our sample). Comparisons with Fort Bragg data are somewhat problematic because a different diagnostic instrument was administered in that study. Nonetheless, the markedly higher levels of Conduct Disorder and Schizophrenia, as well as the slightly higher frequencies of other major disorders in our sample are intriguing and will be explored further over time.

Children and Youth Meeting Criteria
for Multiple Disorders

The two structured diagnostic interviews used in this study (DISC 2.1 and K-SADS) assess whether children and youth meet criteria for a selected set of psychiatric diagnoses. The child or youth can meet criteria for zero, one, or more than one psychiatric diagnosis. The instruments do not prioritize the diagnoses for which criteria are met or provide a standardized and reliable mechanism for determining what the most important diagnosis is for a given individual. To complicate matters further, separate and independent data sets are collected from the parent and the child. Data from the child interviews, compared with the parent diagnostic interviews, reflect varying levels of concordance for specific diagnoses and the number of diagnoses for which criteria are met. The diagnostic data presented in Table 7.2 were collected from the parent. Future publications will address the themes of concordance, ranking of diagnostic findings in individual children and youth, and significance of multiple diagnostic findings.

Table 7.3 presents psychiatric diagnostic data collected from parent respondents only and summarizes the frequencies of diagnoses per case for the DISC 2.1 and the K-SADS. As Table 7.3 shows, only seven subjects in the total sample met criteria for 10 or more psychiatric diagnoses. This very low frequency of diagnoses above 10 or more was consistent for all counties in the study. Across all counties, the average number of diagnoses per subject was approximately two (overall mean = 1.88), with San Mateo subjects receiving slightly fewer (San

Table 7.3 Multiple Diagnoses of Disorders From Parent Report (DISC & K-SADS)

Number of Diagnoses	Santa Cruz n	Santa Cruz %	San Mateo n	San Mateo %	San Francisco n	San Francisco %	Total Sample n	Total Sample %
0	75	25.00	112	38.89	85	34.00	272	32.46
1	69	23.00	67	23.26	62	24.80	198	23.63
2	58	19.33	44	15.28	32	12.80	134	15.99
3	34	11.33	20	6.94	25	10.00	79	9.43
4	26	8.67	14	4.86	11	4.40	51	6.09
5	19	6.33	14	4.86	11	4.40	44	5.25
6	8	2.67	4	1.39	8	3.20	20	2.39
7	7	2.33	6	2.08	5	2.00	18	2.15
8	2	0.67	2	0.69	6	2.40	10	1.19
9	0	0.00	2	0.69	3	1.20	5	0.60
10 or more	2	0.67	3	1.04	2	0.80	7	0.84
M	2.06		1.65		1.93		1.88	
SD	2.01		2.14		2.36		2.17	
N	300		288		250		838	

Mateo mean = 1.65, Santa Cruz = 2.06, and San Francisco = 1.93). The vast majority of subjects overall (and again consistently within each county) met criteria for four or fewer diagnoses. Of the total sample, 32.46% of children and youth did not meet criteria for any diagnosis. Although variable across counties, this category was large in each county sample (Santa Cruz = 25.00%, San Mateo = 38.89%, and San Francisco = 34.00%). Interestingly, findings are remarkably similar across the next three frequency tiers. Nearly 24% of the sample in each county met criteria for only one diagnosis. Frequencies of diagnoses become quite small beyond the level of five or more diagnoses. Additional data analyses are planned to compare the concordance of these findings with diagnostic information collected from the child or youth. We also will analyze diagnostic frequencies as a function of age group, gender, and other demographic and family composition patterns. We are interested in the children and youth who did not meet diagnostic criteria in terms of comparative social functioning; history of service use across all sectors of care, including the juvenile justice system; clinical diagnostic records; and school attendance, performance, and achievement.

Baseline Status on Psychosocial Functioning,
Symptom, and Service Satisfaction Measures
by County and Overall Sample

Table 7.4 presents baseline descriptive statistics for children and youth in each county sample and the overall sample of subjects. Included in Table 7.4 are baseline (Wave 1) data collected using standardized measures of social functioning, global psychosocial functioning, symptoms of depression and other psychological states, and overall satisfaction with services received prior to the baseline interview. Measures used to collect this set of data included the CBCL, the C-GAS, the BDI, the CDI, and a single-item measure of overall service satisfaction. Service satisfaction was from a more extensive assessment of service satisfaction that we administered to the children, youth, and their families.

Table 7.4 depicts remarkable similarity across counties on all the baseline status measures. This baseline consistency of average values and variance provides strong evidence that the three samples provide an excellent opportunity for comparative study of the different services that exist in the three counties. Wave 2 data (collected one year after Wave 1) are now available for analysis and future publications are planned to address the question of differential effectiveness of the two demonstration counties (Santa Cruz and San Mateo) compared with the San Francisco sample.

Wave 1 data presented in Table 7.4 indicate that children and youth in all three counties were significantly impaired in terms of psychosocial competencies and functioning, level of depressive and other debilitating psychological symptoms, global psychosocial functioning, and frequency of functional problems. Across all three counties average global satisfaction with services received, prior to Wave 1 data collection, was 2.88 (SD = 1.28). The satisfaction scale allowed ratings ranging from 1 ("delighted") to 7 ("terrible"). Average level of satisfaction was positive and above the midpoint of the rating scale. This level of satisfaction, although slightly negatively skewed, has sufficient range and variance to allow for detection of differential levels of satisfaction, compared

Table 7.4 Baseline Status on Psychosocial Functioning, Symptoms, and Service Satisfaction Measures by County and Total Sample

	Santa Cruz			San Mateo			San Francisco			Total		
	n	*M*	*SD*	*n*	*M*	*SD*	*n*	*M*	*SD*	*n*	*M*	*SD*
CBCL (*T*-scores)												
Total Problem Behavior	288	63.25	10.65	268	63.47	10.57	241	64.60	11.24	797	63.73	10.81
Internalizing Behavior	288	59.93	11.89	268	61.02	11.63	241	60.81	12.38	797	60.56	11.95
Externalizing Behavior	288	62.20	11.83	268	62.33	11.34	241	63.42	11.94	797	62.61	11.70
Total Social Competency	223	36.96	8.08	228	36.18	8.48	197	36.36	7.80	648	36.50	8.13
C-GAS	289	56.57	12.61	271	57.06	15.46	237	56.53	14.23	797	56.73	14.01
Overall Service Satisfaction 1 (Delighted) - 7 (Terrible)	286	2.94	1.29	259	2.82	1.29	241	2.87	1.26	786	2.88	1.28
Ages 11 through 20 BDI	181	9.67	8.37	194	11.94	10.59	126	10.25	9.42	501	10.62	9.47
YSR (*T*-scores) Total Problem Behavior	194	57.13	11.09	234	57.81	11.71	149	57.64	11.06	577	57.54	11.32
Ages 5 through 10 CDI (*T*-scores)	69	48.45	8.18	27	45.11	7.32	75	50.76	8.99	171	48.94	8.60

with this baseline, at follow-up if the systems of care produce such differential effects over time.

In future publications, we will present analyses of the psychosocial functioning, symptom, and satisfaction measures in the context of the total study data, including psychiatric diagnostic information, service use and cost, school achievement, and family history and composition.

Current Status and Future Directions of the UCSF Child Services Research Group Research Program

The research team continues to evaluate the ongoing implementation of the California System of Care Model in the original 4 counties and in 15 additional counties that have been funded by the state or federal government. Concurrently, we are completing the collection of service use and cost data for the three counties that participated in the Clinical Epidemiology in Three Systems of Care study. In the latter investigation, we have completed collection of the full protocol at Waves 1 and 2 for the entire sample in all three counties. Data analyses are in progress to compare counties and individuals across the two data collection waves. These data will then be integrated with service use and cost data when these variables are available for analysis in the summer of 1996. We are seeking funding to support a third wave of data collection and to allow the research team to refine measures of service use and cost.

To date, our research efforts in a series of complementary investigations have yielded a rich array of data for analysis and application of findings to health policy related to children and adolescents suffering from SED. We are fortunate to have a creative and tenaciously dedicated research team; committed and steadfast research partners at the state and county levels; and an inspiring cohort of children, youth, and their families who served as research subjects. These three groups of participants have worked in a milieu of rapport and cooperation to achieve significant progress toward our research goals. All this effort and achievement was made possible by the support from those funding the research—including especially the Cal-DMH, NIMH, and SAMHSA.

When we began our research program, our goals were to systematically understand what was then a promising service system reform for

youth with SED. Our initial goals were to describe the youth who received care and to understand the costs and outcomes of care. We have
made considerable progress toward each of these goals. Just as the California System of Care Model is expanding to additional counties within
the state at an explosive pace, however, so too is our knowledge base
regarding these efforts. Increasingly, we are documenting the social and
political processes that have created this expansion as well as the essential characteristics of the care systems. Below we describe our research
findings to date as well as the implications and the future directions that
derive from these results.

1. Going to Scale: Reform of Mental Health Services to Children and Youth in California Counties

The mix of a CASSP planning grant along with a pioneering demonstration in Ventura County greatly enhanced the capacity of Cal-DMH
and a group of California counties to embark on a uniquely successful
reform of mental health services for children and youth suffering from
SED. The California System of Care Model has now been implemented
in 19 of the 57 counties in a state now populated by over 30 million
persons, including 7 million children. Over half of the children in the
state are served by care systems that are implementing this model. Implementation of the model has lead to specification of the target population, improved collaboration between the sectors providing
significant educational and human services to the target population,
improved collaboration with the juvenile court and the juvenile justice
system, increased family participation in planning and implementing
services, greatly enhanced evaluation of service system effectiveness,
and increased use of evaluative data for program development. This is
the single largest effort in youth served, repeated replications, and
scope of services provided in the nation that is dedicated to replicating
and implementing a single System of Care Model that is based on
CASSP principles. A combination of modest but essential state, federal,
and local county investments has permitted a dramatic reorientation of
the scope, nature, and type of services provided to youth with SED in
the largest state in the United States. Over the past decade, the system
of care movement in California has outlasted the initial grants and programs that provided for its implementation.

The California System of Care Model is one of only a few system reforms for children with SED that is entering its second decade and also rapidly expanding to new sites. No other single system of care effort, to our knowledge, has grown to this degree. As the model expands to new counties and environments, there exists considerable potential for the degradation of the principles that allowed the initial counties to succeed. Outcomes and efficiencies achieved in the first replications may not continue in new sites for a range of reasons. Consequently, our research team is embarking on a study of the essential components of the System of Care Model to understand what elements seem tied most directly to success.

2. Characteristics of the Youth Served in the California System of Care Model

An essential component of the California System of Care Model is a focus on carefully selecting the population of youth targeted to receive scarce public resources. Our research efforts have described the demographic, diagnostic, and functional characteristics of the youth served in these care systems. Our key findings to date include

Demographic Characteristics of the Youth Served

- Risk of out-of-home placements is associated with ethnic minority status; history of abuse and neglect; speaking a language other than English; and a clinical diagnosis of Affective, Conduct, or Attention Deficit Disorder.
- The System of Care Counties are providing services to between 1% and 2% of the youth residing in the county.

The youth served in the system of care counties tend to be older, male, and ethnically diverse. Although African Americans are overrepresented in the service systems relative to the county child populations and Asian Americans are underrepresented, these patterns are similar to those in other studies of mental health utilization. There is no evidence to date that major barriers to accessing care exist for any specific ethnic group.

Diagnoses of Youth Served

- Diagnoses provided by the treating clinician indicate that Disruptive Behavior Disorders are the most prevalent diagnoses followed by Affective Disorders.
- Diagnoses obtained through research criteria and independent structured interviews follow a similar pattern to those given by the treating clinician. Behavior Disorders are the most frequent diagnoses followed by Affective Disorders, Anxiety Disorders, and Attention Deficit/Hyperactivity Disorder.
- With the exception of Depression, severe mental disorders are rare in this population. The prevalence of Schizophrenia is approximately 5% by both research and clinical diagnostic criteria.
- All youth received a diagnosis from a treating clinician. Across three study counties, however, about a third of the youth (32.5%) did not meet research criteria for any diagnosis on the structured interviews.

Social Functioning, Adaptation, Symptom Expression,
and Global Psychosocial Functioning

- Across three study counties (San Mateo, Santa Cruz, and San Francisco) the level of functioning as measured by behavioral checklists is low. The mean CBCL scores are in the borderline clinical range. The average *T* score places these youth in the lowest 10% of the distribution of a national normative sample.
- Other functioning scales indicate high levels of depression and low overall global functioning. Importantly, these scales were not administered directly after admission to the service systems. Levels of functioning, as reflected on these measures, would likely be lower at the point of service system enrollment.

Our research team has learned a great deal about the youth who are enrolled in the care systems. In general, youth are male, older, conduct disordered, and functionally impaired. In short, the youth who are expressing the most external signs of distress are those who are receiving services. It is also clear, given estimates of population prevalence of SED in a community (ranging from 3% to 20%), that the service systems are not providing care to all those in the community who may require such care. These results are not surprising given that the care systems are focusing on youth who are either in out-of-home placement or at risk for such placement. Managers of these care systems are attempting to broaden the population they serve to include younger children as well as more youth whose level of internal distress may be severe but who do not express their problems externally. This expansion of the original target population poses a "catch-22" dilemma: The service systems are designed to reduce costs associated with out-of-home placements and reducing these costs drives the political and social support behind the programs. Nonetheless, program managers realize the potential value of more preventive efforts that may not result in immediate impacts on service system costs. This dilemma is posing a real challenge to service and research efforts.

Finally, although we have already analyzed a considerable amount of information regarding the youth served in these care systems, much more remains to be done. Our existing data set from the NIMH-funded study contains extensive information regarding the social, economic, and familial backgrounds of the youth served. The relationships of these factors to diagnosis, levels of impairment, costs of care, and outcomes constitute the next step in our description of the populations of youth served in these care systems. Finally, all 19 county care systems that we work with are currently administering CBCL, YSR, and other functioning scales to youth at admission to the programs. These scales are being administered both for their potential clinical utility in the assessment process and for the data they provide regarding the level of functioning of the youth served. We anticipate learning even more about the youth served in these care systems over the next year.

3. Cost Avoidance and Cost Savings

The documentation of cost avoidance and savings has resulted in a number of research reports. The findings indicate that large and significant cost avoidance and savings are being realized in California counties implementing the System of Care Model for children and youth suffering from SED. Reduced placements in restrictive levels of care such as state hospital admissions, group home placements, and special education residential placements primarily account for these realizations. The most central aspect of this work has been the documentation of lower, inflation-adjusted per capita expenditures and rates of group home placements in the system of care counties than in the state as a whole. Per capita expenditures in the original AB377 system of care counties are approximately half the state per capita rate. Given that over half a billion dollars is spent on group homes in California, the potential savings for the state are dramatic if the state as a whole could follow the pattern demonstrated by the system of care counties. Key findings pertaining to cost avoidance and savings include the following:

- For the 6 years from February 1989 to January 1995, the state of California could have saved a total (in nominal, non-inflation-adjusted dollars) of $1.1 billion in group home costs *if the state of California had followed the trend of the System of Care Demonstration Counties instead of the existing trend in the state.*

- The demonstration counties have generated lower per capita inflation-adjusted rates of expenditures and per capita group home placements than California as a whole. The evaluation results provide evidence that an integrated system of care can reduce group home placements.

- Foster home expenditures are lower for the counties replicating the innovative system of care than for California as a whole. Expenditures for special education residential placements are either at the state rate or, in two counties, lower. State hospital expenditure and utilization rates are below the state rate in two of the demonstration counties and slightly higher in one of the demonstration counties.

- The cumulative evidence supports the conclusion that the replication counties are utilizing restrictive levels of care at lower rates than would be expected given statewide patterns.

- Using mathematical models that are conservative in their estimation procedures, we have calculated that on average the effect of the system of care implementation is a savings of $114,600 for San Mateo, $62,500 for Santa Cruz, and $312,400 for Riverside for each quarter of the intervention.

The political and programmatic implications of our results on the cost savings accrued by the California System of Care Model have been profound. More than any single factor emerging from our research, this attention to costs played a critical role in the continued development of the model and its expansion to additional California counties. There remain, however, considerable gaps in our knowledge of costs of services. The costs we tracked to this point focus on aggregate level indicators of county expenditures for restrictive levels of care rather than the costs of services to the individual youth enrolled in the systems. We are in the process of collecting individual-level cost data in the three service systems as a part of our NIMH-funded research.

4. Quality Monitoring and Outcomes of Care

The California System of Care Model requires systematic monitoring of service program implementation, measurement of service effectiveness, and change in service recipient functional status with reference to baseline data. Historically, the collection of routine outcome data in the system of care counties has focused on educational performance and juvenile justice recidivism. In addition, as reported in this chapter, several of the counties have participated in federally funded services research activities. Funding available for these studies has allowed individual- and family-level data collection and follow-up using standardized instruments and independent assessments. We are currently undertaking analyses of Wave 2 follow-up data; these data will be integrated with the results from Wave 1 and with data on service use and cost that are currently being collected on the research samples. This chapter does, however, report on outcomes pertaining to educational attainment, juvenile justice recidivism, and client satisfaction. Our findings to date include the following:

- Youth enrolled in the California System of Care Model have good records of school attendance and are beginning, for the first time, to perform at grade level following enrollment in the system of care. Although it will be necessary to improve our research design in this area, the initial results are very promising. School attendance, performance, and achievement are considered to be critical to long-term adaptation and social functioning.

- The avoidance of future rearrests and recidivism into the juvenile justice system for those youth who have been arrested is an essential goal of the California System of Care Model. Results to date indicate a reduction across system of care counties in the number of juvenile charges filed and sustained from the year preceding treatment to the year following treatment. Approximately half of the youth who had sustained charges prior to treatment have avoided rearrest in the year following discharge from the treatment programs.

- In this chapter, we reported baseline findings for one of several measures of service satisfaction included in the research program. At baseline, we collected satisfaction with services at the inception of the new systems of care. The baseline findings, therefore, assessed level of satisfaction with care received prior to system of care reform efforts in the counties. Although generally positive satisfaction was found at baseline, results indicated that there was considerable room for improvement. The full research protocol includes additional measures of satisfaction with the several components of care typically encountered by participants and their families in the community. A report of the service satisfaction findings will be published with the analysis of Wave 2 data through which the effect of the implementation of the system of care can be determined.

Since 1989, county-level evaluators have met to plan and implement standardized approaches to effectiveness measurement. The UCSF CSRG has taken the lead in organizing the county evaluators and providing technical assistance to them as they plan and implement evaluation activities. Two years ago, when new system of care legislation was passed in California (AB3015), new evaluation requirements for the collection of individual-level outcome data were mandated. Consequently, the UCSF CSRG research team, in collaboration with leaders from Cal-DMH, has overseen the implementation by evaluation personnel in 19 counties of measurement and evaluation strategies that produce a continuous flow of evaluative information about client status and outcomes of care, including client satisfaction. These outcome data are collected periodically on all youth enrolled in the care systems and use the best existing data collection tools, such as the CBCL and the YSR. These tools have been carefully implemented to provide timely internal feedback to clinicians and program administrators. Consequently, local program managers now have a wide range of outcome measures that along with information on client characteristics and service costs provide powerful system management tools. This evaluation and outcome monitoring process is moving toward statewide implementation. Over the next 2 years, these data will be available for detailed analysis and will constitute an extraordinarily rich 19-county database on the outcomes of care for the youth enrolled in these systems.

Finally, through our federally funded research project, we have collected two waves of data that describe the one-year outcomes of youth served in three counties. These data are currently being analyzed and will be available over the next year. We also hope to receive funding to examine the longer-term outcomes of the youth in our sample. The 840 youth in our initial sample constitute an important cohort that can be followed longitudinally to determine long-term outcomes.

Conclusion

Child mental health services research is in its infancy and significant gains have been made in a relatively short period of time. Already, however, the future of the field is in doubt, in part because of a lack of continued and consistent support by a range of funding agencies. Our work could not have been undertaken without the excellent support that we received from Cal-DMH and NIMH. Building a cumulative knowledge base in a rapidly evolving field takes time, and a lack of programmatic support for system of care research will hinder the development of information essential to inform policy and practice over the long haul. Research resources are limited and many other related research endeavors, such as population epidemiology and clinical research, compete with services research for funding. Even within the mental health services research field, child-oriented projects compete with the adult-oriented projects for resources. This competition for too few resources creates ultimately harmful tensions in the services research field. It is tempting to judge the fledgling efforts in the child and adolescent services domain by the standards of more developed fields, even though the early stages of even the most well-established areas of inquiry seem unsophisticated when viewed in retrospect.

Our research efforts in California provide evidence of how a programmatic, long-term commitment to research can go hand in hand with the development and expansion of system reform. Over a decade ago, the state of California embarked on a major reform of its child mental health services system. This reform is being implemented in the context of systematic and independent evaluation research. In addition, the service systems in each county are investing in focused program evaluation being undertaken in a standardized, collaborative enterprise developed with the technical assistance and consultation of our research team. This reform and services research agenda has grown from 1 to 19 counties and has attracted the attention of a national audience of program administrators and services research scientists. The Center for Mental Health Services division of SAMHSA has recognized these pioneering efforts through its funding of service systems development in eight counties.

It is no longer unreasonable to expect that within a 10-year time frame all 58 California counties will be participating in this reform. Importantly, the process of service reform and services research pertaining to these reforms is never static. Service systems are continually evolving and changing as we learn what is and is not effective. External political and social pressures play a role in this development. Ultimately, however, the key role of programmatic services research in the evolution of these programs cannot be overlooked. Similarly, our research efforts build over time with our learning from the successes and failures of prior efforts. A healthy developmental process for the growth of systems of care and service systems research, like any developmental process, requires patience, time, care, partnerships, commitment, and sustenance. The data presented in this chapter are positive and encouraging regarding the costs and effects of the California System of Care Model. We expect to provide more detailed and complete external documentation of whether the System of Care Model produces high-quality care at lower cost with increased accountability to the service recipients, their families, and to the public. We also expect, based on prior experience, great resistance to these reforms from those who favor the current multibillion dollar investment in hospitals, residential facilities, and categorical strategies for funding and delivery of care. Change will come only from the accumulation, over time, of a scientific knowledge base strong enough to create more rational federal, state, and local policies for our nation's youth.

References

Achenbach, T. M., & Edelbrock, C. S. (1983). *Manual for the Child Behavior Checklist and Revised Child Behavior Profile.* Burlington: University of Vermont, Department of Psychiatry.

Achenbach, T. M., & Edelbrock, C. S. (1986). *Manual for the Teacher's Report Form and Teacher Version of the Child Behavior Profile.* Burlington: University of Vermont, Department of Psychiatry.

Achenbach, T. M., Edelbrock, C., & Howell, C. T. (1987). Empirically based assessment of the behavioral/emotional problems of 2 and 3 year old children. *Journal of Abnormal Child Psychology, 15,* 629-650.

Achenbach, T. M., McConaughy, S. H., & Howell, C. T. (1987). Child/adolescent behavioral and emotional problems: Implications of cross-informant correlations for situational specificity. *Psychological Bulletin, 101,* 213-232.

American Psychiatric Association. (1987). *Diagnostic and Statistical Manual of Mental Disorders* (3rd ed., Rev.). Washington, DC: American Psychiatric Association.

Attkisson, C. C., Dresser, K. L., & Rosenblatt, A. (1991, April 29). *Service systems for youth with severe emotional disorder: Systems of care research in California.* (Presented as invited testimony at the hearing, Close to home: Community-based mental health services for children, before the Select Committee on Children, Youth, and Families, U.S. House of Representatives.) Washington, DC: Government Printing Office.

Attkisson, C. C., Dresser, K., & Rosenblatt, A. (1995). Service systems for youth with severe emotional disorder: System of care research in California. In L. Bickman & D. Rog (Eds.), *Children's mental health service systems: Policy, services, and evaluation* (pp. 236-280). Thousand Oaks, CA: Sage.

Attkisson, C. C., & Rosenblatt, A. (1993). Enhancing school performance of youth with severe emotional disorder: Initial results from system of care research in three California counties. *School Psychology Quarterly, 8*(4), 277-290.

Attkisson, C. C., & Rosenblatt, A. (1996). *The Child Services Research Group: Bibliography and record of public service.* San Francisco: University of California, San Francisco, Child Services Research Group (Suite 1450, 44 Montgomery Street, San Francisco, CA 94104-4602).

Attkisson, C. C., Rosenblatt, A., & Dresser, K. L. (1990, October). *Assessing systems of care for severely emotionally disturbed youth in three California counties.* Paper presented at the annual meeting of the American Public Health Association sponsored by the Mental Health Section of APHA, New York.

Barber, C. C., Rosenblatt, A. B., Harris, L., & Attkisson, C. C. (1992). Use of mental health services among severely emotionally disturbed children and adolescents in San Francisco. *Journal of Child and Family Studies, 1,* 183-207.

Beck, A. T., Ward, C. H., Mendelsohn, M., Mock, J. E., & Erbaugh, J. K. (1961). An inventory for measuring depression. *Archives of General Psychiatry, 4,* 561-571.

Bickman, L., Guthrie, P. R., Foster, E. M., Lambert, E. W., Summerfelt, W. T., Breda, C. S., & Heflinger, C. A. (1994). *Final report of the outcome and cost/utilization studies of the Fort Bragg evaluation project* (Vol. 1). Nashville, TN: Vanderbilt Institute for Public Policy Studies, Center for Mental Health Policy.

Box, G. E. P., Jenkins, G. M., & Reinsel, G. C. (1994). *Times series analysis, forecasting and control* (3rd ed.). Englewood Cliffs, NJ: Prentice Hall.

Brandenburg, N. A., Friedman, R. M., & Silver, S. E. (1990). The epidemiology of childhood psychiatric disorders: Prevalence findings from recent studies. *Journal of the American Academy of Child and Adolescent Psychiatry, 29,* 76-83.

Burchard, J. D., & Clarke, R. T. (1990). The role of individualized care in a service delivery system for children and adolescents with severely maladjusted behavior. *Journal of Mental Health Administration, 17,* 48-60.

Burns, B .J., Costello, E. J., Angold, A., Tweed, D., Stangl, D., Farmer, E. M. Z., & Erkanli, A. (1995). Children's mental health service use across service sectors. *Health Affairs, 14*(3), 147-159.

Catalano, R. (1981). Contending with rival hypotheses to correlation of aggregate time series. *American Journal of Community Psychology, 9,* 667-679.

Catalano, R., & McConnell, W. (1993). *Do civil commitments reduce violence in the community? A time-series test* (Working Paper No. 2-93). Berkeley: University of California, Institute for Mental Health Services Research.

Catalano, R., & Serxner, S. (1987). Time series designs of potential interest to epidemiologists. *American Journal of Epidemiology, 126,* 724-731.

Children's Mental Health Services Act of 1987. California Welfare and Institutions Code §§ 5565.10-5565.40.

Children's Mental Health Services Act of 1992. California Welfare and Institutions Code §§ 5850-5883.

Cohen, P., O'Conner, P., Lewis, S., Velez, N., & Malachowski, B. (1987). Comparison of DISC and K-SADS-P interviews of an epidemiological sample of children. *Journal of the American Academy of Child and Adolescent Psychiatry, 26,* 662-667.

Cook, T. P., & Campbell, D. T. (1979). *Quasi experiments: Design and analysis issues for field settings.* Chicago: Rand McNally.

Costello, A. J., Edelbrock, C. S., Dulcan, M. K., & Kalas, R. (1984). *Testing of the NIMH Diagnostic Interview Schedule for Children (DISC) in a clinical population* (Contract No. RFP-DB-81-0027). Rockville, MD: National Institute for Mental Health, Center for Epidemiologic Studies.

Costello, E. J. (1989). Developments in child psychiatric epidemiology. *Journal of the American Academy of Child and Adolescent Psychiatry, 28,* 836-841.

Costello, E. J., Edelbrock, C. S., & Costello, A. J. (1985). Validity of the NIMH Diagnostic Interview Schedule for Children: A comparison between psychiatric and pediatric referrals. *Journal of Abnormal and Child Psychology, 13,* 579-595.

County Welfare Directors Association, Chief Probation Officers Association of California, and the California Mental Health Directors Association. (1990, Spring). *Ten reasons to invest in the families of California: Reasons to invest in services which prevent out-of-home placement and preserve families* (Prepared and published by the authors through a grant from the Edna McConnell Clark Foundation).

Day, C., & Roberts, M. C. (1991). Activities of the Child and Adolescent Service System Program for improving mental health services for children and families. *Journal of Clinical Child Psychology, 20,* 340-350.

Dresser, K. L., Clausen, J. M., Rosenblatt, A., & Attkisson, C. C. (1995, March). *Evaluation of the Child and Adolescent Service System Program: A review of documents.* Paper presented at the 8th Annual Research Conference for Children's Mental Health, Tampa, FL.

Feltman, R., & Essex, D. (1989). *The Ventura Model: Presentation package.* (Available from Randall Feltman, Director, Ventura County Mental Health Services, 300 Hillmont Avenue, Ventura, CA 93003)

Fisher, P. W. (1991). *Post Traumatic Stress Disorder Module for the DISC 2.1.* (College of Physicians and Surgeons of Columbia University, 722 West 168th Street, New York: NY)

Greenbaum, P., Dedrick, R. F., Kutash, K., Brown, E., Lardiery, S., Pugh, A. M., & Friedman, R. M. (in press). National Adolescent and Child Treatment Study (NACTS): Outcomes for youth with emotional and behavioral disabilities. In M. H. Epstein, K. Kutash, & A. Duchnowski (Eds.), *Community-based programming for children with serious emotional disturbance and their families: Research and evaluations.* Austin, TX: PRO-ED.

Jastak, S., & Wilkinson, G. S. (1984). *Wide Range Achievement Test-Revised.* Wilmington, DE: Jastak Associates.

Jordan, D. D., & Hernandez, M. (1990). The Ventura Planning Model: A proposal for mental health reform. *Journal of Mental Health Administration, 17,* 26-47.

Katz-Leavy, J. W., Lourie, I. S., Stroul, B. A., & Zeigler-Dendy, C. (1992). *Individualized services in a system of care.* Washington, DC: Georgetown University Child Development Center, CASSP Technical Assistance Center.

Kaufman, A. S., & Kaufman, N. L. (1990). *Kaufman Brief Intelligence Test manual.* Circle Pines, MN: American Guidance Service.

Kovacs, M. (1991). *The Children's Depression Inventory.* North Tonawanda, NY: Multi-Health Systems.

Madsen, J., Dresser, K. L., Rosenblatt, A., & Attkisson, C. C. (1994). *Evaluation of the California implementation of the NIMH Child and Adolescent Service System Program.* San Francisco: University of California, San Francisco, Child Services Research Group.

Madsen, J., Rosenblatt, A. B., & Attkisson, C. C. (1994). Youth in California state psychiatric hospitals. In C. J. Liberton, K. Kutash, & R. M. Friedman (Eds.), *A system of care for children's mental health: Expanding the research base: Conference Proceedings from the 6th Annual Research and Training Conference* (pp. 339-344). Florida Mental Health Institute, Research and Training Center for Children's Mental Health.

National Institute of Mental Health. (1983). *Program announcement: Child and Adolescent Service System Program.* Rockville, MD: Author.

Public Health Services Act of 1992. Title V, Part E, Section 561 et seq. Comprehensive Community Mental Health Services for Children and Adolescents with a Serious Emotional Disturbance. 42 U.S.C. §§ 290 et seq.

Rosenblatt, A., & Attkisson, C. C. (1992). Integrating systems of care in California for youth with severe emotional disturbance. 1: A descriptive overview of the California AB377 Evaluation Project. *Journal of Child and Family Studies, 1,* 93-113.

Rosenblatt, A., & Attkisson, C. C. (1993a). Assessing outcomes for sufferers of severe mental disorder: A review and conceptual framework. *Evaluation and Program Planning, 6,* 347-363.

Rosenblatt, A., & Attkisson, C. C. (1993b). Integrating systems of care in California for youth with severe emotional disturbance. 3: Answers that lead to questions about out-of-home placements and the California AB377 Evaluation Project. *Journal of Child and Family Studies, 2,* 119-141.

Rosenblatt, A., & Attkisson, C. C. (in press). Integrating systems of care in California for youth with severe emotional disturbance. 4: Educational attendance and achievement. *Journal of Child and Family Studies.*

Rosenblatt, A., Attkisson, C. C., & Fernandez, A. (1992). Integrating systems of care in California for youth with severe emotional disturbance. 2: Initial group home utilization and expenditure findings from the California AB377 Evaluation Project. *Journal of Child and Family Studies, 1,* 263-286.

Scientific Computing Associates. (1994). *Forecasting and time series analysis using the SCA statistical system* (Vol. 1). Oak Brook, IL: Author.

Shaffer, D., Fisher, P., Piacentini, J., Schwab-Stone, M., & Wicks, J. (1989). *Diagnostic Interview Schedule for Children (DISC-2.1).* New York: New York State Psychiatric Institute.

Shaffer, D., Gould, M. S., Brasic, J., Ambrosini, P. J., Fisher, P., Bird, H. R., & Aluwahlia, S. (1983). A Children's Global Assessment Scale (CGAS). *Archives of General Psychiatry, 40,* 1228-1231.

Snowden, L. (1987). *Reaching the underserved: Mental health needs of neglected populations.* Beverly Hills, CA: Sage.

Stroul, B. A., & Friedman, R. M. (1986). *A system of care for severely emotionally disturbed children and youth.* Washington, DC: Georgetown University Child Development Center, CASSP Technical Assistance Center.

Sue, S. (1977). Community mental health services to minority groups: Some optimism, some pessimism. *American Psychologist, 32,* 616-624.

VanDenBerg, J. E., & Grealish, E. M. (1996). Individualized services and supports through the wraparound process: Philosophy and procedures. *Journal of Child and Family Studies, 5,* 7-21.

Ventura County Children's Mental Health Services Demonstration Project. (1988). *Final report on the Ventura County Children's Mental Health Demonstration Project: A 3-year update and addendum to the Two Year Report on the Ventura Model for Interagency Children's Mental Health Services.* (Available from Randall Feltman, Director, Ventura County Mental Health Services, 300 Hillmont Avenue, Ventura, CA 93003)

Woodcock, R. W. (1977). *Woodcock-Johnson Psycho-Educational Battery: Technical report.* Allen, TX: DLM Teaching Resources.

Conducting Randomized Clinical Trials in Children's Mental Health

Experiences and Lessons From One Venture

ELIZABETH M. Z. FARMER

BARBARA J. BURNS

HELEN B. GUILES

LENORE BEHAR

DAN I. GERBER

Since the early 1980s, there has been a move in both the philosophy and practice of children's mental health services away from traditional outpatient and inpatient treatment toward community-based individual-

AUTHORS' NOTE: This research was funded by a grant from the National Institute of Mental Health (MH48053). The first author was supported, in part, by an NIMH NRSA postdoctoral fellowship (MH19117). The authors thank the administrative and clinical staff members from Blue Ridge and Smoky Mountain Area Mental Health Programs for their invaluable help in completing this project and their assistance in reviewing previous drafts of this chapter. We extend particular thanks to Marty Hydaker, Ron Yowell, Angela Ward, Jim Efstation, and Connie Hays.

ized care. One of the incentives for this move clearly has been economic. Another incentive has been the lack of demonstrable effectiveness of traditional services in producing desired changes. In an era of shrinking budgets, youth with challenging and multiple problems, and increasing attention to new treatment approaches, interest about what works remains high.

Randomized clinical trials are an efficient way to attempt to answer the question of what works (Bickman, 1992; Boruch & Wothke, 1985; Campbell & Stanley, 1966). In the current world of mental health services, however, many of the conditions necessary for a randomized clinical trial are difficult to attain (e.g., ability to randomly assign participants, confidence that differences outside of the focal treatment will be randomly distributed across participants, precise administration and measurement of the intervention, an adequate control group, and a finite set of outcomes that can be measured adequately; see Bickman, 1985, 1992; Boruch, McSweeny, & Soderstrom, 1978; Burns, 1994). Although such requirements have always made randomized trials difficult for studies of mental health treatments, the current move toward community-based, individualized treatment has exacerbated the difficulties. But despite obstacles, the randomized clinical trial remains one of the most parsimonious ways to assess the efficacy and effectiveness of treatment. Therefore, finding ways to carry out sound randomized trials in the mental health field should help to advance the field beyond a reliance on rhetoric and increase our knowledge of what works.

In this chapter, we focus on one randomized clinical trial in which we encountered many of the problems common to such studies but worked through these problems to successfully complete the study. The Assessing Coordinated Care (ACC) study examined the effectiveness of case management for youth with serious emotional disturbance (SED). The sample for the study included youth who were participating in the Robert Wood Johnson Foundation's Mental Health Services Program for Youth (RWJF MHSPY) demonstration in two counties of western North Carolina. The intervention involved the addition of a case manager to a youth treatment team. In this chapter, we discuss obstacles that arose, apparent reasons for these difficulties, solutions, and potential prevention of such problems in future research. We view the specific issues raised in the ACC study in the broader perspective of randomized trials carried out in public mental health centers.

North Carolina's
Children's Initiative

In early 1990, North Carolina was selected as one of eight states to receive funding through the RWJF MHSPY (Beachler, 1990; England & Cole, 1992). To simplify communication, the North Carolina site was named the Children's Initiative. The RWJF MHSPY was designed as a multisite demonstration to improve community-based services and interagency collaboration to serve children and adolescents with SED. The North Carolina Children's Initiative included the 11 westernmost counties of the state. This region of the state is characterized by mountainous geography, rural development, and relatively high rates of poverty. The 11 counties are served by two area mental health programs—the Blue Ridge Area Program, which serves 4 counties, including the region's only city (Asheville, pop. 60,000), and the Smoky Mountain Area Program, which serves 7 counties.

Prior to the start of the Children's Initiative, the Smoky Mountain and Blue Ridge Area programs had begun working toward the creation of a full continuum of services for youth with SED. But although most of the elements of a continuum were in place, the services did not exist in sufficient volume to meet the needs of the target population. The target population was defined as youth who (a) had a psychiatric diagnosis, (b) displayed substantial functional impairment, and (c) were currently in out-of-home placements or at imminent risk of such a placement. The Children's Initiative had three interconnected goals to better serve these children and adolescents: (a) to develop and expand a comprehensive system of services, including previously missing components, to facilitate the least restrictive placements possible; (b) to facilitate delivery of these services through a new interagency organizational structure designed to overcome interagency barriers to service delivery; and (c) to develop a state and local partnership to address interagency issues of financing and to maximize drawdown of federal funds. The Children's Initiative was thus designed to address the multiagency needs of youth with SED at various levels.

Case management was seen as the backbone of the Children's Initiative. The RWJF MHSPY emphasized case management as a key ingredient of successful community-based treatment for youth with SED. In addition, North Carolina's experience of serving youth with SED and aggressive behavior through the Willie M. Program (Behar, 1985, 1986; Keith, 1988) led to a familiarity with and a belief in case management. Each youth's case manager was responsible for managing and facilitating the child-specific treatment team, coordinating intervention activities, and ensuring that all team members had input into the intervention plans and any revisions. In short, the case manager was responsible for overseeing, facilitating, and coordinating the youth's care.

The Assessing Coordinated Care Study

The ACC study was designed in conjunction with the Children's Initiative but funded separately through the National Institute of Mental Health (NIMH). The ACC study had two distinct but connected foci: (a) to assess the impact of case managers for youth with SED, and (b) to assess changes in the service system brought about by the Children's Initiative (Burns, Farmer, Angold, Costello, & Behar, in press; Morrissey, Johnsen, & Calloway, in press). This dual focus paralleled the Children's Initiative's emphasis on change and coordination at a variety of levels to serve youth with SED. This chapter is focused on the first of these components—the randomized clinical trial of case management.

A calculation of resources that would be available through the Children's Initiative and of the number of children who would be eligible for inclusion suggested that there would be case management slots for only about half the youth who entered the Children's Initiative. This circumstance provided an opportunity to systematically examine the influence of case management for children and youth with SED.

Youth who entered the ACC study were randomized either to the experimental condition—a treatment team *with* a case manager—or to the control condition—a treatment team *without* a case manager. This design was intended to explore (a) what services were provided by the case manager; (b) how the presence of a case manager affected team behavior, service provision, and client and family outcomes; and (c) whether, and by whom, case management activities would be carried out for youth in the control group.

Recruitment for the study began in summer 1991. To be eligible for the ACC study, a youth first had to be accepted into the Children's Initiative. Youth were screened by the intake clinician at the time of referral to one of the mental health centers to determine eligibility (i.e., psychiatric diagnosis, functional impairment, and unstable residential placement). There were three additional criteria for study inclusion. First, the youth had to reside in either Haywood or Buncombe counties. These two counties were home to approximately 60% of the population in the 11-county Children's Initiative region. This restriction was intended to simplify the research process by providing an adequate sample while limiting the number of community agencies and mental health centers that would need to be involved. Haywood County was served by the Smoky Mountain Center, Buncombe County by the Blue Ridge Center. Second, the youth had to be at least 8 years old. This restriction was imposed because it is not clear that children younger than 8 can provide adequate information on the psychiatric interview included in the research protocol. Third, the youth could not be the sibling of another study participant. This condition was added to reduce the interview burden on the parent. By the end of sample recruitment, 167 youth were included in the study.

The research team was based primarily in the Raleigh-Durham-Chapel Hill (Triangle) area of North Carolina (approximately 250 miles from the research site); a research study coordinator, secretary, and interviewers were located on-site in Haywood County. In addition, a research study director (located in Chapel Hill) acted as liaison between the mental health centers, on-site research staff, and the research team in the Triangle.

Youth were referred to the research study at the time of entry into the Children's Initiative. The Children's Initiative project coordinator at each mental health center telephoned the on-site research study coordinator, who then contacted the parent (or legal guardian), explained the study, and invited the family to participate. If the parent agreed, the research study coordinator assigned the youth, using a list of random numbers, to either the control or experimental group. The youth and a parent were interviewed as soon as possible after admission to the Children's Initiative. Both completed the Child and Adolescent Psychiatric Assessment (CAPA) (Angold & Costello, 1995; Angold et al., 1995; Angold, Prendergast, Cox, Rutter, & Harrington, 1993) and Child and Adolescent Services Assessment (CASA) (Burns, Angold, Magruder-Habib, Costello, & Patrick, 1992; Farmer, Angold, Burns, & Costello, 1994). Parents also completed the Child and Adolescent Burden Assessment (CABA) (Patrick, Angold, Burns, & Costello, 1992). Parents were contacted by phone at 3-month intervals to provide information on recent service use and behavioral symptoms. In addition, data were collected every 3 months from treatment team members about case management activities. Parents and youth were reinterviewed in a follow-up one year after they entered the program. Ninety-five percent of families who were asked to participate agreed to do so. Of these, 89% completed both the baseline and follow-up interviews.

Problems, Solutions, and the Prevention of Problems in Randomized Clinical Trials

The ACC study was based on a rather simple randomized design in which all participants received one aspect of state-of-the-art treatment—a multiagency treatment team. The key difference between the groups was the addition of a case manager to this treatment team for youth in the experimental group. Randomization and intensive interviewing were done by research staff. Clinical staff were required to complete a one-page summary every 3 months to provide information about the number of hours they had spent working with or on behalf of a designated child and what types of activities they engaged in during these hours.

Despite the relative simplicity of this design and implementation, at least five issues arose during the study that threatened its viability and created tension between the research staff and mental health center staffs. In the following section, we discuss the nature and content of these conflicts, apparent reasons for their appearance, solutions reached to continue the project, and ways that such problems might have been prevented (and, perhaps, could be prevented in future studies).

Control Group Treatment

Issue. The first issue to arise was over the nature of the intervention itself. The research design called for a comparison of treatment teams with case managers to those without case managers. As noted above, calculations of available resources suggested that there would be case managers for approximately half of the youth who would be eligible for the Children's Initiative. Hence, this scarce resource needed to be allocated in some way. This scarcity provided an opportunity to explore questions about the utility, necessity, and consequences of adding a case manager to a multiagency team. From the researchers' perspectives, the absence of a case manager in half of the teams made it possible to see what differences occurred in the presence of a case manager and whether (and by whom) activities that are currently thought of as case management activities would be carried out for youth in the control group.

The mental health center staffs expressed concern about this design. They argued that they could not go ahead with treatment teams in which there was no identified case manager because of the threat of such an arrangement to the interagency collaboration that was at the heart of the RWJF MHSPY directive. The mental health centers were the lead local agencies in applying for and receiving the RWJF MHSPY funding. Because of RWJF's emphasis on interagency coordination and cooperation, the centers had devoted a great deal of time and effort to community relations to get other child-serving agencies on board. The mental health centers recognized that there were few tangible incentives that they could offer other agencies to encourage their support and participation. Interagency work was regarded by many as a time-consuming enterprise that increased the number of meetings that needed to be attended, added more paperwork, and reduced agency autonomy. To help convince other agencies of the benefits of participating in this model, the mental health centers stressed that the other agencies would save time and resources because of the case management provided by the centers. Thus, the provision of case management by the mental health centers was seen as a cornerstone of the developing relationships between the centers and other agencies.

This conflict about the control condition appeared to arise for two primary reasons: (a) the lack of temporal synchrony of the demonstration project and the research project, and (b) an objection to the concept of randomization. In terms of timing, the Children's Initiative began serving children in summer 1990. Planning and community relations work took place during 1989 and 1990. ACC funding did not begin until spring 1991. Therefore, during the entire pre-RWJF period of community relations work, the research study was not a factor. During the planning and start-up periods and the first year of the Children's Initiative, the child-serving agencies became accustomed to an interagency structure in which the mental health centers provided case management for youth. To shift this arrangement in mid-1991 to include a "no-case-manager group" would have been seen as a significant change in responsibility and activities by all involved agencies. It is important to note that not all Children's Initiative clients received case management prior to the ACC study; decisions about who received this service were made jointly by staffs of the mental health centers and other agencies.

Delays in funding postponed the start of the ACC study until nearly a year after the commencement of the Children's Initiative. This delay was beyond the control of the mental health centers and the research group. On the other hand, planning for the ACC study was conducted as the community relations and start-up of the Children's Initiative were progressing. In addition, the shortage of case management resources was anticipated during the planning phase of the Children's Initiative. Frank discussions of this shortage may have made the benefit of participation less clear to other agencies, but it also would have quelled unrealistic expectations about the demonstration by these agencies. Inclusion of the research study in initial discussions of interagency collaboration may have placed the mental health centers in a more tenable position and would have prevented a change in intervention for the research study. The most logical way to have done this would have been to include research staff in the conversations and meetings required to build community relations. The study's on-site research study coordinator did participate in such conversations, but this did not occur until late spring 1991, nearly a year after the Children's Initiative had started. Such participation may have been too little too late. Expanding such participation would have served at least three purposes: (a) it would have prepared other community agencies for the protocol and anticipated demands of the research study; (b) it would have given all agencies a clear idea of who was responsible for which aspects of the protocol; and (c) it would have given the other agencies a better sense of the scope and goals of the RWJF MHSPY, their roles in the Children's Initiative and the ACC study, and the linkages between these endeavors.

Resolution. The issue of the control condition was resolved and internal validity for the ACC study was preserved, but the result was not completely satisfactory to either the mental health centers or the research project. The compromise resulted in a modification of the control group condition. Rather than having a control group with *no* case manager, the revised model contained a control group for which the youth's primary mental health clinician served as the case manager. Primary clinicians thus had case management responsibilities added to their previous set of duties and caseloads. This compromise, as we will discuss below, led to other difficulties for the mental health centers. From the research perspective, it reduced the distinction between the intervention and control groups. This led to an increased risk of Type II error, an inability to fully answer the question of how case management responsibilities would be covered or divided in the absence of a designated case manager, and greater concern about specifying and documenting differences in the treatment received by the two groups. In retrospect, this compromise did not actually alter the initial intent of the control condition. Findings from the ACC study show that designating a clinician as a case manager did not increase the amount of time that the clinician actually spent on case management activities (Burns et al., in press). Hence, the original comparison continued in practice, if not in official designation.

Randomization

Issue. A randomized trial, by its nature, interferes with normal clinical practice. In normal clinical practice, mental health staff members are aware of the available options for serving clients and are accustomed to choosing between these options. In a randomized trial, the parameters of available options and the authority to choose between them become the domain of the research study. This general shift in authority and division of labor created a number of tensions. The most central of these conflicts, however, involved randomization itself—both the concept and the process.

As discussed above, randomization was not a comfortable concept for the mental health staff members. Limited resources for case management were a normal part of the mental health centers' operating environments, so the shortage of case management slots in the Children's Initiative demonstration was not an unusual clinical reality. What was unusual was that the allocation of this scarce resource was not being made by the clinical staff. Throughout the research study, mental health staff complained that case management was being "wasted" on clients who did not need it and was not available for clients who truly did. Given the definition of the group targeted for the Children's Initiative—youth with SED, functional deficits, and an unstable residential placement—it is unlikely that any of these youth were wasting case management slots. The resistance to randomization seemed to be based on several factors: (a) clinical staff appeared to firmly believe in the importance and utility of case management (i.e., that certain clients needed case management and could not be treated effectively without it), and (b) randomization removed some of the clinicians' autonomy and power. They were not allowed to use clinical judgment to decide who needed case management but instead were told which youth would receive it. In addition, the combination of randomization and the compromise about the control group's case management resulted in clinicians' feeling forced into the role of case manager.

Problems also arose around the process of randomization. Before a youth could be assigned to the experimental or control group, the youth's parent or guardian had to consent for the child to participate. In most cases, such consent was obtained very quickly (on the same day as the child was admitted to the Children's Initiative). But there were cases in which obtaining consent took substantially longer (either when a parent was difficult to reach or when the youth was in the custody of another agency). Many youth entered the Children's Initiative at a point of crisis, and clinical staff members often felt that the youth's presenting problems required immediate action. In usual practice, an intake worker would assign the case to whoever was on call, had room to accept new clients, or had expertise in the area of most immediate need. In many cases, a case manager would be the person assigned to the case (to get a picture of what was going on, to get in touch with other agencies involved with the youth, and to organize other clinical services). Given the research design, there was concern that this immediate response would contaminate the control group and invalidate the randomization.

Resolution. Although the practical issues were partially resolved, the concern about the concept of randomization was never completely alleviated. Clinical staff remained convinced that the "wrong" clients were taking up case management slots and researchers remained convinced that case management was appropriate for all Children's Initiative participants. Two agreements were reached that helped to reduce this friction. First, the research team agreed that individual youth could be withheld from the study if it was felt that they absolutely needed a case manager (i.e., that randomization to the control group would represent a substantial risk to their well-being). To our knowledge, this exemption was used in only two cases. Second, the research staff agreed that immediate or emergency services could be provided without waiting for a youth to be randomized. This provision recognized that clinicians and researchers work under very different time imperatives. Although a delay of several hours or even days was not a significant problem for the research staff, such a delay could be catastrophic for the provision of appropriate clinical services. As soon as the youth was enrolled and randomized, however, the youth would be treated according to the research protocol.

Conflicts over randomization probably cannot be avoided completely in clinical trials. If a treatment has attracted enough attention to warrant a clinical trial in a real-life setting, it is likely that providers are aware of the treatment and have formed an opinion about it. This was clearly true in the ACC study. Belief in the importance of case management and concerns about its allocation via randomization resulted in two compromises that recognized the authority and clinical requirements of the mental health center staffs without jeopardizing the research study. If, however, the centers had frequently used their "right" to withhold subjects whom they determined to need case management, the research study would have been presented with potential sample biases and, thus, another problem to address. An alternative strategy to prevent such conflict would have been to randomize on the basis of clinician preference (Bradley, 1993). Such an approach may have increased cooperation and enthusiasm, but it risks the introduction of substantial selection bias.

One key to minimizing such conflicts is to allow sufficient time to thoroughly explore the concept and process of randomization with clinical staff before the research study begins. Delays in funding the ACC study meant that lead time was considerably shorter than originally planned. Prestudy discussions of the need for a randomized trial to assess the effectiveness of the targeted intervention could have helped to make clinical staff a part of the research process and reinforce the value of the study for the field. Such conversations also could explore potentially problematic situations (such as the need for emergency services) so that procedures for handling such situations are in place before the study begins. Finally, delays in obtaining consent added a level of frustration that fueled underlying discontent with the study. Procedures should be outlined in advance to facilitate obtaining consent from other agencies for youth in their custody. Clinical and research teams should arrive at an agreement of how long consent can be delayed before the youth is no longer eligible for the study. Collaboration on these early decisions may reduce subsequent conflicts. It is important that these conversations include clinical staff, not just administrative staff, so that all relevant stakeholders and participants are included.

Monitoring the Intervention

Issue. Once the intervention has been agreed on and the issues of randomization have been addressed, the next potential difficulty involves monitoring the implementation of the intervention. Regardless of how well the study is designed, if it is not carried out with strict adherence to the design, it will be seriously compromised and potentially undermined (Burns, 1994). The question of how to monitor is thus crucial but also potentially could cause conflicts. In essence, the researchers seem to be saying that they do not trust the clinical team to adhere to the research protocol. The need for careful monitoring does not suggest any malfeasance by or distrust of the clinical staff, however. Rather, it underscores the importance of appropriate implementation of the intervention and recognizes the many potential obstacles to such implementation (e.g., lack of time, competing clinical demands, inadequate introduction to the research protocol or aims, poorly designed protocol).

   In the ACC study, research staff carefully monitored the number of youth referred to the study and the randomization of these participants. Once randomization had been communicated to the mental health centers, however, monitoring of subsequent activities was initially very sparse. It was recognized that lack of monitoring could lead to problems. Early plans called for just annual monitoring of the intervention, however, because of obstacles to carrying out more frequent monitoring. The primary obstacle was the relatively new and underdeveloped management information systems (MIS) in the mental health centers at the start of the project and the absence of a way to collect relevant data without imposing substantial burdens on center staffs.

This lack of monitoring led to several problems, the most serious of which was the belatedly detected use of a waiting list for youth in the experimental group. For a period of approximately 6 months, one of the mental health centers did not have any available case manager slots. Hence, youth were assigned to the experimental condition, but they were not assigned to a case manager. While they were on the "case manager waiting list" they received whatever services were considered necessary by their clinician. In effect, they were receiving the control group condition.

Problems related to monitoring seemed to stem from a number of factors. First, during the initial phase of the project, much of the research staff's concern focused on the rate of recruitment. Rates of recruitment were therefore monitored carefully, but subsequent treatment was unmonitored. Second, the initial research design did not take into account some of the realities of clinical work. Staff shortages resulting in waiting lists are normal conditions in public mental health centers. Short treatment periods and variety between clients in the intensity of treatment are accepted as a normal part of working with difficult youth and families who move frequently, have few resources, and regard treatment as a priority only during times of crisis. Third, the geographic distance between the research site and the academic research staff meant that visits to the centers were infrequent and brief. Fourth, the mental health center staffs were not aware that they were jeopardizing the research. They were providing a large amount of data to the research project and therefore felt that their activities were quite evident to the researchers. When the researchers did not raise questions or objections, the staffs of the mental health centers assumed that their activities were acceptable.

Resolution. The monitoring problems were remedied after the initial year of the study. The research staff took greater responsibility for being aware of what was happening clinically. Procedures were put into place to make this change possible. MIS data were monitored to examine service delivery. Biweekly conference calls involved representatives of the mental health centers; the state mental health, developmental disabilities, and substance abuse office; the on-site research study coordinator; and the research study director. In addition, the research study director began making more frequent (approximately monthly) visits to the on-site research office and mental health centers. These visits and calls encouraged non-crisis-oriented discussions of research issues, relieved the mental health center staffs from the responsibility of monitoring the research component, and made it possible to prevent problems. As part of this change in communication, both the research and mental health staffs became perhaps overly cautious—asking each other about issues that were relatively minor. This caution helped set the tone for this new communication style, however, because it meant that many of the questions that were raised were not problems. Both sides realized that raising an issue did not necessarily mean that something had to be fixed or changed.

Preventing the problems caused by insufficient monitoring is, in theory, quite simple. In practice it is more complicated. Weisz and colleagues (Weisz, Donenberg, Han, & Kauneckis, in press) advocate the use of manuals to structure treatment and to facilitate careful monitoring. But given the enormity of the task, monitoring tends to be focused on areas that are viewed as potentially problematic or that have in the past been problematic. The key is to identify critical activities and aspects that are essential for successful completion of the study and then to determine ways to monitor these things. For the ACC study, this meant that the research staff needed to fully monitor the randomization of participants and had to be certain that, once randomized, participants in each group were being exposed to the intended intervention. Monitoring of randomization was never a problem because it was carried out by the research study coordinator and reviewed regularly by the investigators. As discussed above, monitoring the intervention was problematic during the first year of the study but was substantially improved during the final 2 years. Other aspects of the intervention (such as length of treatment, hours of treatment, variety of treatment, etc.) were never monitored. In fact, the research staff wanted to affect *only* the variable of interest (i.e., case management) rather than to interfere with the entirety of clinical practice. Data on the various dimensions of dose were collected but were not used by the research project staff to direct or influence the provision of treatment.

Despite the difficulties associated with monitoring, the ACC study contained two elements that may be essential to successful monitoring. First, the study had high visibility at the sites by having an on-site research study coordinator who was a member of the research staff and whose office was located in one of the mental health centers. It would have been useful to have had an office in each center and to divide this person's time between sites. This person helped to make the research study a part of the broader clinic, gave a face to an otherwise amorphous imposition, and provided information to the research team about activities and changes in the centers. Second, a contact person was designated at each center. In both centers, these were the project coordinators for the Children's Initiative. These liaisons could answer any questions about individual youth, staff assignments, or other changes at the centers that might affect the research study. Without such a contact person, monitoring (and implementation) would have been difficult, if not impossible.

Staff Dissatisfaction

Issue. Because a randomized trial changes usual practice in some fashion and often increases paperwork, it is not surprising that staff members often express irritation with the study. For the ACC study, this was particularly apparent among clinicians who, as discussed above, did not like being assigned case management responsibilities. Case managers also felt that the study was creating larger than usual caseloads. For both groups, complaints about the amount of paperwork were common. A more serious concern was staff turnover that could be attributed to the study. It appeared that the study served as "the last straw" for several staff members who were frustrated by changes and caseloads brought about by the Children's Initiative.

These dissatisfactions (expressed in both the mild form of complaining and the more extreme form of departing) appeared to arise from two factors. First, the research study did impose new requirements, involved a loss of clinical autonomy, and required more paperwork than usual. Perceptions of imposition were particularly high for the ACC study because staff members confused the demands of the research study with the requirements of the Children's Initiative. Most of the increased paperwork would have occurred whether or not the ACC study had existed. The addition of case management responsibilities to clinicians' normal caseloads was viewed as a substantial and burdensome change by staff members, however, and was directly attributable to the ACC study. Second, the study became a scapegoat for the perceived dissonance between individuals' view of what their job ideally should be and the reality of what it actually entailed. Randomization was a very visible deviation from usual practice. Thus, it was easy for staff members to attribute a wide variety of grievances to the impositions of randomization.

Resolution. The ACC study included several approaches to reduce clinical staff dissatisfaction and enhance the probability of success for both clinical and research aims. During the first year of the study, a member of the research team met with clinicians and case managers to explain the study and to emphasize its importance to the broader field of children's mental health services. Midway through the study, two researchers met with the case managers and clinicians at each mental health center in focus groups. The groups' input provided the research staff with an overview of the problems and issues that each group perceived and included a good deal of valuable information about the process of providing services in the particular settings. In response to clinical staff complaints about the amount of paperwork and researchers' concerns that the study's one-page forms were not being completed in a timely fashion, the Children's Initiative project coordinators at each center volunteered to meet with individual staff members to assist in the completion of these forms.

It is unclear whether it is possible to conduct a randomized study without some objections by people involved. It does seem possible, however, to try to minimize these difficulties. First, it appears absolutely essential to involve clinical staff in the project to the greatest extent possible. This requires a firm commitment to the study by the center's administration so that enthusiasm and commitment are encouraged and expected of all staff members. It also requires meetings with the clinical staff as soon as possible to help make them a part of the process. As new clinical staff are hired, it is important that the research staff take responsibility for introducing them to the study to ensure that all staff are familiar with the research design, requirements, and importance. It is also important to ensure that staff resources are sufficient to meet the staffing needs of the study. There is some appeal to staffing key positions (in this study case managers and clinicians) with individuals who are hired specifically for the study and are supported by it. Such an approach gives the study substantial control over the size of caseloads, qualifications of staff, training, and completion of data forms. This approach potentially changes a study from an examination of effectiveness to one of efficacy, however, thus jeopardizing its external validity. Perhaps a reasonable compromise is to provide funding to hire necessary additional staff members who will be formally hired, trained, and supervised by the mental health center. This ensures adequate staff size, increases authenticity, and provides the centers with a tangible payback for their participation.

Slow Recruitment

Issue. Slow recruitment appears to be a widespread problem in randomized trials of mental health interventions in clinical settings (Clark et al., 1994; Evans et al., 1994). Slow recruitment may be based on inaccurate or optimistic projections of the eligible population or recruitment rates. It also is influenced by the logistics and requirements of participating (e.g., eligible individuals who refuse to participate, missed opportunities to recruit some individuals, exclusionary criteria that were not adequately assessed in projections). In extreme cases, difficulties with recruitment can result in an inadequate sample (Sechrist, West, Phillips, Redner, & Yeaton, 1979). In less extreme cases, an adequate sample is eventually recruited, but at a later date than anticipated. In the ACC study, recruitment was expected to be completed in 12 months (12-14 subjects per month). In reality, it took 19 months to recruit the required number of participants.

Although the reasons for this slow recruitment are specific to the ACC study, they are illustrative of common issues. First, because the ACC study began recruiting nearly a year after the Children's Initiative began, youth who entered the Children's Initiative during its early months were not eligible for the study. This was a substantial loss to the ACC study because the Children's Initiative had a high rate of intake during these early months when communities referred a backlog of children with unmet needs. Second, recruitment could happen only as quickly as youth entered the Children's Initiative. Slow intake was attributable to a number of factors: The centers could admit only as many children as they had staff resources to serve; staff turnover lowered capacity throughout much of the study recruitment phase; and during summer months, few children were referred to the Children's Initiative. Third, in its most serious manifestation, the capacity issue resulted in a waiting list for case management. Because participants on the waiting list had not received the intended intervention, they had to be dropped from the sample and replaced with new recruits. Finally, exclusionary criteria limited the rate of recruitment. In the ACC study, young children (i.e., younger than 8) and siblings of study subjects were formally excluded from the sample.

Resolution. Given the regularity with which recruitment problems occur in randomized clinical trials, investigators should expect slow recruitment and should include strategies in their study plan to minimize the problems caused by it. First, studies should be designed to recruit two to three times as many subjects as are needed. This may involve the use of more sites than are necessary or allowing additional time for recruitment. If recruitment goes more quickly than these precautions allow for, the shortened recruitment time will be a welcome announcement to the participating sites. Second, steps should be taken to make certain that every eligible participant has the best possible chance of being recruited. This may mean having a research staff member present the research to the families (rather than relying on the clinician for initial introduction), devoting extra effort to contacting families and obtaining consent, and offering sufficient rewards or payment to participants.

Conclusions

The ACC study was fairly typical of randomized clinical trials in the types of issues and problems it encountered (Bickman, 1990; Kazdin, 1992). The five issues discussed here were the nature of the intervention, concerns about randomization, staff dissatisfaction, adequate monitoring, and slow recruitment. In the more technical language of randomized trials, the ACC study encountered obstacles to internal validity, treatment fidelity, random assignment, and study completion. All of these issues were resolved in the ACC study so that the study could be completed successfully. It is improbable that all of these problems could have been prevented. It does appear, however, that they could have been minimized and could be minimized in future studies.

Experiences from the ACC study in comparison with other randomized trials suggest that several ingredients are central to making such studies run as smoothly as possible.

1. A great deal of work needs to go into the start-up phase. Several of the problems that occurred could have been minimized if the study design had been incorporated into early community relations work among the agencies participating in the Children's Initiative. This pre-study phase also is a critical period for developing a good working relationship with relevant agency administrators and bringing the service providers into the research endeavor. Developing positive perceptions and relationships with key participants and stakeholders should be well worth any brief delay in study start-up.

2. Once the initial relationships have been established, it is crucial to maintain them for the length of the study. The impositions of the study, absence of most members of the research team from the sites, daily requirements of clinical practice, and addition of new clinical staff members all make the continued nurturance of these relationships essential. Maintaining the balances between intrusiveness and visibility, collaboration and supervision, and objectivity and empathy is not easy for either service providers or researchers. Such relationships must be based on trust, respect, and a general belief that both clinical and research efforts are important aspects of successfully serving clients.

3. The monitoring of study procedures is crucial. Monitoring must focus on key aspects of the study that, if not handled correctly, will jeopardize the entire project. Arrangements to obtain necessary data should be in place before recruitment begins. Although monitoring by both the mental health center staff and research staff is ideal, it is necessary to specify who ultimately is responsible for making sure that the study is going as planned. In our experience, the final oversight should be the responsibility of the research team (via one designated member). Issues such as length of treatment and other aspects of dose of treatment

should be considered carefully in advance and monitored throughout to ensure that the planned intervention is implemented in a uniform manner (Burns, 1994; Taube, Morlock, Burns, & Santos, 1990; Teague, Drake, & Ackerson, 1995). In longitudinal studies, it is important to continue monitoring the intervention after recruitment has ended. A variety of factors, both inside and outside the mental health center, may change in ways that affect the randomization or treatment of participants.

4. The design must reflect clinical realities. Procedures that seem simple in the abstract may present significant difficulties in practice. Discussions in the prestudy period should bring some of these potential problems to light so that they can be addressed proactively.

In sum, communication, competent liaisons, and the development and maintenance of good working relationships are what make it possible to address and resolve the issues that arise in randomized clinical studies. The goal, of course, is to prevent as many of these problems as possible with a well-designed study, adequate planning, and sufficient monitoring. Our experiences with community-based randomized studies suggest that these precautions do not guarantee the absence of problems. Rather, they prevent disaster and, together with good relationships, provide a base for resolving the issues that arise to allow successful completion of randomized studies.

References

Angold, A., & Costello, E. J. (1995). A test-retest reliability study of child-reported psychiatric symptoms and diagnoses using the Child and Adolescent Psychiatric Assessment (CAPA-C). *Psychological Medicine, 25,* 755-762.

Angold, A., Prendergast, M., Cox, A., Harrington, R., Simonoff, E., & Rutter, M. (1995). The Child and Adolescent Psychiatric Assessment (CAPA). *Psychological Medicine, 25,* 739-753.

Angold, A., Prendergast, M., Cox, A., Rutter, M., & Harrington, R. (1993). *The Child and Adolescent Psychiatric Assessment (CAPA).* Durham, NC: Duke University Medical Center.

Beachler, M. (1990). The mental health services program for youth. *Journal of Mental Health Administration, 17*(1), 115-121.

Behar, L. (1985). Changing patterns of state responsibility: A case study of North Carolina. *Journal of Clinical Child Psychology, 14*(3), 188-195.

Behar, L. (1986, May-June). A state model for child mental health services: The North Carolina experience. *Children Today*, pp. 16-21.

Bickman, L. (1985). Randomized experiments in education: Implementations lessons. In R. Boruch (Eds.), *Randomized field experiments* (pp. 39-53). San Francisco: Jossey-Bass.

Bickman, L. (1990). Study design. In Y. Ying-Ying & M. Rivest (Eds.), *Preserving families: Evaluation resources for practitioners and policy makers* (pp. 132-166). Newbury Park, CA: Sage.

Bickman, L. (1992). Designing outcome evaluations for children's mental health services: Improving internal validity. In L. Bickman & D. J. Rog (Eds.), *New directions for program evaluation: Evaluating mental health services for children* (pp. 57-68). San Francisco: Jossey-Bass.

Boruch, R. F., McSweeny, A. J., & Soderstrom, E. J. (1978). Bibliography: Illustrative randomized field experiments. *Evaluation Quarterly, 4*, 655-695.

Boruch, R. F., & Wothke, W. (Eds.). (1985). *Randomization and field experimentation*. San Francisco: Jossey-Bass.

Bradley, C. (1993). Designing medical and educational intervention studies. *Diabetes Care, 16*, 509-518.

Burns, B. J. (1994). The challenges of child mental health services research. *Journal of Emotional and Behavioral Disorders, 2*(4), 254-259.

Burns, B. J., Angold, A., Magruder-Habib, K., Costello, E. J., & Patrick, M. K. S. (1992). *The Child and Adolescent Services Assessment (CASA)*. Durham, NC: Duke University Medical Center.

Burns, B. J., Farmer, E. M. Z., Angold, A., Costello, E. J., & Behar, L. B. (in press). A randomized trial of case management for youths with serious emotional disturbance. *Journal of Clinical Child Psychology*.

Campbell, D. T., & Stanley, J. C. (1966). *Experimental and quasi-experimental designs for research*. Skokie, IL: Rand McNally.

Clark, H. B., Prange, M. E., Lee, B., Boyd, L. A., McDonald, B. A., & Stewart, E. S. (1994). Improving adjustment outcomes for foster children with emotional and behavioral disorders: Early findings from a controlled study on individualized services. *Journal of Emotional and Behavioral Disorders, 2*(4), 207-218.

England, M. J., & Cole, R. F. (1992). Building systems of care for youth with serious mental illness. *Hospital and Community Psychiatry, 43*(6), 630-633.

Evans, M. E., Armstrong, M. I., Dollard, N., Kuppinger, A. D., Huz, S., & Wood, V. M. (1994). Development and evaluation of treatment foster care and family-centered intensive case management in New York. *Journal of Emotional and Behavioral Disorders, 2*(4), 228-239.

Farmer, E. M. Z., Angold, A., Burns, B. J., & Costello, E. J. (1994). Reliability of self-reported service use: Test-retest consistency of children's responses to the Child and Adolescent Services Assessment (CASA). *Journal of Child and Family Studies, 3*(3), 307-325.

Kazdin, A. E. (1992). *Research design in clinical psychology*. Needham Heights, MA: Allyn & Bacon.

Keith, C. R. (1988). Community treatment of violent youth: Seven years of experience with a class action suit. *Journal of the American Academy of Child and Adolescent Psychiatry, 27*(5), 600-604.

Morrissey, J. P., Johnsen, M. C., & Calloway, M. O. (in press). Evaluating performance and change in mental health systems serving children and youth: An interorganizational network approach. *Journal of Mental Health Administration*.

Patrick, M., Angold, A., Burns, B., & Costello, E. J. (1992). *The Child and Adolescent Burden Assessment*. Durham, NC: Duke University Medical Center.

Sechrist, L. B., West, S. G., Phillips, M. A., Redner, R., & Yeaton, W. (1979). Some neglected problems in evaluation research: Strength and integrity of treatments. In L. Sechrest, S. G. West, M. A. Phillips, R. Redner, & W. Yeaton (Eds.), *Evaluation studies review annual* (Vol. 4, pp. 15-35). Beverly Hills, CA: Sage.

Taube, C. A., Morlock, L., Burns, B. J., & Santos, A. B. (1990). New directions in research on assertive community treatment. *Hospital and Community Psychiatry, 41*(6), 642-647.

Teague, G. B., Drake, R. E., & Ackerson, T. H. (1995). Evaluating use of continuous treatment teams for persons with mental illness and substance abuse. *Psychiatric Services, 46*, 689-695.

Weisz, J. R., Donenberg, G. R., Han, S. S., & Kauneckis, D. (in press). Child and adolescent psychotherapy outcomes in experiments versus clinics: Why the disparity? *Journal of Abnormal Child Psychology*.

The Stark County Evaluation Project

Baseline Results of a Randomized Experiment

LEONARD BICKMAN
WM. THOMAS SUMMERFELT
JENNIFER M. FIRTH
SUSAN M. DOUGLAS

In this chapter, we describe the methods and baseline data of a study designed to assess the extent to which a comprehensive system of individualized care leads to improvements in the clinical functioning of children with severe emotional disturbance (SED). The Stark County Mental Health Board, in Stark County, Ohio, has developed an innovative system of care to provide comprehensive and managed mental health services to children and adolescents served in the public sector.

AUTHORS' NOTE: First and foremost, we would like to extend our gratitude to the participants of the Stark County Evaluation who gave of their time and experiences. We acknowledge the efforts of our Stark County Advisory Committee members: A. Leslie Abel, David Boyle, Beth Dague, Robert Klaehn, Cleo Lucas, John McCall, Jon Thomas, and David Willis. Data collection and preparation of this chapter were supported by the National Institute of Mental Health Research Grant #RO1-MH48988 and Training Grant #T32MH-19544 to Dr. Leonard Bickman.

The Stark County Evaluation Project (SCEP) was developed to evaluate this system of care. This mental health services research project is distinctive in that (a) randomized experimental design was used to study the effectiveness of the system, and (b) interactive computerized interviews (Summerfelt, 1992; Summerfelt & Hodges, 1992) were used for primary data collection. The purpose of this chapter is to examine these two unique features of this study.

A pivotal Office of Technical Assessment report (Saxe, Cross, Silverman, Batchelor, & Dougherty, 1987) concluded that existing mental health services for children are fragmented. Even where services are available, the lack of coordination between programs compromises the effectiveness of the interventions (Stroul & Friedman, 1986). Given the developmental complexity and multiple needs of children and adolescents with emotional or behavioral problems, services must be both available and coordinated (Behar, 1988). In addition, it is believed that these youth are best treated in the least restrictive, most normative environment that is clinically appropriate (Friedman & Duchnowski, 1990). Alternatives to the fragmented system of care have been widely discussed by experts in this field (Friedman & Duchnowski, 1990). There is a strong consensus about the need for a managed and comprehensive system of care and the critical elements of such a system (see Friedman, Chapter 2, this volume; Stroul, 1996).

The Fort Bragg System of Care

In pursuit of improved mental health systems for children and adolescents, the Department of the Army funded the Fort Bragg Child and Adolescent Mental Health Demonstration Project through an $80 million contract with the state of North Carolina. The demonstration began operating in June 1990, providing a full continuum of mental health services. To assess the effectiveness of the demonstration on multiple levels, an independent evaluation of the demonstration was conducted by Vanderbilt University. The evaluation project studied almost 1,000 children in a 5-year period in both the demonstration site and two comparison sites. The results of this study have been reported extensively (Bickman, 1996a, 1996b, 1996c; Bickman et al., 1995). The evaluators concluded that although children at the demonstration received more comprehensive services in less restrictive settings in a high-quality continuum of care, the clinical outcomes were similar to those of the comparison sites that had no continuum of care. Moreover, the costs to treat children at the demonstration were much higher.

System of Care in the Public Sector

Although the Fort Bragg study answered many questions about a continuum of care system for children, it had some limitations. Many of these were addressed by SCEP. These limitations involved issues of design, target group selection, service system characteristics, special attributes of Fort Bragg, and funding of the system.

First, although pretest equivalence between the demonstration and comparison sites was found in the Fort Bragg evaluation, the design was quasi-experimental, making it more difficult to provide conclusive statements about causal relationships. Our SCEP study replicates many of the strong methodological features of the Fort Bragg study and, in addition, uses a randomized design.

Second, the Fort Bragg study examined a population of military children and families that may differ from a civilian population and limit the generalizability of the findings. The families in the Fort Bragg study were primarily two-parent families of middle income. Because these families were privately insured and were of middle income, this sample was considered to be similar to most of the families in the United States. But questions were raised about how the results would compare if the study had targeted youth in a publicly funded population (Friedman & Burns, 1996).

Third, the Fort Bragg intervention was characterized as a managed continuum of care and not a system of care. A system of care includes the active participation of multiple public agencies. The Fort Bragg demonstration did not involve multiple public agencies. In contrast, Stark County is recognized as a leader in the introduction of systems of care into the community (Stroul, 1992) and has been rated as one of the top systems of care out of 30 sites participating in the Center for Mental Health Services Children's Services Demonstration program (MACRO International, 1996).

Fourth, the Fort Bragg intervention was unique compared with interventions in the civilian setting. For example, no limits were placed on expenditures for individual treatment and few problems were experienced regarding coordination of services between agencies, as most services were provided or arranged by the demonstration project's clinic with only one funding source. Concerns also have been raised that the Fort Bragg demonstration was evaluated too early in its history, before it had time to stabilize (Friedman & Burns, 1996). In contrast, the Stark County system has been developed over the past 20 years.

Finally, the Fort Bragg evaluation was a special demonstration developed with federal funding. Stark County's system of care was developed with few external funds, as is typical with most system-of-care reforms in communities. Our Stark County study extends both the external and internal validity of the Fort Bragg evaluation. In summary, the maturity of the Stark County system of care and the use of a randomized design increase the internal validity of our study. Increased internal validity provides more confidence for forming causal attributions regarding the effectiveness of the system of care model. In addition, because the Stark County system of care is more typical of what is implemented in most state or community efforts, the generalizability of our findings is increased.

Stark County System of Care and the Evaluation Project

History of the Evaluation Project

This project was originally proposed to the National Institute of Mental Health (NIMH) in February 1990, to evaluate the clinical outcomes of children and their families being served in four of the sites participating in the Robert Wood Johnson Foundation's Mental Health Services Program for Youth (RWJF MHSPY) (Beachler, 1990). That proposal was not funded. The proposal was revised to include only one site as a randomized experiment. The review committee deferred decision, requesting more information on the commitment of the site. In January 1991, the project received a fundable score, but a few weeks later, the site had to withdraw from the RWJF project for several reasons. NIMH allowed us to find a replacement site. We contacted several sites and experts in the field and conducted interviews with potential sites during a conference in the summer of 1991. The criteria for selection included

(a) existence of a mature system, (b) inability to serve all clients so that random assignment from a waiting list was ethical, (c) enthusiastic support for an external and objective evaluation, and (d) ability to deal politically with possible negative results of the evaluation. The Stark County system of care met all these criteria.

Theoretical Underpinnings of the Stark County System of Care

The ultimate goal of the Stark County system of care is to provide high-quality care for children and youth with severe mental health problems that ultimately will lead to improvements in the clinical functioning of the children served and in the functioning of their families. High-quality care as defined by the program incorporates the Child and Adolescent Service System Program (CASSP) philosophical framework of a system of care (Stroul & Friedman, 1986)—that is, a child-centered, family-focused system that offers a comprehensive and coordinated network of mental health and other necessary services organized in a coordinated network. This system model includes a managed system of individualized care. The system of care philosophy emphasizes four ingredients:

- Organizing interagency agreements to ensure that coordination will occur, one coordinated system of care will result, and efforts will go beyond the mental health system to identify needy clients
- Implementing case management to ensure that each child and family receives, and continues to receive, the necessary set of individualized services and care
- Adding services and modifying existing ones to ensure a comprehensive array of services, including educational, vocational, health, recreational, home-based, and support services as well as mental health treatment
- Developing financing mechanisms to streamline and improve the management of care of individuals served through the system

The implementation of these four ingredients is hypothesized to lead to a system of care that is more comprehensive, efficient, and coordinated than existing systems or nonsystems that lack these ingredients. These improvements in the system are believed to lead to improvements in the quality of care provided to children and their families.

High-quality care is believed to be care that is managed, individualized, and provided in the most appropriate and least restrictive settings. Furthermore, high-quality care supports continuity of services and treatment and is responsive to the needs of the child and family. In turn, high-quality care is hypothesized to lead to improved child clinical outcomes, (e.g., reduced psychopathology, enhanced social functioning, better school performance) and improved family outcomes (e.g., reduced family strain and improved family functioning).

Description of the System's Target Population

Enrollment criteria for the Stark County system of care included youth aged from birth to 20 years with a serious emotional disturbance (SED) or a *DSM-III-R* mental health diagnosis and current placement or risk of placement outside the family. In addition, at least one of the following had to be present: (a) involvement with three or more child-serving systems or living in a family involved in more than three child-serving systems, (b) current placement in residential treatment facility, (c) placement in multiple residential facilities (three or more), or (d) two or more psychiatric hospitalizations or current placement in a psychiatric facility. Youth fitting these criteria defined the target population for the system of care. The target population for SCEP was a subset of these youth and is described in the next section.

The system serves approximately 300 children at any one time. The point of entry into the system of care is the Child and Adolescent Service Center (C&A). Families can be self-, school, or court referred. The C&A clinic conducts initial assessments, develops a treatment plan, and coordinates the delivery of services. A menu of services available in the C&A clinic is presented in Table 9.1. Services that are available outside the system of care are described under the heading "Standard Care."

Aims of the Evaluation Project

We did not attempt to test the complete system of care model, although the model does provide the theoretical basis for predictions that can be tested. Rather, we tested whether clinical outcomes are positively associated with the system of care provided to a subsample of subjects. As discussed in the introduction, this chapter is focused on design and baseline data collection issues that preclude the examination of the impact of a system of care. Because funds for this study were much more limited than those for Fort Bragg, SCEP was focused on clinical and functional outcomes and did not go into any depth about costs, quality, or implementation analysis of the system of care. Fortunately, other sources of information are available from site visit reports (Stroul, 1992) and an evaluation that Stark County is participating in as part of the Children's Mental Health Services project funded by the Center for Mental Health Services (MACRO International, 1996). Specifically, SCEP focused on five key questions:

- What is the impact of a comprehensive system of care on the clinical functioning of children with SED and on the functioning of their families?
- What are the individual child and family factors that influence the outcomes?
- Are gains made through the system more enduring than those realized through standard care regimes? At what rate do gains grow or decay?
- How do the patterns of service utilization differ between the system and standard care. For example, do children leave care earlier? Do they reenter the system more or less frequently? Do they move between levels of care more frequently?
- Are there patterns of service utilization (within and across treatment conditions) that are predictive of positive, enduring changes in outcome?

Design and Data Collection Methods for the Evaluation Project

SCEP used a longitudinal experimental design. To date, few prospective longitudinal studies or randomized experiments of children's mental health service systems have been completed. The longitudinal data will allow exploration of treatment patterns and transition rates. Four follow-up interviews are scheduled for 6, 12, 18, and 24 months following the collection of baseline data; at each follow-up, respondents are asked to complete a battery of instruments administered by phone and mail. When combined with the intake interview and service utilization data, this schedule of follow-up interviews will provide a rich data set

Table 9.1 Description of Services Available in Stark County

Service	System of Care (Experimental)	Standard Care (Control)
Comprehensive Intake	Multifactored, comprehensive intake assessments and treatment planning.	Not available.
Outpatient Services	Services include assessment; individual, group, or family therapy; and alternative school outreach services.	Community outpatient centers, such as Catholic Community League, and private practices.
Prevention and Early Intervention	Programs and services targeting at-risk youth that provide information to parents, operate preschool programs to prevent dropout, and sponsor peer support groups.	Not available.
Case Management	Services include assessment, advocacy, monitoring and planning of services for youth and their families.	Not available.
Home-Based Services	Two types of services are available to families: therapeutic in-home emergency service (short-term) and intensive home-based services (long-term).	Not available.
Day Treatment or Partial Hospitalization	Collaborative program between the education and mental health systems that serves youth (ages 5-17) with severe emotional, behavioral, or social problems.	Day treatment is available to children and youth under standard services.
Crisis Services	Services include a 24-hour hotline, face-to-face outreach services, home-based therapists and case managers, and use of observation beds at the center.	Crisis Intervention Center services can be used in emergency situations.

to address the research aims of the project. (To date, baseline data and the first follow-up have been completed for all participants, together with some of the subsequent follow-ups for the first-enrolled participants.)

Table 9.1 Continued

Service	System of Care (Experimental)	Standard Care (Control)
Child and Family Advocacy Program	A coalition between the crisis center and C&A that provides assessments of sexual abuse, therapeutic services, and group treatment.	The Child and Family Advocacy Program is available to children and youth under standard care.
Substance Abuse Services	Services include individual counseling, family and group therapy, and access to medical services.	Quest services can be used for alcohol and drug screens.
Youth Sex Offenders Program	A joint program of the Stark Family Court and C&A, this program provides a diagnostic assessment, counseling and psychotherapy, and group therapy to offenders and those at high risk of offending.	The Youth Sex Offender program is accessible to all youth in the Stark County area under standard care.
Respite Services	Tri-County Easter Seals provides in-home respite care for families needing assistance with the physical and emotional demands of caregiving.	Respite services provided by the Tri-County Easter Seal Society are available under standard care.
Residential Services	Inpatient psychiatric services are primarily provided by local hospitals with specialized child or adolescent psychiatric units. All residential treatment centers (RTCs) are located outside the county through the child welfare system.	The Department of Human Services operates group homes. Services from local hospitals and RTCs outside the county are also available.
Wraparound Funds	Flexible funds made available to case managers to purchase services individually tailored for each child.	Not available.

Recruitment

To recruit participants for SCEP, names and contact information were obtained from either the county office of the Ohio Department of Human Services (DHS) or C&A. Caseworkers at DHS nominated children who they thought were in the need of mental health services. On the basis of a contact with the child's primary caretaker, an intake worker at C&A rated the youth on the need for services using a clinical assessment tool developed by C&A. It is important to note that the Vanderbilt staff did not decide whether the child was eligible for services is critical: Eligibility was determined by the C&A intake worker following the agency's usual guidelines. As mentioned previously, all those eligible for services were not included in the evaluation, due to such factors as emergency status; not meeting criteria for age, SED, or IQ; being identified as a youth sex offender; being a sibling of an SCEP participant; being already enrolled in the system of care; or living outside the county.

Once a parent or guardian gave permission to be contacted, a Vanderbilt staff member called the parent or guardian. Following a standardized script, the SCEP research staff explained the study, determined interest in receiving mental health services, and obtained oral agreement to participate. During this initial contact, parents were read the following statement: "If you and your child agree to participate in the study, your child will be randomly assigned either to get expanded services at the Child and Adolescent Service Center or to receive services from other providers in the local community." Once parents agreed to participate, a staff member completed the telephone version of the Child and Adolescent Functional Assessment Scale (CAFAS) (Hodges, 1994) and arranged for an in-person interview.

Random Assignment
Process

After the parent and child completed baseline data collection, the interviewer then used a computer program that randomly assigned the family to either the system of care at C&A or other community services that the parents had to arrange on their own. The randomization process had the following properties: (a) randomization was conducted by the evaluators before the family became a client of C&A services; (b) receipt of system services was independent of the decision to participate in research, that is, if parents did not want to participate in the study, they could wait for services like any other family; (c) all eligible children had the same chance to receive system services; and (d) families were informed of their treatment condition at the latest possible point to reduce the threat of differential attrition. Random assignment occurred after all initial data were collected, thus eliminating differential attrition from the initial data collection stage.

It should be stressed that the randomization procedure was developed in collaboration with the authorities in Stark County after extensive study and negotiation. Several strategies were considered, but the one presented here was seen to be the most fair, least cumbersome, and most ethical. Because C&A staff did not feel that they could refuse to provide services once a family had become clients, the random assignment process occurred at the initial inquiry phase with the family. The only incentive to participate in the study was that if selected for the experimental group, services would be provided without the usual wait. In addition, participating families in the control group could be treated in the system by simply withdrawing from the study. If this occurred, an effort was made to continue to collect outcome data. In the analyses, youth from these families were treated as members of the control group—that is, we followed an intention to treat procedure in the analysis.

There was one other way in which control participants could receive services through the system of care that the county insisted be included in the design. Children assigned to the control group could enter the experimental group and remain in the study if they had four out-of-home placements after being assigned to the control group and were about to experience a fifth placement. This circumstance has been very rare; to date, no child in the control group has entered the treatment group this way.

Baseline Data Collection Procedures

The primary data collection effort was focused on children's psychopathology, clinical functioning, and family characteristics. At baseline, this effort was managed by a Vanderbilt-employed site coordinator and an assistant site coordinator in Canton, Ohio. The data on children, between the ages of 4 and 17 years, included measures of psychiatric status, behavior problems and social competence, level of functioning, self-perception, and school adjustment and achievement. Family data included measures of caregiver perceptions of self-efficacy and the need for mental health services for their child, family attitudes toward mental health professionals, family functioning, family life events, and family resources. All computerized interviews were conducted in the family's home or in the site office. Home visits were scheduled at times convenient to the families, and child care support was available.

During the in-person interview, the parent first completed the consent and release forms. Then, the research staff determined the reading ability of the parent by assisting the parent on a tutorial on how to operate the computer. If the parent could read the questions and told the site coordinator the answers without prompting, then the interviewer left parents to complete the computerized interview on their own. If the parent was not able to read the questions, a staff member read the questions aloud, giving only predetermined explanations. The computerized interview with the parent was designed to last approximately 1 to 1.5 hours.

During the initial face-to-face contact with children ages 9 to 11, a staff member asked for oral assent from the child (no written consents were obtained for this age group). After the child agreed to participate, the staff member showed the child the computerized tutorial. Next, the interviewer gave the computerized interview designed for this age group. Adolescents (ages 12-17) signed their own consent forms, completed the tutorial with the research staff, and then completed the computerized interview. If children were 5 to 8 years old, only the parent was interviewed. As with the procedure with parents, when it was determined that a youth had difficulty reading, the interview was read aloud by research staff.

The parent was paid $30 and reimbursed for any mileage or baby-sitting expenses. For adolescents ages 12 to 17, parental permission was secured to pay the adolescent $20 directly. If the child was between 9 and 11, the parent or caretaker received $50 with the understanding that the child was to receive $20.

After the initial interview, C&A was informed of those families with priority for services (experimental group) and those who were not to be served in the system (control group). In addition, if the interview was completed between October and May, the research staff mailed a school packet to a teacher nominated by the family as being most familiar with the youth. A provider questionnaire also was sent to mental health providers named by the parent. A postinterview phone call was completed at 30 days to determine if the child had received mental health services since the interview.

All follow-up data collection interviews were completed using computer-assisted telephone interviews and mailed packets. This process required the alteration of our data collection package. The most notable change was that no diagnostic interviews were administered after baseline. There is some evidence that problem checklists function just as well in detecting clinical status change in a longitudinal services research project as do research diagnostic interviews (Bickman & Lambert, 1996).

The Measurement of Child and Family Outcomes

The primary source of mental health outcome data was the youth and their families. The instrument package utilized was designed to be (a) comprehensive, providing information on a number of child and family variables; (b) standardized; and (c) feasible, asking respondents to provide a large but not excessive amount of information. Table 9.2 describes the instruments used in the study.

Data at baseline were collected using a combination of an interactive, computerized interview, a paper-and-pencil checklist, and an interviewer-rated assessment. The computerized interviews included diagnostic assessment of child psychopathology (i.e., P-CAS, CAS, DISC, DICA), social functioning (i.e., CAFAS, SPP, Social Competence from CBCL and TRF), child and family background, family perceptions (MHN, MHE, MHA), family resources (FRS), and family functioning (FAD, A-FAD). The paper-and-pencil checklist (i.e., CBCL) was also used to assess child psychopathology. Additional data were collected from youth service providers and teachers.

In the development of this entire package, each instrument went through a series of pilot tests and was used in the data collection for the Fort Bragg evaluation with close to 1,000 families. Several instruments were adapted for use in this project and altered to eliminate duplication of items and to enhance readability. The instrumentation package was reviewed by members of national family advocacy organizations as well as African American and Hispanic mental health experts for possible cultural biases.

Table 9.2 Instruments Included in Wave 1 Interview

Title	Acronym and Author	Respondent	Domain
Child and Adolescent Functional Assessment Scale	CAFAS (Hodges, 1990, 1994)	Interviewer rated based on reports	Clinical impairment
Mental Health Needs	MHN (Kelker, 1987)	Parent	Perceived need for services
Mental Health Efficacy	MHE (Bickman, Earl, & Klindworth, 1991)	Parent	Efficacy in interacting with the service system
Attitudes Toward Mental Health Professionals	MHA (Fischer & Turner, 1970)	Parent	Attitudes toward mental health professionals
Family Assessment Device	FAD & A-FAD (Epstein, Baldwin, & Bishop, 1983; Miller, Epstein, Bishop, & Keitner, 1985)	Parent and youth	Family functioning
Family Resource Scale	FRS (Dunst & Leet, 1987)	Parent	Household resources
Child Behavior Checklist	CBCL (Achenbach, 1991a)	Parent	Social competence and behavior problems
Child Assessment Schedule	PCAS & CAS (Hodges, Kline, Stern, Cytryn, & McKnew, 1982)	Parent and youth	Psychiatric diagnoses and symptoms
Diagnostic Interview Schedule for Children	DISC (Shaffer et al., 1989)	Parent and youth	Psychiatric diagnoses
Diagnostic Interview for Children and Adolescents	DICA (Reich & Welner, 1990)	Parent and youth	Psychiatric diagnoses
Self-Perception Profile	SPP (Harter, 1985)	Youth	Global self-worth
Life Events Survey	LES (Moseley & Lex, 1990)	Youth	Difficult events in life
Teacher Report Form	TRF (Achenbach, 1991b)	Teacher	Social competence and behavior problems
School Survey	(SCEP, 1993)	Teacher	School behavior and services
Provider Survey	(SCEP, 1993)	Provider	Treatment and provider characteristics

Data Analysis

The analyses of initial data focused on pretreatment differences between groups. The use of random designs in community research is generally believed to be difficult to implement (e.g., see Farmer, Burns, Guiles, Behar, & Gerber, Chapter 8, this volume). This initial investigation was an attempt to test the validity of this perception. The results provide a means to verify the randomization process and to identify factors that may need further consideration in subsequent longitudinal analyses. Because the randomized design was a critical feature of SCEP, the assessment of its success is crucial.

It is well recognized that when researchers test multiple hypotheses that all bear on a single issue (e.g., 142 comparisons of group equivalence in this section), the individual probabilities of those tests may not be appropriate indicators of statistical significance. The most popular adjustment for multiple testing of hypotheses is the Bonferroni procedure. The Bonferroni procedure, which is easily understood, is the result of dividing the predetermined alpha level by the number of comparisons (e.g., in this section, the Bonferroni adjusted level would be alpha at .05/142 or .0004). We use the Bonferroni adjustment in our baseline comparisons of the treatment conditions.

Results

Recruitment Data

More than 1,300 families applied directly or were referred to SCEP by agencies in Stark County, with 419 youth being considered eligible to participate in the evaluation. Of those eligible, 350 agreed to participate (83.5%). There were 925 youth who were determined ineligible to participate in the evaluation according to SCEP criteria. Figure 9.1 illustrates those families potentially eligible to participate as well as those excluded by SCEP criteria.

Examining Initial Group Equivalency

Demographics. The demographic characteristics of the experimental and control groups were virtually identical, as shown in Table 9.3. The

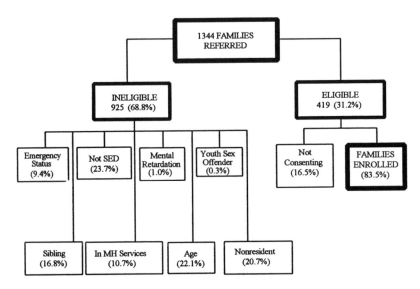

Figure 9.1. Characterization of the SCEP Recruitment for Eligible and Ineligible Groups (for the ineligible breakdown, youth can be considered in more than one exclusionary criterion)

mean age was 11 years with an almost even split between teens and preteens. As in the served population, males and whites were over-represented in the study sample.

Diagnosis. In this analysis, no diagnosis eliminated a youth from receiving other diagnoses except when Oppositional Defiant and Conduct Disorder were both present (i.e., Oppositional Defiant was omitted). Thus, youth could receive more than one diagnosis at baseline. As presented in Table 9.4, no differences between the groups were found in the presence of parent-reported diagnoses (P-CAS). Practically all of the youth received a diagnosis (97%), with over two-thirds receiving a diagnosis other than an adjustment disorder. Table 9.5 presents the presence of diagnoses by youth report (CAS). After applying the Bonferroni adjustment, there were no differences by treatment condition in the rates of diagnoses as determined by youth report. In addition, no differences were found when both the parent and youth reports were combined.

Table 9.3 Demographic Characteristics by Treatment Condition

Group (N)	Experimental (171)	Control (179)	Difference by Group?
Mean Age (SD)	11.09 (3.65)	11.14 (3.48)	No
Age Group	52.0% adolescent	51.2% adolescent	No
Sex	63.7% male	61.9% male	No
Race	73.5% white	75.7% white	No

Symptom Levels. An examination of symptom scale scores from both the P-CAS and CAS (parent and youth reports, respectively) indicated that both conditions are comparable except for the youth-reported symptoms related to depression. In a univariate test of significance, those in the experimental condition were more likely to have higher numbers of major depressive symptoms ($p = .02$), but when the Bonferroni adjustment was applied, this difference disappeared.

Problem Checklist Psychopathology. The CBCL was used as another means of measuring psychopathology in youth. According to the caregiver report, the two groups were identical on global measures of behavior problems, as shown in Table 9.6. Similarly, the two treatment groups were comparable on the more narrowly defined scales. The majority (71%) of children and adolescents in both groups scored in the clinical range (means above the cutoff of 63) on total behavior problems and externalizing behavior problems; about half of each group scored in the clinical range on internalizing problems. This is consistent with the literature in that caregivers are more likely to underreport internalizing symptoms (Chambers et al., 1985; Hodges, Gordon, & Lennon, 1990; Kovacs, 1983). As a consequence, subsequent data collection points have included the Youth Self Report (Achenbach, 1991c) to gain a more complete clinical picture. No differences between treatment conditions were found for scales of the TRF ($n = 205$).

Impairment. The CAFAS was used to measure impairment in functioning, as reported by the caregiver. Severe impairment (indicated by a total mean greater than 30) was reported for children across both groups. This suggests that the average youth in either group experi-

Table 9.4 Percentage of Parent-Reported Diagnoses by Treatment Condition
($N = 345$)

	Experimental	Control	$p(\chi^2)$
Any Diagnosis	96.5	97.7	.49
Major Diagnosis	68.8	73.7	.32
Oppositional Defiant	28.2	33.7	.27
Attention Deficit	20.6	17.1	.41
Conduct Disorder	20.6	26.3	.21
Separation Anxiety	2.9	5.7	.21
Overanxious	2.9	5.1	.30
Major Depression	8.2	5.1	.25
Dysthymia	16.5	10.3	.09
Phobia	8.2	8.0	.94
Obsessive-Compulsive	0.0	0.0	—
Enuresis	7.7	12.0	.18
Encopresis	2.4	5.1	.17
Post-Traumatic Stress	4.7	5.1	.85
Eating Disorder	0.0	0.0	—
Mania/Hypomania	0.6	0.6	.98
Substance Dependence and Abuse	1.2	1.1	.97
Adjustment Disorder	32.4	28.6	.45

NOTE: The $p(\chi^2)$ is based on χ^2 for ordinal variables. The presence of a diagnosis other than Adjustment Disorder constituted the presence of a "Major Diagnosis." Dashes indicate that there were no endorsements of that category.

enced either severe impairment in one life area or moderate impairment in two or more life areas. There were no differences in CAFAS scores by treatment condition.

Social Competence and Self-Perception. The social competence scales from the CBCL and TRF as well as scores from the Self-Perception Profile for children and adolescents were analyzed. No differences in these scales were found between treatment conditions.

Family Factors. There were no differences found on caregivers' perceived self-efficacy in interacting with children's mental health services,

Table 9.5 Percentage of Child-Reported Diagnoses by Treatment Condition ($N = 245$)

	Experimental	Control	$p(\chi^2)$
Any Diagnosis	75.4	78.9	.52
Major Diagnosis	50.8	49.6	.85
Oppositional Defiant	13.1	13.0	.98
Attention Deficit	5.7	1.6	.09
Conduct Disorder	18.9	21.1	.66
Separation Anxiety	5.7	4.1	.54
Overanxious	4.9	7.3	.43
Major Depression	9.8	2.4	.02
Dysthymia	13.1	8.1	.21
Phobia	6.6	7.3	.82
Obsessive-Compulsive	0.0	0.8	.32
Enuresis	1.6	3.3	.41
Encopresis	2.5	2.4	.99
Post-Traumatic Stress	4.9	7.3	.43
Eating Disorder	0.0	0.0	—
Mania/Hypomania	0.0	0.0	—
Substance Dependence and Abuse	3.3	5.1	.36
Adjustment Disorder	32.8	41.5	.16

NOTE: The $p(\chi^2)$ is based on χ^2 for ordinal variables. The presence of a diagnosis other than Adjustment Disorder constituted the presence of a "Major Diagnosis." Dashes indicate that there were no endorsements of that category.

perceived need for mental health services for the children, attitudes about seeking help from mental health professionals, familial resources, or family functioning. Likewise, adolescents did not differ in reported negative life events or family functioning by treatment condition.

Risk Factors. Familial risk factors such as family composition, income level, receipt of public assistance, and previous use of mental health services by youth in the study are presented in Table 9.7. In the univariate comparisons, two differences were found between treatment conditions. Families in the control group were more likely to be single-parent families and to have received public assistance in the past 6 months. If

Table 9.6 Means of CBCL Scale Scores by Treatment Condition

	Experimental		Control			
	Mean	SD	Mean	SD	ES	p(F)
Broad Band Scales						
Total Problem	68.0	9.9	67.4	9.4	0.05	0.56
Total Externalizing	68.4	9.6	67.9	10.1	0.05	0.57
Total Internalizing	63.5	12.2	62.6	10.4	0.08	0.40
Narrow Band Scales						
Withdrawn	62.9	11.1	62.2	9.5	0.07	0.48
Somatic	60.0	10.3	59.6	9.5	0.04	0.53
Anxious/Depressed	64.9	11.1	62.9	9.3	0.19	0.06
Social Problems	63.0	10.6	63.8	10.0	0.07	0.52
Thought Problems	63.7	9.6	63.7	9.2	0.00	0.92
Attention Problems	66.4	10.8	66.6	10.4	0.02	0.90
Delinquency	67.0	9.0	67.1	9.2	0.01	0.97
Aggressive	69.3	11.8	68.6	11.8	0.06	0.53
Sex Problems	56.2	8.7	57.3	10.5	0.11	0.53

NOTES: Effect size (ES) is the difference between experimental and control means expressed in standard deviations. The $p(F)$ is the univariate probability of F.

the adjustment for multiple tests is considered, the two groups were equivalent with respect to this set of risk factors.

Feedback Regarding Interview Process. There were no differences found in respondents' attitudes toward computers in general or toward the interview used in this study. Across both groups, the vast majority of respondents said that they preferred the computerized over a written interview (91.6%). Some respondents experienced initial difficulty using the interactive interview (10.2%). These initial difficulties included manipulating the mouse, using the scroll bars to view "hidden" text, and using the keyboard. The interview had an initial tutorial section aimed at identifying these problems so that the evaluation staff could remedy these difficulties. In the rare case that respondents still could not adequately respond to the interview (most of these cases involved reading ability), the evaluation staff read questions and recorded responses in a standardized manner.

Table 9.7 Family Risk Factors by Treatment Condition

	Experimental	Control	$p(\chi^2)$
Single-Parent Family	49.7	62.4	.02
Siblings	81.9	80.3	.71
Below Poverty Level	59.2	67.8	.10
Public Assistance	76.0	87.1	.01
Previous Mental Health Service Use by Youth	76.0	74.7	.77

NOTE: The $p(\chi^2)$ is based on χ^2 for ordinal variables.

Discussion

In this chapter, we set out to examine two unique features of SCEP. The first focused on the ability of researchers to implement a randomized design to test community-based programs. The second focused on the feasibility of using interactive computerized interviews for primary data collection. A significant issue related to the implementation of a randomized design that had profound impact on the current study was participant recruitment. This issue will be considered when discussing the use of random assignment in community-based research.

Random Assignment

The results of the extensive baseline comparisons between the experimental and control groups demonstrate the success of the design in creating similar groups of children. Although there were some differences on a few variables, given the large number of comparisons there were no differences beyond what one would expect by chance. Thus, there is reason to believe that the treatment groups were equivalent on both the measured and unmeasured variables.

We are not aware of any previous researchers attempting to use a randomized design to evaluate a child and adolescent mental health system (as opposed to the study in Chapter 8, this volume, focused on case management). We suspect that two factors have inhibited researchers from attempting this design. First, there are logistic difficulties in finding a community that is able and willing to cooperate.

Second, and related to the first factor, are ethical issues about the use of random assignment to services, particularly when youth are involved.

As noted in the introduction, the funding of this project was unusual in that we had the commitment of funds before we had a site. Thus, we were able to interview administrators from several communities who were interested in having an evaluation of the system of care.

Having found a cooperative community, our implementation of the design was not a simple matter. An advisory committee was developed to help monitor the study. The committee consisted of representatives of all the public child-serving agencies in the community. Their participation was critical, especially with respect to working out the details of the design and troubleshooting. In retrospect, the addition of parent representatives would have provided a valuable perspective.

The random assignment procedure was based on several principles. We felt, and the advisory committee agreed, that the control of the random assignment should be in the hands of the researchers. To avoid bias, we used a computer program to make random assignments. Another principle was to make the assignment as late as possible to minimize postassignment attrition. To accomplish this, assignments were made after the baseline data collection was completed. Thus, we had baseline data on all persons who took part in the assignment process.

As noted earlier, there are ethical concerns about randomized designs. The first concern raised by the C&A agency staff was that they did not want to deny services to their clients. This was resolved by obtaining informed consent to participate in the research before the families were clients of the agency. We also had to assure the community that certain categories of children would not be asked to participate in the study. Thus, emergency cases and youth sex offenders were not included in the study. The former were excluded because of the concern that these children required immediate care. Youth sex offenders were excluded because they were few in number and there was a perceived risk that if they did not receive services, they might commit another offense. The exclusion of these children does reduce the external validity of the study, but this was a trade-off that had to be made.

Another ethical consideration involved the conditions under which children assigned to the control group could receive services from the system. As noted earlier, there was an escape clause that allowed children who had experienced multiple out-of-home placements to be served in the system. This option was never used but was seen as a necessary measure. It should be noted that as part of the informed consent process, families were told that they could leave the study at any time. Thus, if they wanted system services, they could approach C&A for services and wait to be served in the system.

The legality and ethics of randomized designs have been widely debated (Boruch, in press). In general, there are no legal reasons forbidding randomized designs. The ethical issues can be addressed from several perspectives. First, all eligible families had an equal opportunity to participate in the study. Second, the only possible disadvantage for families who chose not to participate is that they might have had to wait somewhat longer for services, because evaluation participants selected for the system had a higher priority for services. The larger ethical issue centers on the choice not to conduct a study, using the strongest design possible, for services of unknown effectiveness. If it was known that the system had a superior effect, then there would be no reason to conduct an evaluation. But because all the major stakeholders agreed that we did not know if a system of care was indeed more effective, it then became morally responsible to evaluate these services. To continue to deliver services of unknown effectiveness to children who have significant problems raises other ethical issues, issues that may be more important than the type of evaluation design.

Participant Recruitment

It is common knowledge that field experiments are usually delayed because the persons who agree to participate in the study are usually substantially fewer than anticipated during the research design phase (Hedrick, Bickman, & Rog, 1993). There are many reasons for this problem. For new programs, administrators tend to overestimate the need for a program to help justify its funding. It has been said that immediately following the ribbon cutting the number of clients appears to be half of what was expected (Boruch, in press). We tried to anticipate this problem by conducting a "pipeline study" as part of the evaluation planning. Pipeline studies are designed to estimate the number of clients in the pipeline so that an accurate estimate of the number of eligible participants can be made.

To conduct a pipeline study, the investigator needs to know (a) the number of persons that apply or are referred or recruited per month, (b) the relevant characteristics of those persons, (c) the eligibility criteria for the program, (d) the number of new clients per month that the program can admit (that is, the experimental group cannot be larger than the capacity of the program), (e) the eligibility criteria for the study, and (f) the percentage of eligible clients who will agree to participate in the study. All this information is needed to accurately estimate participant flow; a pipeline study is only as good as the data on which it is based.

We were able to get good estimates for the number of persons who were screened at intake to C&A. This was fortunate, as many programs do not keep screening information. We also had some information on the characteristics of those potential clients such as age and sex. But we did not have information on some of the characteristics that were critical to the pipeline study. Figure 9.1 presents the information needed to conduct a pipeline study for this project. We needed estimates for the number of youth who were (a) emergency cases, (b) not considered SED, (c) sex offenders, (d) mentally retarded, (e) siblings of someone receiving services at C&A, and (f) residents of Stark County. With the help of the staff of the several agencies, we estimated the percentages in each category. It was difficult to account for the multivariate nature of these characteristics, however, for a youth could have more than one characteristic. We knew the capacity of the program was limited by the number of case managers in the program, but we did not know the percentage of the eligible clients who would agree to participate in the study. On the basis of our previous research, we estimated that 80% would agree to participate, actually very close to the obtained rate of participation (83.5%).

In addition to conducting a pipeline study for planning purposes, it is critical to monitor the process of recruitment. On the basis of our pipeline study, we felt that we had a sufficient number of clients in the time frame budgeted for participant recruitment. Nonetheless, once we started collecting data we found our estimates overly optimistic. At our initial rate of recruitment, it would have taken 5 years to reach the desired number of participants. When we saw that we were not recruiting at a sufficient rate, we quickly traced our slow recruitment to a miscommunication with the intake staff. In their screening process, intake staff rated each potential client on a scale of 1 to 10 for severity of mental health problems. We requested clients between 6 and 9 (10 was an emergency case). Initially, very few clients were rated in this range. When we spoke with the intake staff, it appeared that the importance of the study to the agency had not been fully explained to them. Subsequently, the intake supervisor attended our monthly advisory committee meetings to observe the commitment of the leadership in the community to implementing this study.

Although our recruitment rate increased subsequent to reaching a better understanding with the intake staff, it was still not sufficient. Many advisory committee meetings were spent trying to discover the cause of our hindered recruitment rate. In hindsight, a review of Figure 9.1 makes the answer deceptively simple. We grossly underestimated the percentage of children who lived out of the county, had siblings who were in services at C&A, or were already receiving mental health services somewhere else. Collectively, these three factors accounted for as much as 48% of our ineligibles.

Although pipeline studies are important to conduct, the precision of the data and the assumptions the investigator must make in field situations can strongly influence the feasibility of the planned research study. Even with superb cooperation from the community, it took us much longer (and therefore cost much more) to collect our baseline data. Based on our own and others' experiences, being conservative in the estimation of recruitment rates would be beneficial.

Interactive Computerized Interviewing in the Real World

Although a more rigorous psychometric study of the computerized assessments we used is under way, the feasibility of using such technology in research was demonstrated in this study. Computerized interactive interviews have many advantages. They are less expensive, quicker, and more reliable (i.e., interrater reliability is not an issue as there is only one interviewer and that interviewer also does not suffer from intrarater unreliability). Respondents in this study enjoyed the interview. Most stated that they preferred the computer over a written or person-administered interview. Although the computerized interview needs to be more fully investigated psychometrically, this technology may hold promise for research and clinical practice in children's mental health. One advantage to this methodology is the reduction in costs of administration and data manipulation. Another is reduction in time to process interview responses. The reduced costs of data collection and speed of data manipulation would enable us to collect data more frequently, possibly assisting us in better understanding the impact of mental health problems on youth and their families over time.

We believe that the randomized design and our data collection procedures were successfully implemented and will set the stage to answer the SCEP research questions presented in this chapter.

References

Achenbach, T. M. (1991a). *Manual for the Child and Behavior Checklist and 1991 profile*. Burlington: University of Vermont, Department of Psychiatry.

Achenbach, T. M. (1991b). *Manual for the Teacher Report Form and 1991 profile*. Burlington: University of Vermont, Department of Psychiatry.

Achenbach, T. M. (1991c). *Manual for the Youth Self Report and 1991 profile*. Burlington: University of Vermont, Department of Psychiatry.

Beachler, M. (1990). The mental health services program for youth. *Journal of Mental Health Administration, 17*, 115-121.

Behar, L. (1988). An integrated state system of services for seriously disturbed children. In J. G. Looney (Ed.), *Chronic mental illness in children and adolescents* (pp. 131-158). Washington, DC: American Psychiatric Press.

Bickman, L. (1996a). A continuum of care: More is not always better. *American Psychologist, 51*, 689-701.

Bickman, L. (1996b). Implications of a children's mental health managed care demonstration project. *Journal of Mental Health Administration, 23*, 107-117.

Bickman, L. (1996c). Implications for evaluators from the Fort Bragg evaluation. *Evaluation Practice, 17*, 51-67.

Bickman, L., Earl, E., & Klindworth, L. (1991). *Vanderbilt Mental Health Service Efficacy Questionnaire*. Unpublished manuscript.

Bickman, L., Guthrie, P., Foster, E. M., Lambert, E. W., Summerfelt, W. T., Breda, C., & Heflinger, C. A. (1995). *Managed care in mental health: The Fort Bragg experiment*. New York: Plenum.

Bickman, L., & Lambert, E. W. (1996). *Comparison of multiple methods of obtaining outcome data on psychopathology for services research*. Paper presented at the 9th Annual Research Conference, A System of Care for Children's Mental Health, Tampa, FL.

Boruch, R. (in press). Randomized field tests for planning and evaluation: A practical guide. In L. Bickman & D. Rog (Eds.), *Applied social research methods series*. Thousand Oaks, CA: Sage.

Chambers, W. J., Puig-Antich, J., Hirsch, M., Paez, P., Ambrosini, P. J., Tabrizi, M. A., & Davies, M. (1985). The assessment of affective disorders in children and adolescents by semistructured interview: Test-retest reliability of the K-SADS-P. *Archives of General Psychiatry, 42*, 696-702.

Dunst, C. J., & Leet, H. E. (1987). Measuring the adequacy of resources in households with young children. *Child: Care, Health and Development, 13*, 111-125.

Epstein, N. B., Baldwin, L. M., & Bishop, D. S. (1983). The McMaster Family Assessment Device. *Journal of Marital and Family Therapy, 9*, 171-180.

Fischer, E. H., & Turner, J. L. (1970). Orientations to seeking professional help: Development and research utility of an attitude scale. *Journal of Consulting and Clinical Psychology, 35*, 79-90.

Friedman, R. M., & Burns, B. J. (1996). The evaluation of the Fort Bragg Demonstration Project: An alternative interpretation of the findings. *Journal of Mental Health Administration, 23*, 128-136.

Friedman, R. M., & Duchnowski, A. J. (Eds.). (1990). Children's mental health services [Special issue]. *Journal of Mental Health Administration, 17*(1).

Harter, S. (1985). *Manual for the Self-Perception Profile for Children.* Denver: University of Denver Press.

Hedrick, T. E., Bickman, L., & Rog, D. J. (1993). *Planning applied social research.* Newbury Park, CA: Sage.

Hodges, K. (1990). *The Child and Adolescent Functional Assessment Scale.* Unpublished manuscript.

Hodges, K. (1994). *The Telephone Interview Version of the Child and Adolescent Functional Assessment Scale.* Unpublished manuscript.

Hodges, K., Gordon, Y., & Lennon, M. P. (1990). Parent-child agreement on symptoms assessed via a clinical research interview for children: The Child Assessment Schedule (CAS). *Journal of Child Psychology and Psychiatry, 31*, 427-436.

Hodges, K., Kline, J., Stern, L., Cytryn, L., & McKnew, D. (1982). The development of a child assessment interview for research and clinical use. *Journal of Abnormal Child Psychology, 10*, 173-189.

Kelker, K. A. (1987). *Working together: The parent-professional partnership.* Families as Allies Project, Research and Training Center to Improve Services for Seriously Emotionally Handicapped Children and Their Families, Portland, OR.

Kovacs, M. (1983). *The Interview Schedule for Children (ISC): Interrater and parent-child agreement.* Unpublished manuscript.

MACRO International. (1996). *The National Comprehensive Community Mental Health for Child and Families Program Evaluation: Report from year one, Stark County, OH.* Atlanta, GA: Author.

Miller, I. W., Epstein, N. B., Bishop, D. S., & Keitner, G. I. (1985). The McMaster Family Assessment Device: Reliability and validity. *Journal of Marital and Family Therapy, 11*, 345-356.

Moseley, J. C., & Lex, A. (1990). Identification of potentially stressful life events experienced by a population of minority youth. *Journal of Multicultural Counseling and Development, 18*, 118-125.

Reich, W., & Welner, Z. (1990). *Diagnostic Interview for Children and Adolescents (rev.): Child version DICA-R-C (DSM-III-R version).* St. Louis, MO: Washington University, Division of Child Psychiatry.

Saxe, L., Cross, T., Silverman, N., Batchelor, W. F., & Dougherty, D. (1987). *Children's mental health: Problems and treatment.* Durham, NC: Duke University Press. (Originally published by Office of Technology Assessment, U. S. Congress, Washington, DC)

Shaffer, D., Fisher, P., Piacentini, J., Schwab, C., Stone, M., & Wicks, J. (1989). *Diagnostic Interview Schedule for Children: DISC-2. 1C, Child Version.* Unpublished manuscript.

New York: New York State Psychiatric Institute, Department of Child and Adolescent Psychiatry.

Stark County Evaluation Project. (1993). [Unpublished instruments]. Nashville, TN: Vanderbilt University, Center for Mental Health Policy.

Stroul, B. A. (1992). *Profiles of local systems of care for children and adolescents with severe emotional disturbances.* Washington, DC: Georgetown University Child Development Center, CASSP Technical Assistance Center.

Stroul, B. A. (1996). *Children's mental health: Creating systems of care in a changing society.* Baltimore, MD: Paul H. Brookes.

Stroul, B. A., & Friedman, R. M. (1986). *A system of care for severely emotionally disturbed youth.* Washington, DC: Georgetown University Child Development Center, CASSP Technical Assistance Center.

Summerfelt, W. T. (1992). *The development of a computerized version of the Child Assessment Schedule: An initial study.* Unpublished master's thesis, Eastern Michigan University, Ypsilanti.

Summerfelt, W. T., & Hodges, V. K. (1992, March). *Test-retest reliability of an interactive computerized interview with adolescents: The computerized Child Assessment Schedule.* Poster presented at the 5th Annual Research Conference, A System of Care for Children's Mental Health, Research and Training Center for Children's Mental Health, University of South Florida, Tampa.

Methodological Challenges in Cross-Cultural Research of Childhood Psychopathology

Risk and Protective Factors

GLORISA CANINO

HECTOR R. BIRD

IAN A. CANINO

Assessing Childhood Psychopathology Cross-Culturally

The Need for Multiple Informants

Childhood diagnoses, even when made in the context of a given culture, cannot be made on the basis of observations obtained from a single informant or from informants in a single setting. Adults are assumed to be accurate reporters of their own emotions and behaviors in different contexts, such as their home, their place of work, or their interpersonal functioning; therefore, the report made by an adult is generally relied on as a single, valid source of information for both clinical and research purposes. By contrast, because of broad variations in cognitive and developmental level, children traditionally are considered to be less dependable in their ability to describe their own behaviors; in their capacity for self-observation and introspection; and in the skill with which they can deal with spatial and temporal sequencing to accurately report onset, severity, or duration of symptomatology. For these reasons, an accurate assessment of a child must rely on data from multiple informants, generally the schoolteacher, the parent, and the child himself or herself, each being assumed to illuminate with greater precision different facets of the child's behavior and emotional life (Bird, Gould, Rubio-Stipec, Staghezza, & Canino, 1991; Edelbrock, Costello, Dulcan, Calabro-Conover, & Kala, 1986; Kashani, Orvaschel, Burk, & Reid, 1985; Loeber, Green, Lahey, & Stouthamer-Loeber, 1989; Reich, Herjanic, Welner, & Gandhy, 1982).

If, within a culture, contextual variations are important in childhood assessment, they may be even more important to consider when children from different cultures are compared. One way of ascertaining the patterns of child disturbance that are most strongly influenced by social forces or culture and those that are more likely to be shaped by genetic, biological, or cognitive processes is by comparing rates and correlates of psychiatric disorders across different cultures or ethnic groups (Weisz et al., 1987). Similarities and differences in rates of psychiatric disorder across different cultures are potentially informative, particularly when they are not attributable to differences in diagnostic definitions or method of ascertainment.

Lack of Consensus in Case Definition

The task of comparing rates of disorder in children across cultures is hampered by a lack of consensus as to the most valid definitions of childhood psychopathology. Although *DSM-III-R* and *DSM-IV* improved classification by making criteria more descriptive and operational, still many diagnoses have not been validated empirically. As Rutter and Shaffer (1980) have noted, the behavioral and emotional components of psychiatric disorders also are observed in normal children. If the state of the art is a lack of consensus on the definition of "caseness," deciding what constitutes a case in different cultural groups poses an even greater challenge. Another difficulty faced by investigators is the choice of research models and diagnostic tools that are culturally sensitive. When a different language is involved, as happens with migrant Hispanic groups, issues of translation and diagnostic equivalency compound the problem.

Disentangling Socioeconomic
Status From Culture

A major methodological difficulty faced by researchers in the mainland United States who are attempting to investigate the effects of culture or ethnicity in children's risk for psychopathology is finding ways to disentangle the effects of culture from those of low socioeconomic status (SES), migration, or other types of stresses to which children from different ethnic groups are subjected. In addition, researchers investigating the risk for psychopathology in Hispanic children must deal with a lack of consensus regarding the definition of what constitutes the Hispanic culture. Hispanic children may originate from cultures as diverse as that of a mulatto from the Caribbean to that of a mestizo from southern Mexico. Membership in this broadly defined group of Hispanic children may identify specific risk factors for psychopathology or may be associated with different rates of psychiatric diagnosis. Unfortunately, there is a paucity of studies in which groups of children from different Hispanic backgrounds are compared.

When a cultural group is studied in its country of origin, some of the foregoing challenges are more easily addressed. For example, most island Puerto Ricans or Mexicans residing in Mexico are not faced with the stressors associated with migration or minority status. Similarly, cultural heterogeneity is usually not an issue because in Puerto Rico and in Mexico, most residents are respectively Puerto Rican or Mexican and not of other Hispanic heritage. There also is greater heterogeneity of SES in these countries, in contrast to the range of SES found for Hispanics or other ethnic minorities in the United States, who tend to be overwhelmingly of low SES. Thus, it is much easier to disentangle the effects of SES or stressors associated with migration or minority status from those of culture vis-à-vis the risk for psychopathology when studying Hispanics—or persons from any other cultural group—in the context of their culture of origin. Comparisons can be made between children in their culture of origin and those who migrate, to evaluate how migration, acculturation, prejudice and alienation, and poverty affect the risk for psychopathology. Still, even when the possibility of cross-country comparisons exists, all the issues are not resolved. Issues related to the choice of research design; definition of caseness; assessment tools; and translation of existing, state-of-the-art instruments remain.

What follows is a review of the existing research on the environmental and cultural factors shaping the risk for psychopathology in children focusing on Hispanic children in the mainland United States and on the island of Puerto Rico, and on the critical research gaps and methodological challenges faced when studying this cultural group.

Cross-Cultural Childhood Psychiatric Epidemiology: Research and Methodological Considerations

Cross-Cultural Similarities in Prevalence Rates of Overall Psychopathology

The results of a psychiatric epidemiology study carried out in Puerto Rico in 1985 (Bird et al., 1988) revealed that 49.5% of children and adolescents in the community met *DSM* diagnostic criteria for one or more diagnoses, including those with or without impairment. Prevalence rates were estimated in two ways: using the computer algorithms of the Diagnostic Interview Schedule for Children (DISC) administered by child psychiatrists, and by clinician judgment. Rates also were estimated based on the clinical judgment of these same psychiatrists who administered the DISC. With both methods of case ascertainments, the rates of psychiatric disorder were equally high. Nevertheless, most of the children who met *DSM* criteria, but were not functionally impaired, were not considered to be in need of mental health services by the child psychiatrist who evaluated them, their parents, or their teachers (Bird et al., 1990). Prevalence rates were significantly lowered to 17% when moderate to severe impairment (as ascertained by the Children's Global Assessment Scale; Shaffer et al., 1983) in addition to *DSM* criteria was used in the definition of caseness. Recent data from four sites (Georgia, Connecticut, New York, and Puerto Rico) reported by the Collaborative Agreement for Methodologic Research for Multi-Site Epidemiologic Surveys of Mental Disorders in Child and Adolescent Populations (the MECA study) showed similar results to those obtained in Puerto Rico (Shaffer et al., 1996). The data from both studies and the four different communities studied suggest that many or most of the children who meet criteria for *DSM* disorders may not be functionally impaired and that a measure of impairment is imperative in the estimation of population prevalence rates for children. The data also suggest that prevalence rates of overall psychopathology in children do not seem to vary cross-culturally. Other studies in which *DSM* criteria as well as impairment in functioning were used to estimate prevalence rates also have reported rates ranging from 16 to 20% (Anderson, Williams, McGee, & Silva, 1987; Costello, 1989; Costello et al., 1988; Offord et al., 1987; Velez & Ungermack, 1989; Verhulst, Berden, & Sanders-Woudstra, 1985; Verhulst, Koot, & Berden, 1990).

Cross-Cultural Differences
in Specific Rates

Although it seems that overall prevalence is similar across studies, cultural differences in the rates of specific disorders, specific areas of symptomatology, or the associated risk factors of specific disorders need to be evaluated. For example, in the 1985 Puerto Rico study (Bird et al., 1988), prevalence rates of alcohol and drug use, as well as conduct disorders, in the child and adolescent population were considerably lower than those obtained in other epidemiological studies in the mainland United States or other parts of the world. These findings were confirmed several years later (1992) when data from Puerto Rico were compared to three other sites as part of the MECA study (Shaffer et al., 1996). This study employed the same methodology, with identical case ascertainment methods (DISC 2.3), and a household probability sample in an attempt to reduce the influence of local variables (see Lahey et al., 1996). Despite the methodological similarities, Puerto Rican children had substantially lower rates of substance abuse and conduct disorders. Their lower rates were attributed to cultural and contextual factors related to strong family ties and parental and community supervision typical of Puerto Rican families with children ages 9 to 17 and not as common in the U.S. communities that were studied.

Gender differences in the prevalence of behavioral problems as measured by the Teacher Report of the Child Behavior Checklist (Achenbach et al., 1980) were observed in the Puerto Rican child epidemiology survey. In this study, there was no significant gender and culture interaction in parental reports for children ages 4 to 16, yet teachers reported significantly more behavioral problems in boys than in girls. In the U.S. sample, this gender differential also was observed, but to a lesser extent. Boys obtained significantly higher problem scores than girls in teacher ratings in both cultures. In the adult population of the island, significantly more females scored in the clinical range for depression on self-report than among women in the United States (Canino et al., 1987). In addition, greater male-to-female ratios for the diagnoses of alcohol (Canino, Burnam, & Caetano, 1992) and drug abuse (Canino, Anthony, Freeman, Shrout, & Rubio-Stipec, 1993) were observed in the adult population of the island as compared to the U.S. mainland. Traditional societal values in the Puerto Rican culture that stress sex role differentiation may be related to these findings.

Epidemiologic studies of Mexican American children and adolescents consistently point to higher rates of depressive symptomatology among mainland U.S. Hispanic children and adolescents as compared to non-Hispanic whites, African Americans, or youth from Mexico (Roberts, in press; Roberts & Sobhan, 1992; Swanson, Linskey, Quintero-Salinas, Pumariega, & Holzer, 1992; Weinberg & Emslie, 1987). It is not clear whether the higher rates are the result of lower socioeconomic status of this ethnic group, acculturation into U.S. culture, or the stressors associated with minority status.

Recent reports have yielded conflicting results on these issues. Roberts (in press) showed that Mexican American students from two communities in New Mexico reported significantly more depressive, anxiety, and suicidal symptoms than students of Anglo origin. Odds ratios analyses adjusted by age, gender, perceived physical health, and father's educational level eliminated the differences in the rates of symptomatology between the two ethnic groups. The author was unable to conclude that low socioeconomic status was mainly responsible for the high depressive scores of Mexican American students because data from another study indicated opposite results (Roberts & Sobhan, 1992). In this study, Roberts and Sobhan (1992) analyzed data on depressive symptomatology from a national probability population household survey of 2,200 adolescents, ages 12 to 17. The results showed that Mexican American adolescents reported significantly more depressive symptoms as compared to Anglo, African American, and Mexican-origin adolescents and continued to have higher levels of depressive symptomatology even after adjusting for age, gender, perceived health, and socioeconomic status. In addition, no significant interactions emerged. The authors stressed the complexities involved in disentangling ethnicity as a risk factor from other risks or correlates of psychopathology, particularly in view of the fact that in two different samples of Mexican American youth, the results of multivariate analyses differed.

Similarities and Differences in Risk Factors of Psychopathology Among Hispanic Groups

One of the few studies that provide data that specifically address risk factors of psychopathology in the Hispanic population is the previously mentioned psychiatric epidemiology study carried out in Puerto Rico (Bird, Gould, Yager, Staghezza, & Canino, 1988). The study showed the following variables to be strongly associated with risk for psychopathology in Puerto Rican children: low socioeconomic background, male gender, 6 to 11 years of age, school failure, poor medical history, and the presence of stressful life events within 6 months of the interview. Nevertheless, these factors are not different from those typically found in most studies investigating the risk factors of childhood psychopathology (Rutter, 1989).

Studies of Mexican American adolescents (Roberts, in press; Roberts & Sobhan, 1992) also have found an association between risk for depressive symptoms in this population and factors such as male gender, low SES, and perceived poor physical health. The same correlates of depression were identified for the other two ethnic groups investigated in these studies (African American and non-Hispanic whites). Of interest was the fact that acculturation to U.S. society, as measured by greater use of the English language by Mexican American adolescents, was inversely related to depressive symptomatology. The higher the acculturation, the lower the depressive symptoms in this group. This finding recently was contradicted in a study by Swanson et al. (1992), however. In this study, U.S. Mexican Americans reported significantly more depressive symptoms, suicidal ideation, and drug use than adolescents living in Mexico. Differences in results between the studies may be due to the fact that Swanson et al. (1992) compared children from schools in a border town of Mexico with children from schools in Texas. The Mexican schools have significantly higher dropout rates (at least 40%) than the U.S. schools, and it is usually the children at greater risk who leave school. This may explain the lower rates of depression found in adolescents living in Mexico and the fact that low acculturation was related to fewer depressive symptoms.

The paucity of research regarding risk factors of psychopathology in Hispanic children has left many questions unanswered. For example, how are the high levels of stress that many mainland U.S. Hispanics experience related to the high prevalence rates of depressive and other symptomatology reported for these populations? Hispanic children in the United States are subjected to migration and inner-city life stressors such as acculturation, prejudice, culture shock, disruption of support systems, inadequate schools, and life in high crime areas, as well as to the stress associated with frequent family violence.

The presence of psychosocial factors and stressful life events in children has been frequently associated with increased risk for psychopathology and poorer prognosis (Compas, Davis, Forsythe, & Wagner, 1987; Compas, Malcarne, & Fondacaro, 1988; Goodyear, Wright, & Altham, 1988; Rutter, 1981). Violent or traumatic events may predispose the child to post-traumatic stress disorder (PTSD) as well as depression and disruptive disorders (Egeland, Jacobvitz, & Sroufe, 1988; Rutter, 1981; Siegel & Brown, 1988).

The unique characteristics in the way that children and adolescents from a specific cultural background are affected by stress has not been explored adequately and is an important, but neglected area of investigation. For example, the relationship between exposure to violence and vulnerability to externalizing disorders, such as conduct and oppositional disorders, needs to be investigated not only for Hispanic children but also for minority inner-city children and all children who are constantly exposed to community and family violence. Often, inner-city minority children exhibit aggressive behavior that may be syntonic with the environment in which they live; physical violence may be a survival skill in a subculture in which truancy and other types of misbehavior are part of everyday life. In-depth analysis for differentiating between what is adaptive "antisocial behavior" and what constitutes a true psychiatric disorder among these special populations is greatly needed.

Similarities and Differences in Protective Factors

The term *protective factor* stems from the related notion of resilience (Rutter, 1987) and is "the term used to describe the positive role of individual differences in people's response to stress and adversity" (p. 316). The essential component of this concept is that the vulnerability or resilience becomes evident only in interaction with the risk factor. Protection lies not in the evasion of the risk but in the successful mastery and adaptive changes that stem from successful coping. Much of what has been written focuses on individual protective mechanisms and very little has been explored regarding how culture and environment can serve as a protective mechanisms.

Garmezy (1985) concluded that there are three main types of protective factors: (a) personality factors, (b) family cohesion and absence of discord, and (c) the availability of external support systems that can reinforce coping efforts. The last two factors appear to be strongly related to culture and will be discussed further below.

As previously stated, there is evidence that alcohol and drug use disorders are rare among island Puerto Rican children (Bird et al., 1988; Shaffer et al., in press). Higher rates of family disintegration and alienation sometimes found in the families of children with drug abuse or dependence are observed less frequently in Puerto Rico compared to other cultural settings. Strict parental supervision and regulation of children's peer group activities are protective factors against youth delinquency and use of drugs (Wilson, 1974, 1980). Hispanic families generally are characterized precisely by this strict parental supervision and regulation of children's activities (Bird et al., 1989).

The emphasis on family cohesion and extended kinship networks in the Puerto Rican culture may serve as a protective mechanism against the development of some types of externalizing problems in children. This extended kinship system may reduce the risk of problems following certain life events such as parental death, divorce, or maternal hospitalization. Chain reactions of negative events in other less supportive or extended family systems could result in dramatic changes in child care or in institutionalization of the child. The extended kin system and the family cohesion characteristic of Hispanic families protects against these long-term negative consequences by providing support to the remaining parent and thus ensuring the continuity of care and relationships for the child.

Another protective factor against the use of drugs among island Hispanic children may be a strong negative attitude in the Puerto Rican society against the use of illicit drugs. Szalay, Canino, and Vilov (1992) compared attitudes toward drugs of adolescent island Puerto Ricans, Puerto Ricans living in New York, and Anglos. The results of the study showed that negative attitudes toward drugs were significantly greater among island youth as compared to the New York Puerto Rican or Anglo adolescents.

Rutter (1987) observed that changes in the individual's circumstances are strongly related to changes in resilience. In fact, this is what we hypothesize happens regarding the risk of drug use when Hispanics migrate to the United States. The changes in cultural values associated with the process of acculturation, as well as the stressors and alienation associated with minority status, seem to place Hispanics in the United States at considerably greater risk for drug use and abuse as compared to Hispanics in their country of origin.

In one of the few studies comparing Puerto Rican children on the island with Puerto Rican children on the mainland, Velez and Ungermack (1989) studied the drug use patterns of Puerto Rican children in two New York City schools. The New York children were matched with island children on age and socioeconomic status. Prevalence rates of illicit drug use among Puerto Rican adolescent islanders 11 to 17 years of age were found to be significantly lower than corresponding prevalence values for their U.S. mainland counterparts. Length of residence in New York was strongly associated with the risk of drug use and abuse—the longer the stay, the greater the risk. These data are similar to those reported by Swanson et al. (1992) that showed significantly lower prevalence rates of drug use among Mexican youth as compared to Mexican American youth living in Texas. Further analyses of these data revealed that children and adolescents with both parents born in Mexico had significantly lower rates of drug use than their peers who had one or both parents born in the United States. These results are consistent with other national studies of drug use in the United States (De la Rosa, Kholsa, & Bouse, 1990; National Institute on Drug Abuse, 1987).

Data from a number of adult studies that examined the role accul-turation plays substance use patterns among different Hispanic groups confirm those obtained with children and adolescents. Most of the stud-ies consistently show that acculturation by Hispanics to U.S. culture is significantly related to an increase in substance use and substance-related disorders (Burnam, 1989; Burnam, Hough, Karno, Escobar, & Telles, 1987; Caetano, 1986; Ortiz & Medina-Mora, 1987).

Cultural Sensitivity of Diagnostic Tools

The adequacy of a diagnostic instrument in a given culture does not guarantee its reliability or validity in another, even given a faithful translation (Bravo, Woodbury-Fariña, & Canino, 1993; Brislin, Looner, & Thorndike, 1973). Unless the assessment tool used for diagnosing children is developed in the culture for which it is intended, the use of diagnostic instruments requires a comprehensive translation and adap-tation process. The resultant instrument must be capable of identifying phenomena similar to the original version, but in a dissimilar sociocul-tural context.

In most instances, researchers from developing countries are forced to use diagnostic instruments developed in other cultures. Lack of re-search funding or expert personnel precludes the possibility that diag-nostic tools can be developed specifically for their population. This is particularly true in the case of population psychiatric epidemiology research, which often requires the use of structured psychiatric inter-views, such as the DISC, that can be administered by lay interviewers. The DISC has been in the process of development in the United States for more than a decade, but to date all of the psychometric work needed on the instrument has not been completed (Sheffer et al., 1996).

Similar problems are encountered by researchers in the United States who have minority populations in their sample. Even though most di-agnostic instruments have been developed by U.S. researchers, the test-ing of the instrument's psychometric properties usually does not include a large enough sample of minority populations to draw conclu-sions about the instrument's validity and reliability for different sub-groups.

In Puerto Rico, we have used a comprehensive cross-cultural model to adapt and translate a number of diagnostic instruments for children and adolescents, particularly the DISC.2, the CBCL, and a number of other instruments designed to measure impairment and risk for psychopathology. This model involves testing the instrument for equivalency in five dimensions: (a) cultural, (b) semantic, (c) technical, (d) criterion, and (e) conceptual (for more detail, see Bird et al., 1989, 1991; Bravo, Canino, Rubio-Stipec, & Woodbury-Fariña, 1991; Flaherty, 1987). Adequate ethnographic information is needed to permit the measurement of possible "culture-specific syndromes" or particular ways Hispanic children may have of expressing certain psychiatric symptomatology. This ethnographic research also could provide cultural interpretations in case differences in prevalence rates are observed in the different ethnic or cultural groups studied.

Researchers who decide to adapt or translate an instrument developed in one culture to use it in another must first decide if most of the instrument's constructs have face validity for that particular culture. For example, ideally, impairment measures should provide indicators of the child's psychosocial functioning or adaptation in the most important areas of a child's life, including the school, the family, the community, and friends. A measure that provides objective criteria separating these important domains is necessary because it is possible that a child may show adaptational problems in one area and not in another. Intervention and prevention can then be focused in the problem area identified. Yet adaptation is defined by the way the person's role performance conforms to the expectations of his or her referent group. Measures are thus based on behaviors or roles that are normative to a given society or context (Katsching, 1983). Given this contextual definition, one would expect the construct to vary across different cultural and socioeconomic groups. We have evidence from the 1985 Puerto Rican survey (Achenbach et al., 1990) that supports this statement. Even after matching children for age, sex, and SES, differences between Puerto Rican and Anglo children were observed, especially for CBCL Social Competence. Social competence scores reported by adolescents and their parents and teachers were considerably lower for the Puerto Rican sample than for the Anglo sample. The only exception were items that measured frequency of contacts with friends and getting along with family and siblings. These last results may reflect the importance placed on close family ties and good interpersonal relations in the Puerto Rican culture (Canino & Canino, 1982). Furthermore, reports of involvement in sports, hobbies, organizations, or jobs were significantly lower for Puerto Rican children. The lack of resources of low-income neighborhoods common in the island and the high unemployment rates that limit the availability of jobs, particularly for the younger age groups, probably account for these findings as opposed to concluding that Puerto Rican children are less socially adapted. Any measure of impairment must be carefully evaluated in a culturally sensitive way to avoid bias.

Directions for Future Research

Combining ethnographic and empirical approaches is essential to better define what constitutes a case, particularly when using a psychiatric nosology that may be overinclusive in diagnosing children and adolescents in the community. We have discussed the possible protective mechanisms that seem to be associated with finding unacculturated Hispanic children less vulnerable to drug use and addiction. It also is possible that the low prevalence rates may be affected by particular response styles of systematic underreporting of illicit drug use that Hispanic populations may have regarding highly stigmatizing and illegal behavior. Ethnographic research would be helpful in investigating these response styles. In addition, this type of research would help to establish the various cultural definitions of illness or cultural significance of key symptoms and the possible existence of culture-bound syndromes in children and adolescents. The unique ways in which culture may shape the risk for psychopathology in Hispanic children are generally unknown. We do not know whether the phenomenologies of different disorders are similar across groups. Manson, Shore, and Bloom (1985), for example, found great variations in the phenomenology of emotion as well as in the language in which it is expressed among Hopi Indians, which has important implications for the definition of depression among this group. Similar research needs to be conducted among Hispanic populations.

Comparisons of the rates obtained in epidemiologic studies carried out in other regions of the world cannot be made because of differences in methods of ascertainment, in the age range of the children, and in the type of populations studied. Large cross-cultural population studies of mental disorders in children and adolescents that use the same instruments and methods across settings are needed to determine more precisely whether there are specific childhood disorders that are more likely to be affected by cultural differences. The recently funded study by the National Institute of Mental Health (NIMH), known as UNO-CCAP, promises to provide this much-needed data. This collaborative effort between four universities and NIMH, combined with a very similar study to be carried out concomitantly in Puerto Rico, could serve as a basis addressing the extent to which societal context and culture influences the prevalence and correlates of mental disorders in children and the extent to which genetics may play a role. Two priorities—(a) the use of additional instruments or items and ethnographic methods to explore the specific cultural symptomatic expressions of psychopathology, and (b) the use of common instruments and methods of ascertainment in cross-cultural research—are equally important.

In addition, epidemiologic research should evaluate whether the presence of multiple stressors places Hispanic and other minority children in the United States at greater risk for certain types of psychopathology than other children less exposed to multiple stressors. Investigating the association between specific stressors and specific symptomatology is necessary. Multivariate strategies to compare the contributions of diverse types of stressors and risk factors would facilitate the testing of competing hypotheses. For example, four-way comparisons of (a) Hispanic children exposed to various stressors with (b) those not exposed and (c) non-Hispanic children exposed and (d) not exposed would be necessary to evaluate the contributions of stress and culture or stress and context in increasing the risk for psychopathology in children. Equally important is the exploration of possible cultural mechanisms that may protect children in a particular group against the risk for certain disorders. The cultural mechanisms involved, for example, in the hypothesized protection that the Hispanic culture offers against drug use, should be empirically investigated. These studies should be carried out using household probability community samples. School-based studies are most frequently reported in Hispanic populations in the United States. Given the high school dropout rate of Hispanics, both in the United States and in their culture of origin (exceeding 30% of the population), and the fact that the dropout population is at higher risk for mental disorders, school-based studies underestimate the true prevalence of disorders and may provide misleading information about risk factors.

Given the present difficulties encountered in defining a case in child psychiatry and psychology, epidemiologic research with children and adolescents should use multiple definitions of psychopathology. Finally, a longitudinal perspective is essential to evaluate the interactions of biological and social developmental factors with culture and social class.

References

Achenbach, T. M., Bird, H., Canino, G., Phares, V., Gould, M., Rubio-Stipec, M. (1990). Epidemiological comparisons of Puerto Rican children and U.S. Mainland children: Parent, teacher, and self reports. *Journal of the American Academy of Child and Adolescent Psychiatry, 29*(1), 84-93.

Achenbach, T. M ., & Edelbrock, C. S. (1983). *Manual for the Child Behavior Checklist and the Revised Child Behavior Profile.* Burlington: University of Vermont, Department of Psychiatry.

Anderson, J. C., Williams, S., McGee, L., & Silva, P. A. (1987). DSM-III disorders in preadolescent children: Prevalence in a large sample from the general population. *Archives of General Psychiatry, 44,* 69-76.

Bird, H. R., Canino, G., Rubio-Stipec, M., Gould, M. S., Ribera, J., Sesman, M., Woodbury, M., Huertas-Goldman, S., Pagan, A., Sanchez-Lacay, A., & Moscoso, M. (1988). Estimates of the prevalence of childhood maladjustment in a community survey in Puerto Rico. *Archives of General Psychiatry, 45,* 1120-1126.

Bird, H. R., Gould, M. S., Rubio-Stipec, M., Staghezza, B., & Canino, G. (1991). Screening for childhood psychopathology in the community using the Child Behavior Checklist. *Journal of the American Academy of Child and Adolescent Psychiatry, 30*(1), 116-122.

Bird, H. R., Gould, M. S., Yager, T., Staghezza, B., & Canino, G. (1989). Risk factors of maladjustment in Puerto Rican children. *Journal of the American Academy of Child and Adolescent Psychiatry, 28,* 847-850.

Bird, H. R., Yager, T. J., Staghezza, B., Gould, M. S., Canino, G., & Rubio-Stipec, M. (1990). Impairment in the epidemiological measurement of childhood psychopathology in the community. *Journal of the American Academy of Child and Adolescent Psychiatry, 29*(5), 796-803.

Bravo, M., Canino, G., Rubio-Stipec, M., & Woodbury-Fariña, M. (1991). A cross-cultural adaptation of a psychiatric epidemiologic instrument: The Diagnostic Interview Schedule's adaptation in Puerto Rico. *Culture, Medicine and Psychiatry, 15,* 1-18.

Bravo, M., Woodbury-Fariña, M., & Canino, G. (1993). The Spanish translation and cultural adaptation of the Diagnostic Interview Schedule for Children (DISC 2.1) in Puerto Rico. *Culture, Medicine and Psychiatry, 17,* 329-344.

Brislin, R., Looner, W., & Thorndike, R. (1973). *Cross-cultural methods.* New York: John Wiley.

Burnam, M. A. (1989). Prevalence of alcohol abuse and dependence among Mexican-Americans and Non-Hispanic whites in the community. In D. L. Spiegler, D. A. Tate, S. S. Aitken, & C. M. Christian (Eds.), *Alcohol use among U.S. ethnic minorities* (NIAAA Research Monograph No. 18, DHHS Publication No. [ADM] 88-1435), pp. 102-128. Washington, DC: Government Printing Office.

Burnam, M. A., Hough, R., Karno, M., Escobar, J., & Telles, C. (1987). Acculturation and lifetime prevalence of psychiatric disorders among Mexican Americans in Los Angeles. *Journal of Health and Social Behavior, 28,* 89-102.

Caetano, R. (1986). Patterns and problems of drinking among U.S. Hispanics. In *Report of the Secretary's task force on black and minority health: Vol. 7. Chemical dependency and diabetes* (pp. 143-186). Washington, DC: U.S. Department of Health and Human Services.

Canino, G., Anthony, J. C., Freeman, D., Shrout, P., & Rubio-Stipec, M. (1993). Drug abuse and illicit drug use in Puerto Rico. *American Journal of Public Health, 83,* 194-200.

Canino, G., Burnam, A., & Caetano, R. (1992). The prevalence of alcohol abuse and/or dependence in two Hispanic communities. In J. Helzer & G. Canino (Eds.), *Alcoholism—North America, Europe and Asia: A coordinated analysis of population data from ten regions* (pp. 131-155). New York: Oxford University Press.

Canino, G., & Canino, I. (1982). Culturally syntonic family therapy for migrant Puerto Ricans. *Hospital Community Psychiatry, 39,* 200-303.

Canino, G., Rubio-Stipec, M., Shrout, P. E., Bravo, M., Stolberg, R., & Bird, H. (1987). Sex differences and depression in Puerto Rico. *Psychological Women Quarterly, 11,* 443-459.

Compas, B. E., Davis, G. E., Forsythe, C. J., & Wagner, B. M. (1987). Assessment of major and daily stressful events during adolescence: The Adolescent Perceived Events Scale. *Journal of Consulting and Clinical Psychology, 55,* 534-541.

Compas, B. E., Malcarne, V. L., & Fondacaro, K. (1988). Coping with stressful events in older children and young adolescents. *Journal of Consulting and Clinical Psychology, 56,* 405-411.

Costello, E. J. (1989). Child psychiatric disorders and their correlates: A primary care pediatric sample. *Journal of the American Academy of Child and Adolescent Psychiatry, 28,* 851-855.

Costello, E. J., Costello, A. J., Edelbrock, C., Burns, B. J., Dulcan, M. K., Brent, D., & Janiszewski, S. (1988). Psychiatric disorders in pediatric primary care. *Archives of General Psychiatry, 45,* 1007-1116.

De la Rosa, M. R., Kholsa, J. H., & Bouse, B. A. (1990). Hispanics and illicit drug use: A review of recent findings. *International Journal of Addictions, 25,* 665-691.

Edelbrock, C., Costello, A. J., Dulcan, M. K., Calabro-Conover, N., & Kala, R. (1986). Parent-child agreement on child psychiatric symptoms assessed via structured interview. *Journal of Child Psychology and Psychiatry, 27,* 181-190.

Egeland, B., Jacobvitz, D., & Sroufe, L. A. (1988). Breaking the cycle of abuse. *Child Development, 59,* 1080-1088.

Flaherty, J. A. (1987). Appropriate and inappropriate research methodologies for Hispanic mental health. In M. Gaviria & J. Arana (Eds.), *Health and behavior: Research agenda for Hispanics* (Simon Bolivar Research Monograph Series, No. 1, pp. 177-196). Chicago: University of Illinois Press.

Garmezy, N. (1985). Stress-resistant children: The search for protective factors. In J. E. Stevenson (Ed.), *Recent research in developmental psychopathology. Journal of Child Psychology and Psychiatry* (Suppl. 4). Oxford, UK: Pergamon.

Goodyear, I. M., Wright, C., & Altham, P. M. (1988). Maternal adversity and recent stressful life events in anxious and depressed children. *Journal of Child Psychology and Psychiatry, 29*, 651-667.

Kashani, J. H., Orvaschel, H., Burk, J. P., & Reid, J. C. (1985). Informant variance: The issue of parent-child disagreement. *Journal of the American Academy of Child Psychiatry, 24*, 437-441.

Katsching, H. (1983). Methods for measuring social adjustment. In T. Helgason (Ed.), *Methodology in evaluation of psychiatric treatment* (pp. 205-218). New York: Cambridge University Press.

Lahey, B. B., Flagg, E. W., Bird, H. R., Schwab-Stone, M., Canino, G., Dulcan, M. K., Leaf, P. J., Davies, M., Brogan, D., Bourdon, K., Horwitz, S. M., Rubio-Stipec, M., Freeman, D. H., Lichtman, J., Shaffer, D., Goodman, S. H., Narrow, W. E., Weissman, M. M., Kandel, D. B., Jensen, P. S., Richters, J. E., & Regier, D. A. (1996). The NIMH methods for the epidemiology of child and adolescent mental disorder (MECA) study: Background and methodology. *Journal of the American Academy of Child and Adolescent Psychiatry, 35*(7), 855-864.

Loeber, R., Green, S. M., Lahey, B. B., & Stouthamer-Loeber, M. (1989). Optimal informants on childhood disruptive behaviors. *Development Psychopathology, 1*, 317-337.

Manson, S., Shore, J. H., & Bloom, J. D. (1985). The depressive experience in American Indian communities: A challenge for psychiatric theory and diagnosis. In A. Kleinman & B. Good (Eds.), *Culture and depression* (pp. 331-368). Los Angeles: University of California Press.

National Institute on Drug Abuse. (1987). *Use of selected drugs among Hispanics: Mexican Americans, Puerto Ricans, Cuban Americans*. Rockville, MD: U.S. Department of Health and Human Services.

Offord, D. R., Boyle, M. H., Szatmari, P., Rae-Grant, N. I., Links, P. S., Cadman, D. T., Byles, J. A., Crawford, J. W., Munroe-Blum, H., Byrne, C., Thomas, H., & Woodward, C. A. (1987). The Ontario Child Health Study: Prevalence of disorder and rates of service utilization. *Archives of General Psychiatry, 44*, 832-836.

Ortiz, A., & Medina-Mora, M. E. (1987). Research on drugs in Mexico. In *Epidemiology of drug abuse and issues among Native American populations* (Community Epidemiology Work Group Proceedings). Washington, DC.

Reich, W., Herjanic, B., Welner, Z., & Gandhy, P. R. (1982). Development of a structured psychiatric interview for children: Agreement on diagnosis comparing child and parent interviews. *Journal of Abnormal Child Psychology, 10*, 325-336.

Roberts, E. R. (in press). Research on the mental health of Mexican origin children and adolescents. In M. Karno & C. Telles (Eds.), *Mental disorders in Hispanic populations: The current state of research*. Washington, DC: National Institute of Mental Health.

Roberts, E. R., & Sobhan, M. (1992). Symptoms of depression in adolescence: A comparison of Anglo, African and Hispanic Americans. *Journal of Youth and Adolescence, 21*, 639-651.

Rutter, M. (1981). Stress, coping and development: Some questions and some answers. *Journal of Psychology and Psychiatry, 22*, 323-353.

Rutter, M. (1987). Psychosocial resilience and protective mechanisms. *American Orthopsychiatric Association, 57*, 316-331.

Rutter, M. (1989). Pathways from childhood to adult life. *Journal of Child Psychology and Psychiatry, 30*, 23-51.

Rutter, M., & Shaffer, D. (1980). DSM-III, a step forward or back in terms of the classification of child psychiatric disorders. *Journal of the American Academy of Child and Adolescent Psychiatry, 19,* 371-394.

Shaffer, D., Fisher, P., Dulcan, M., Davis, D., Piacentini, J., Schwab-Stone, M., Lahey, B., Bourdon, K., Jensen, P., Bird, H., Canino, G., & Regier, D. (1996). The NIMH Diagnostic Interview Schedule for Children (DISC 2.3): Description, acceptability, prevalences, and performance in the MECA study. *Journal of the American Academy of Child and Adolescent Psychiatry, 35*(7), 865-877.

Shaffer, D., Gould, M. S., Brasic, J., Ambrosini, P. J., Fisher, P., Bird, H. R., & Aluwahlia, S. (1983). A Children's Global Assessment Scale (CGAS). *Archives of General Psychiatry, 40,* 1228-1231.

Siegel, J. M., & Brown, J. D. (1988). A prospective study of stressful circumstances, illness symptoms, and depressed mood among adolescents. *Developmental Psychology, 24,* 715-721.

Swanson, J. W., Linskey, A. O., Quintero-Salinas, R., Pumariega, A. J., & Holzer, C. E. (1992). A binational school survey of depressive symptoms, drug use and suicidal ideation. *Journal of the American Journal of Child and Adolescent Psychiatry, 31,* 669-678.

Szalay, L. B., Canino, G., Vilov, S. K. (1992). Vulnerabilities and culture change drug abuse among Puerto Rican adolescents in the United States. *International Journal of Addictions, 28,* 327-354.

Velez, C. N., & Ungermack, J. (1989). Drug use among Puerto Rican youth: An exploration of generational status differences. *Social Sciences and Medicine, 29,* 779-789.

Verlhust, F. C., Berden, G. F. M., & Sanders-Woudstra, J. (1985). Mental health in Dutch children: 2. The prevalence of psychiatric disorder and relationship between measures. *Acta Psychiatrica Scandinavica, 72*(Suppl. 324), 1-45.

Verhulst, F. C., Koot, H. M., & Berden, G. F. (1990). Four-year follow-up of an epidemiological sample. *Journal of the American Academy of Child and Adolescent Psychiatry, 29,* 440-448.

Weinberg, W. A., & Emslie, G. J. (1987). Depression and suicide in adolescents. *International Pediatrics, 8,* 154-159.

Weisz, J. R., Suwanlert, S., Chaiyasit, W., Weiss, B., Achenbach, T. M., & Walter, B. R. (1987). Epidemiology of behavioral and emotional problems among Thai and American children: Parent reports for ages 6 to 11. *Journal of the American Academy of Child and Adolescent Psychiatry, 26,* 890-897.

Wilson, H. (1974). Parenting in poverty. *British Journal of Social Work, 4,* 254.

Wilson, H. (1980). Parental supervision: A neglected aspect of delinquency. *British Journal of Criminology, 20,* 203-235.

Name Index

Subject Index

About the Editors

Carol T. Nixon, MA, is Research Psychologist at First Mental Health in Nashville, Tennessee. She is finishing her doctoral studies at Vanderbilt University in applied social psychology with training in program evaluation and mental health services research. She has been a predoctoral fellow under the Center for Mental Health Policy's NIMH-sponsored training grant in child and adolescent mental health services research. In addition to editing and contributing to the present volume, she also served as coeditor for Volume 2 of the Sage Children's Mental Health Services series, *Families and the Mental Health System for Children and Adolescents: Policy, Services, and Research.* Her current research efforts and interests include stakeholder perspectives of the quality of mental health services, the outcome of long-term care patients discharged to community-based alternatives, the effectiveness of case management, and outcomes associated with managed behavioral healthcare.

Denine A. Northrup, PhD, is a Research Associate at the Vanderbilt Institute for Public Policy Studies, Center for Mental Health Policy, and an NIMH Postdoctoral Fellow in children's mental health services. She received her PhD from Vanderbilt University in applied social psychology, with her master's in clinical psychology. She is currently the Project Manager of an implementation analysis of the transition from the children's mental health demonstration program at Fort Bragg to a new managed care approach for children receiving mental health services. She has also worked with the Tennessee Commission on Children and Youth on the evaluation of the statewide Tennessee Children's Plan. Her research has been focused on family issues in children's mental health services, specifically multiple informant issues, measurement of family issues, and family empowerment.

About the Contributors

Mary I. Armstrong, MSW, MBA, is Director of the Division of State and Local Support in the Department of Child and Family Studies at the Florida Mental Health Institute, University of South Florida. She received her master's degree in social work from Temple University and a master's degree in business administration from the University at Albany of the State University of New York. She has been involved at all levels in the development and administration of community-based service, family support programs, advocacy, and interagency collaboration. She served as Director of the Bureau of Children and Families for the New York State Office of Mental Health for 10 years and was New York's first Director of the Children and Adolescent Service System Program.

C. Clifford Attkisson, PhD, is Professor of Psychology in the Department of Psychiatry at the University of California, San Francisco, and Dean of Graduate Studies and Associate Vice Chancellor for Student Academic Affairs on the San Francisco campus. Previously, he served for 10 years as Associate Dean of the Graduate Division; he has been a member of the psychology faculty at UCSF for 24 years. He earned the PhD degree in 1970 at the University of Tennessee after completing undergraduate work at the University of Richmond in Virginia, his home state. He is a frequent contributor to the scientific literature in his field and is senior editor of three widely cited volumes: *Evaluation of Human Service Programs, Patient Satisfaction in Health and Mental Health Services,* and *Depression in Primary Care.* In addition, he has published numerous articles and book chapters in mental health services research and service system research. His teaching activities and research projects have been focused on human services program evaluation, information systems for the human services, clinical services research, and service systems research. His current research program is a collaborative study of innovative systems of care for children and adolescents who suffer from serious emotional disorder.

Harold R. Baize, Jr., PhD, is a Postdoctoral Fellow at the University of California, San Francisco. He earned his PhD in social psychology at the University of California, Berkeley, where he also studied personality assessment and scaling as a research assistant at the Institute of Social and Personality Research. His personality studies focused on the trait descriptive approach to personality. He served as data manager with the UCSF Child Services Research Group on the NIMH-funded study "Clinical Epidemiology in Three Systems of Care for Youth." He is currently a fellow in the NIMH-funded UCSF Clinical Services Research Training Program, where he is working with large data sets to investigate the impact of changes in mental health service delivery on outcomes for children and adolescents with severe emotional disturbance.

Lenore Behar, PhD, is Chief of the Child and Family Services Section, North Carolina Division of Mental Health, Developmental Disabilities, and Substance Abuse Services. Her doctorate in clinical psychology is from Duke University. She has been a central figure in mental health services for children and their families for more than 20 years, serving on many national boards and as an expert in litigation regarding services for children. Her work on behalf of children has been acknowledged in a series of awards. In 1995 she received awards from the Washington Business Group on Health and the Robert Wood Johnson Foundation's Mental Health Services Program for Youth (MHSPY), and the Nicholas Hobbs Award from the American Psychological Association. She has worked through a series of projects to develop model systems of care for children's mental health. This included her work with MHSPY and her development of a CHAMPUS demonstration to provide comprehensive mental health services to 48,000 children at Fort Bragg. She continues to work with national organizations and foundations to expand and implement community-based, cross-agency efforts on behalf of children. Her recent presentations and publications have addressed issues of delivering and financing mental health care for children and families.

Leonard Bickman, PhD, is Director of the Center for Mental Health Policy at Vanderbilt University and Professor of Psychology, Psychiatry, and Public Policy. He is a nationally recognized leader in mental health services research on children and adolescents. He just completed the evaluation of the largest mental health services demonstration project ever conducted on children and adolescents. The evaluation of the Fort Bragg demonstration was funded by both the U.S. Army and NIMH to study the effects of a full continuum of care provided for military dependents. In addition, he has recently received a competitive renewal from the NIMH to follow the participants of the Fort Bragg study an additional 3 years. He also is collaborating with state and local officials in Ohio in a multiyear, randomized experiment focused on an innovative mental health system for children and adolescents in the public sector. He is a Co-Principal Investigator on the national Use, Need, Outcomes, and Costs in Child and Adolescent Populations (UNO-CCAP) study that was recently funded. His center was awarded the first training grant in child and adolescent mental health services research. He coedited the first monograph on methodological issues in the evaluation of child and adolescent mental health services and is editor of a series on child and adolescent mental health published by Sage. His standing in this field has been recognized by Secretary of Health and Human Services Shalala by his appointment as the only services researcher to the nation's highest advisory council on mental health and substance abuse services (SAMHSA). He is president of the American Evaluation Association.

Hector R. Bird, MD, is Professor of Clinical Psychiatry at Columbia University, College of Physicians and Surgeons and Deputy Director of the Division of Child and Adolescent Psychiatry at the New York State Psychiatric Institute. He has conducted epidemiologic and methodologic research in child psychiatric epidemiology and has published on clinical, epidemiologic, and cross-cultural issues.

Barbara J. Burns, PhD, holds academic appointments at Duke University as Professor of Medical Psychology, Department of Psychiatry and

Behavioral Sciences; Associate Research Professor, Center for Health Policy Research and Education; and Senior Fellow, Center for the Study of Aging and Human Development. She is a Research Fellow at the Cecil G. Sheps Center for Health Services Research at the University of North Carolina at Chapel Hill. She serves as Director of the Psychiatric Epidemiology and Health Services Research Program in the Department of Psychiatry and Behavioral Sciences at Duke and as Co-Director of the Postdoctoral Research Training Program in Mental Health Services and Systems administered through Duke and the University of North Carolina at Chapel Hill. She is a nationally recognized mental health services researcher and policy expert. Her current research includes randomized clinical trials of innovative community services for children and adults with severe mental illness. In these studies, she is investigating outcomes of case management for children and the effectiveness of assertive community treatment and outpatient commitment for adults. With other Duke investigators she also is involved in epidemiological studies of mental health and substance abuse disorders and service use by children living in the Great Smoky Mountains of North Carolina.

Glorisa Canino, PhD, is Professor of Pediatrics and Director of the Behavioral Sciences Research Institute at the University of Puerto Rico, Medical Sciences Campus. She also is consultant at the Administration of Mental Health and Anti-Addiction Services. She is the Principal Investigator under several grants funded by the NIMH and by the National Institute of Alcohol. She has published extensively in peer review journals in the areas of cross-cultural psychiatric epidemiology, instrument development and psychometrics, and the epidemiology of drugs and alcohol among Hispanic populations.

Ian A. Canino, MD, completed his training in adult and child psychiatry at Albert Einstein College of Medicine in New York. He is presently Associate Clinical Professor, Department of Psychiatry at Columbia University. He is the Deputy Director of Child Psychiatry Training and Director of Community Child Psychiatry at the New York State Psychiatric Institute, Division of Child Psychiatry, College of Physicians and Surgeons of Columbia University. His career has been dedicated to the special mental health needs of inner-city culturally diverse children. He has published extensively in this area; has been the recipient of grant awards; and has participated as a lecturer at local, national, and international mental health organizations. He has been the founding member for many national Hispanic organizations and has been actively involved in the American Academy of Child and Adolescent Psychiatry. As a member of other national organizations, he has participated in nominating committees, on boards of advisers, and as consulting editor for journals.

June Madsen Clausen, PhD, is Assistant Professor of Psychology at the University of San Francisco, where she teaches clinical and experimental psychology courses. She is a clinical psychologist with interests in child psychopathology and child maltreatment. She has published scientific articles and technical reports based on her research in the areas of foster care, health psychology, and system of care research with youth who experience serious emotional disorders.

Theodore P. Cross, PhD, is Senior Research Associate at the Family and Children's Policy Center, Florence G. Heller School for Advanced Studies at Brandeis University, and Adjunct Professor in the Department of Psychology at Brandeis. He was Co-Principal Investigator of the evaluation of the Robert Wood Johnson Foundation's Mental Health Services Program for Youth, and Senior Scientist of the Technical Assistance Center for the Evaluation of Children's Mental Health Systems. In his research, he examines systemic interventions in the areas of children's mental health and child abuse. Trained as a clinical psychologist, he maintains a small private practice in child and family therapy.

King E. Davis, PhD, is Professor of Mental Health Policy and Planning at the Virginia Commonwealth University School of Social Work. He holds a PhD from the Florence G. Heller School for Advanced Studies at Brandeis University and also is a licensed clinical social worker. He served as Commissioner of the Virginia Department of Mental Health, Mental Retardation, and Substance Abuse from 1990 to 1994. As commissioner, he was responsible for a statewide behavioral health care system, comprising 15 hospital facilities and 40 local community service agencies. From 1985 to 1987, he was the Galt Visiting Scholar, responsible for developing and implementing collaborative education models between public universities and the Virginia Department of Mental Health. He held full professorships at each of Virginia's three medical schools and departments of psychiatry. He has served on a number of local, state, and national boards and commissions and has published books, articles, and reports in the areas of mental health, fund raising, and social justice. He lectures extensively in the United States, Africa, Mexico, Canada, and the West Indies.

Susan M. Douglas, MS, is a doctoral student in clinical psychology in the Department of Psychology and Human Development at Vanderbilt University. She is working as a research assistant under her adviser, Len Bickman, at the Center for Mental Health Policy at the Vanderbilt Institute for Public Policy Studies. For her dissertation research, she is proposing an integrated assessment model for identifying posttraumatic stress disorder in children and adolescents. During the summer of 1996, she participated in a UNICEF project to reestablish a children's mental health care system in Mostar, Bosnia.

Karyn L. Dresser, PhD, is a social psychologist trained in children's services research. She currently serves as the Research and Evaluation Coordinator for the Family Mosaic Project in San Francisco, teaches at Bay Area colleges, and is a consultant to human service organizations regarding implementing comprehensive integrated systems of care for emotionally disturbed children and youth.

Mary E. Evans, PhD, is Visiting Research Professor, College of Nursing, University of South Florida. Prior to this she was Director of and Principal Research Scientist in the Bureau of Evaluation and Services Research in the New York State Office of Mental Health. She earned her doctorate in sociology from the State University of New York at Albany. She has been working in services research for over 20 years and is currently the principal investigator of three federally funded research demonstration grants in children's mental health services.

Elizabeth M. Z. Farmer, PhD, is a sociologist and mental health services researcher. She is Assistant Professor in the Department of Psychiatry and Behavioral Sciences at Duke University Medical Center.

Her research interests focus on community-based services for children, organization of mental health services, treatment processes and outcomes, and mental health across the life course. Her recent work has included a randomized trial of case management for children, patterns of care and outcomes for youths served through North Carolina's Willie M Program, and analyses of access to care and patterns of care among youths in a general population sample.

Jennifer M. Firth has been involved in mental health services research for 4 years and currently is the Project Coordinator for the Stark County Evaluation Project. While working at the Center for Mental Health Policy at Vanderbilt University, she has served as research analyst on the Fort Bragg Evaluation Project and the Fort Bragg Longitudinal Evaluation. She also has worked as a family interviewer for the Vanderbilt School-Based Counseling Project. Her current research interests include family abuse issues, quality of care, mental health services in educational systems, and family participation in service delivery.

Robert M. Friedman, PhD, is a clinical psychologist who has specialized in research and policy analysis for children and families. He received his BA from Brooklyn College and his MS and PhD from Florida State University. He is currently Professor and Chair of the Department of Child and Family Studies, at the Florida Mental Health Institute, University of South Florida. He also serves as Director of the Research and Training Center for Children's Mental Health. The Research and Training Center is one of two such centers nationally funded by the National Institute on Disability and Rehabilitation Research and the Center for Mental Health Services. He is a researcher, author, policy analyst, and consultant on issues such as clinical services for children and families, the development and evaluation of community-based systems of care, collaborations between mental health and child welfare systems, and prevalence of emotional disorders. He has published and presented more than 125 papers and articles. He is coauthor with Beth Stroul of *A System of Care for Severely Emotionally Disturbed Children and Youth,* which has been widely used across the United States to plan services for children with emotional disorders and their families. He also is coeditor of a special edition of the *Journal of Mental Health Ad-*

ministration on children's mental health services and coeditor of a book entitled *Advocacy on Behalf of Children With Serious Emotional Problems.*

Dan I. Gerber, PhD, is Deputy Area Director and Clinical Director of the Blue Ridge Center for Mental Health, Developmental Disabilities, and Substance Abuse Services in Asheville, North Carolina. He also is a Clinical Assistant Professor in the Department of Psychiatry, School of Medicine, University of North Carolina at Chapel Hill. His PhD is in clinical psychology from Columbia University. He has been very active in developing and implementing North Carolina's 1915(b) Medicaid waiver for children's mental health and has taken a lead in developing community-based services for children.

Helen B. Guiles, BA, holds a degree in psychology from Duke University. She served as Project Coordinator for the Assessing Coordinated Care (ACC) Study, a randomized trial of case management for children with serious emotional disturbance. The ACC study was carried out in conjunction with the Robert Wood Johnson Foundation's Mental Health Services Program for Youth (MHSPY) in western North Carolina. She is currently an artist in Asheville, North Carolina.

Samuel L. Lind, DrPH, is a second-year Postdoctoral Fellow in the Department of Psychiatry at the University of California, San Francisco, where he is responsible for economic analysis of children's mental health service systems for the Child Services Research Group. His research concentrates on the development of comprehensive multivariate time series models that forecast expenditures for the delivery of children's mental health services in California. He earned a doctorate in the School of Public Health at the University of California, Berkeley, in 1995. His undergraduate studies were completed at Ohio Univesity, where he graduated cum laude. He earned an MBA degree in international finance from The Ohio State University. He has held faculty appointments in economics and quantitative methods at Saint Mary's College of California and the University of San Francisco. He has completed several research projects in his field of health economics and econometrics relating to children's mental health services and has presented research papers and discussions that disseminate the results of his analyses at economic and statistical conferences for the Center for Mental Health Services and the National Institute of Mental Health.

Kathleen A. Maloy, JD, PhD, is Senior Researcher with Mathematics Policy Research, Washington, DC, and previously served as Deputy Director of the Center for Mental Health Policy at the Vanderbilt Institute for Public Policy Studies at Vanderbilt University. Before that, she was Senior Policy Analyst at the Mental Health Policy Resource Center in Washington, DC, and also served as Chief Legal Counsel for the Tennessee Department of Mental Health and Mental Retardation. She began her professional career as a legal services attorney. She received her law degree from Boston College Law School in 1979 and her doctorate in health policy in 1990 from Boston University. Her areas of expertise include health care financing and policy, state policymaking, services for children and families, evaluation research, legal rights of people with disabilities, juvenile justice, and Medicaid. Her research has been focused on how states can implement systemwide reform in services to children and families and whether involuntary outpatient commitment represents an effective state mental health policy.

Judith C. Meyers, PhD, is Senior Consultant with the Center for the Study of Social Policy, Washington, DC, and the National Technical Assistance Center for Children's Mental Health at Georgetown University, focusing on improving outcomes for children and families through reforming state and local human services systems. From 1992 to 1994, she was a Senior Associate for Mental Health at the Annie E. Casey Foundation, where she was responsible for grant making in the area of mental health. She had primary responsibility for a multisite initiative to develop mental health systems of care for children in poor urban neighborhoods. From 1989 to 1991, she was Administrator for the state of Iowa's Division of Adult, Children, and Family Services, responsible for the state's child welfare and juvenile service systems. She has a PhD in clinical psychology from the University of Colorado and completed postdoctoral fellowships in psychology and in mental health research and evaluation at Yale University. From 1982 to 1983, she was an AAAS Congressional Science Fellow, working in the office of Congressman David Obey (D-WI). She has held faculty appointments in the Department of Psychiatry at Yale University, the University of Michigan, and the University of New Hampshire, and was a Visiting Lecturer at Harvard Medical School. She served as President of the American Psychological Association's (APA) Division of Children, Youth, and Family Services in 1991 and currently serves on the APA Committee on Children, Youth, and Families.

Abram B. Rosenblatt, PhD, is Assistant Adjunct Professor at the University of California, San Francisco, where he serves as Director of Research for the Child Services Research Group. He is also a Co-Investigator with the NIMH-funded Center for the Study of the Organization and Financing of Services to the Severely Mentally Ill at the University of California, Berkeley. He earned the BA degree in psychology from the University of California, San Diego, and MA and PhD degrees in clinical psychology from the University of Arizona. His current research interests are in the area of mental health services and policy research with an emphasis on services to children with severe emotional disturbance. He is an associate editor of the *Journal of Child and Family Studies* and a member of the editorial board of the *Journal of Emotional and Behavioral Disorders.* He has served on national panels and initial review groups convened by the NIMH and the Center for Mental Health Services pertaining to children's mental health services evaluation and research. His recent scholarly contributions include book chapters and articles in peer-reviewed journals on depression, program evaluation, research methods, quality assurance, juvenile delinquency, outcomes research, integrating economics and psychology in health services research, and the costs and outcomes of services to children with severe emotional disturbance.

Leonard Saxe, PhD, is a social psychologist whose work focuses on the evaluation of mental health interventions and systems. He is Professor of Psychology at the Graduate School and University Center of the City University of New York and Adjunct Professor of Social Welfare at the Florence G. Heller School for Advanced Studies, Brandeis University. He has worked for the Congressional Office of Technology Assessment, where he conducted evaluations of the effectiveness of psychotherapy, treatment for alcoholism, and children's mental health and was Principal Investigator of the Robert Wood Johnson Foundation's Mental Health Services Program for Youth (MHSPY) as well as an ongoing study of the foundation's community-based drug and alcohol prevention program, Fighting Back. He is the author of a text on evaluation research, *Social Experiments: Methods for Design and Evaluation,* as well as several monographs and numerous book chapters and journal articles on the conduct of applied research. He has been a recipient of the American Psychological Association's early career award for Research in the Public Interest.

Wm. Thomas Summerfelt, PhD, is Research Associate at the Center for Mental Health Policy at Vanderbilt University. He is an applied social psychologist with training in clinical psychology, applied social psychology, program evaluation, and mental health services research. He served as chief services analyst in the Fort Bragg Evaluation Project and is currently part of the national UNO-CCAP collaboration. He was both a predoctoral and postdoctoral fellow at the Center for Mental Health Policy under the NIMH-sponsored training grant in child and adolescent mental health services research. His research interests have been focused on defining and measuring quality in mental health services, defining and measuring functioning in children with SED, and linking psychological outcomes to service utilization.